THE LAST
SENTRY

THE LAST SENTRY

The True Story that Inspired
The Hunt for Red October

Gregory D. Young

Nate Braden

Naval Institute Press
Annapolis, Maryland

Naval Institute Press
291 Wood Road
Annapolis, MD 21402

Library of Congress Cataloging-in-Publication Data

Young, Gregory D., 1953–
   The last sentry : the true story that inspired the hunt for Red October /
Gregory D. Young, Nate Braden.
      p. cm.
   Includes bibliographical references and index.
   ISBN 1-59114-992-4 (alk. paper)
   1. Mutiny—Soviet Union.   2. Soviet Union—History, Naval—20th century.
3. Soviet Union—History—1953–1985.   4. Sablin, Valeriæi Mikhaæilovich,
1939–1977.   5. Storozhevoæi (Ship)   I. Braden, Nate, 1968–   II. Title.
DK274.Y68 2005
947.085'2—dc22

                                                            2004030762

12 11 10 09 08 07 06 05   9 8 7 6 5 4 3 2
First printing

To Nina Mikhailovna and Mikhail Valerievich

*Who have borne the burden of the true believer
and paid the price of the idealist.*

Нине и Михаилу
Потому, что Вы несли бремя истинно верующих,
заплатив цену идеалиста.

Sometimes you wait almost half your life for your one moment to come.

VALERY SABLIN
Diary entry, 7 November 1975

CONTENTS

FOREWORD

This book is about an event that happened thirty years ago. It is a story about the fate of a Russian naval officer—a husband and a father. Who was Valery Sablin to us, and how did we view his calling?

Captain Sablin was a romantic. He wanted freedom for his countrymen but was stopped by those who wanted to keep them enslaved.

Valery Sablin was an idealist. He dreamed of a perfect country where the rule of law served the people and stood in harmony with society. His contemporaries did not understand him.

Captain Sablin was a patriot. He dreamed of a strong Russia. To Brezhnev and his circle, such people were a threat. True patriots endangered the Communist system—a system that eventually destroyed him.

Valery Sablin came from a long line of warriors. The honor of a Russian naval officer was his guiding principle. Shameless careerists, far removed from honor, sabotaged his plans.

Captain Sablin was a rebel. The corrupt party elite opposed him because he dared to speak the truth to their faces.

Valery Sablin was a sailor. He went to sea and never came home. What happened to him in his last days is still unknown to us.

Valery Sablin was simply a man who loved his wife and son.

Valera. Dad. We have parted, but you are still with us. We are proud of you.

NINA SABLINA
MIKHAIL SABLIN
St. Petersburg, Russia
May 2004

THE LAST
SENTRY

THE PARADE

He knew his way around a ship; he had been to sea many times. His previous deployments had always been in the service of his Motherland, and this one would be no different. Like the name of the ship on which he served—*Storozhevoy,* Russian for "the sentry"—he too was on watch. He was the last sentry on watch who was still a true believer in the fallen faith of Communism.

Valery Mikhailovich Sablin was an officer of the Soviet Navy. A thirty-six-year-old third rank captain, the equivalent of a lieutenant commander in the U.S. Navy, he was essentially a midgrade officer. After fifteen years of service, he was comfortably set on a promising career path. He was the political officer aboard the destroyer *Storozhevoy,* a type of vessel the Russians called *bolshoi protivolodochniy korabl* (BPK), a large antisubmarine ship. Should the Cold War turn hot, *Storozhevoy* was to sail out into the Atlantic Ocean and engage American and NATO submarines.

The ship's homeport was Baltiysk, near the city of Kaliningrad, and it was assigned to the Baltic Fleet. By the 1970s, the Soviet Navy had no intention of remaining close to its own shores in the event of war. For more than two hundred years, the Russian fleet had been merely an attachment of the army, assigned the mission of guarding its flanks. The country now had a "blue water navy," meaning it could deploy deep into the Atlantic, Pacific, or Indian Ocean and fight far from home. On the evening of 8 November 1975, some of these warships were sitting quietly at anchor in Riga Harbor in parade formation. The occasion was the fifty-eighth anniversary of the Bolshevik Revolution, when Lenin's Communists took control of St. Petersburg in 1917 (the official holiday was 7 November). It was the end of the second day of festivities, and many of the sailors had been given liberty ashore. Following standard operating procedure, two-thirds of each vessel's crew remained aboard at all times in case the ship needed to get under way immediately.

On this night, *Storozhevoy* would indeed get under way immediately, and it would be an emergency of the first order. It would be an unusual deployment in several respects, including the fact that Third Rank Captain Sablin was the only one who knew about it. Although the country was not at war, Sablin was; he had been at war with himself for many years. Now at last he might be able to direct his energies toward his enemy instead of himself. That night, his enemy was five hundred miles to the east, asleep in Moscow. Sablin hoped it was a restless sleep, induced by vodka or pills, because the man in Moscow had much to answer for.

This man with the bushy eyebrows and the low, gravelly voice had hijacked the beloved revolution that meant so much to Valery. He had tightened the screws on the Soviet ship of state, suffocating its crew and crushing its passengers. The Russian people had given much in the name of their 1917 revolution, and for what? So Leonid Brezhnev could enrich himself by pilfering oil contracts? So he could give his sons prestigious jobs for which they were not qualified? So he could fumble around the Kremlin while the military-industrial complex ran at full throttle, spitting out nuclear missiles and armaments at the expense of the civilian economy?

Enough was enough. Sablin reached into the pocket of his officer's tunic and felt the hard metal of the Makarov pistol in his hand. He had fabricated some story to the duty officer about how he needed one, so he had been allowed to get it from the armory. The weapon both reassured him and made him nervous. He truly did not want to use it, but his charisma and reasoning would not be enough to persuade everyone. Sablin looked up at the clock in his stateroom—1700 hours. Five o'clock in the afternoon. It was time to begin.

Today Riga is the capital of an independent Latvia, but in 1975 it was just another city in the Soviet Union. The original inhabitants of this region, known as Letts, settled there a thousand years ago. Unlike their Russian neighbors, Letts have never felt the pull between Asia and Europe; they regard themselves as wholly a product of the latter and have fought several wars to remain so. Surrounded by Russia, Poland, Germany, and Sweden, however, their struggles were not always successful. In 1629, the Swedes conquered Latvia, and in turn lost it to the Russians in 1721. For the next two hundred years, Latvia would remain a vassal state of the tsar, until the chaos caused by the Russian Revolution gave the Letts a chance to declare their independence in 1920.

About three hundred miles northeast of Riga, Tsar Peter the Great turned a swamp into his capital city in 1703, as a permanent testament to where he thought Russia's future lay. St. Petersburg became not only the gateway to the Baltic but also his "window to Europe." Among Peter's other creations was the Russian Navy, which came to view the Baltic as its backyard. For a nation that has traditionally been vulnerable to land attack from all directions, a navy was viewed by many Russians as a luxury, but Peter felt it an essential tool of a great power. His city remained the capital of the Russian empire for 215 years. Shortly after the Bolshevik Revolution, the Communists moved the capital to Moscow, signifying their belief that the Soviet Union no longer sought acceptance from the nations of Europe. Instead, their capital would become the center of world revolution. Under Communist rule, Russians referred to Moscow as simply that, *Tsentr*, the place from which all orders and directions flowed.

One of these orders came in 1940, when Josef Stalin sent the Soviet Army to invade and occupy Latvia, along with its fellow Baltic states of Lithuania and Estonia. This arrangement had been made in collusion with Adolf Hitler. The previous year, the governments of Nazi Germany and Soviet Russia had signed a non-aggression pact, secret provisions of which guaranteed Stalin a free hand in the then-independent Baltic states. They would not see freedom again for another half-century.

If the Latvians were not particularly satisfied with their new status as a Soviet republic, the Russian Navy was, because Riga provided its ships with a new harbor. One of the weaknesses of St. Petersburg as a naval base was its narrow avenue of approach. All shipping had to go through the Gulf of Finland, which was vulnerable to blockade, especially from Finland. Keeping the entire Baltic Fleet there was akin to putting all your eggs in one basket. Riga provided Stalin's warships with another basket.

The port is actually on the banks of the Daugava River, which empties into the Gulf of Riga ten miles to the north. Ships leaving the Daugava must transit this gulf for sixty nautical miles before they reach the Irben Channel, the passageway that eventually leads to the open waters of the Baltic. Because of shoals on its northern side, the navigable portion of this channel is very narrow, often causing traffic jams with the high volume of shipping that goes through it. The lighthouse on Rukhnu Island in the Gulf of Riga acts like a traffic cop, directing outgoing ships to turn west and incoming ships to turn south.

Over the weekend of 8–9 November 1975, most of the traffic was coming south in anticipation of the holiday naval parade. Because of the number of ships taking part, several of them had to be moored at the customs pier in central Riga, normally reserved for commercial traffic. The pier sits on the eastern bank of the Daugava, on the same side of the river as the city center. Clearly visible were the spires of both the St. Peter and Mara churches as well as the cupolas of hundred-year-old government buildings, which could only be reached by traveling the narrow winding cobblestone streets of old Riga.

One of the geographical facts that tends to surprise those who are not residents of the continent is just how far north of the equator Europe sits. Paris is actually north of Seattle, and Germany is about where British Columbia is. At the more northern latitudes, the days are either very short or very long. The sun never really sets in late June; it remains in twilight as it dips just below the horizon, giving northern Russia its famous "white nights." In winter, of course, the opposite is true, and when the sun does take a peek over whatever natural obstacles are hiding it, it casts a long blue twilight on land and water. Depending on your disposition, this can be either very beautiful or very depressing.

This is most certainly true of the Baltic Sea region, which because of its isolation from its fellow waterways is somewhat immune to the wind and currents that create weather in other parts of the world. Socked in by a good fog in late fall or early winter, the absence of light can create an eerie sensation, as if the world is closing in on you.

On Saturday, 8 November 1975, the sun had set at 5:30 in the afternoon, and as the air cooled, the mist rose from the water and spread throughout the city like a night watchman making his rounds. At 11:00 that night, the engines of one of the ships near the customs pier came to life. She was actually moored out in the middle of the Daugava, tethered to a buoy with her anchor dropped. Once she started her engines, she weighed anchor, lurched forward, and struck the stern of the submarine in front of her. The man at the helm was an accomplished seaman, but because nobody expected one of the ships to break parade formation, they were closely moored together.

As the men on the bridge knew, this was the least of their worries. The four-hundred-foot ship now had to turn around in a shallow river crammed with other vessels. The helmsman did so, skillfully putting the bow downriver. The gas turbine engines accelerated, and *Storozhevoy* sailed north toward the Gulf of Riga. Now the real danger began.

The getaway was not entirely clean. Colliding with the sub was a bad break, but as far as anyone else knew, *Storozhevoy* had received special instructions from Naval Headquarters and was simply heading back to its homeport. Still another development had compromised Valery Sablin's secret mission. Half an hour before *Storozhevoy* weighed anchor, one of her officers had jumped ship by crawling down the mooring line on her bow. The submarine *S-263* was moored to the same buoy next to *Storozhevoy,* and the fugitive officer had crawled up her bowline. Once he reached the conning tower, he demanded to see the sub's skipper. He was then brought before *S-263*'s captain, who eyed him skeptically and examined him closely for signs that he had been drinking—it was a holiday, after all. His story seemed incredible. He explained that the political officer on board *Storozhevoy* had locked up the captain in a compartment below decks and taken over the ship.

Now the submarine skipper was even more skeptical. A political officer? One of the official Communist Party watchdogs attached to every unit and vessel in the Soviet armed forces? By definition, they were as loyal as any Communist yet invented. They were stationed aboard ships to prevent exactly the sort of thing this man was now suggesting had occurred. If true, it meant they had to think the unthinkable.

A ship of the Soviet Navy was in mutiny.

The bridge of *Storozhevoy* was dark. The only lights in use were subdued red or blue ones for marking a passageway or reading a chart. A ship at sea could be seen for twelve miles—that was how far you could look out across the water's surface before the curvature of the earth dropped the rest of the world out of sight. At night, even a single white light could be seen at this distance, so it was imperative for a ship's protection that it be completely darkened. Since it is harder for the human eye to contrast red and blue at night, these are the only lights allowed aboard a warship after sunset.

Sablin was on the bridge now, in command of a *Krivak*-class destroyer. As one of the ship's senior leaders, he was a qualified watch officer, which meant he knew the procedures for weighing anchor and leaving port. Additionally, he was proficient in navigation and maneuvering, and he knew how to pilot a ship in open water. He also knew it would only be a matter of time before the rest of the fleet found out. They would come after him. They could not do otherwise.

Sablin was aware that one of his officers had jumped ship and was probably ashore telling anyone who would listen that *Storozhevoy*'s political officer had gone renegade and taken control of his ship. He now had less time than he had anticipated. There were several sailors on the bridge with him: the helmsman at the wheel, a signalman at the radar station, and a radioman at the communications post. They all eyed him nervously, awaiting further orders. There was no turning back now. It really was Sablin's show. At that moment, he was probably the freest man in the Soviet Union. He stared forward into the darkness.

"*Storozhevoy,* all ahead full."

Chapter 1

THE COMMISSAR

Valery Mikhailovich Sablin. He was the Russian version of a kid who grew up in Norfolk, San Diego, and Honolulu—traditional American naval towns where people keep abreast of ship deployments and turn out to see the crews off as they put to sea. The Russian equivalents of these cities are Archangel, Polyarniy, and Severomorsk, places where Valery Sablin spent his youth.

He was born in Leningrad on New Year's Day 1939, the son of a naval officer. When war came to Russia in 1941, his father Mikhail was attached to the Northern Fleet staff. Ships from this fleet dodged German bombers and submarines escorting merchant vessels from the North Atlantic to the port of Murmansk. This was a vital lifeline to the country, supplying aid from the United States and Britain, and First Rank Captain Sablin saw plenty of action. His three sons, Boris, Valery, and Nikolai, came to revere their father and probably knew his medals better than he did: an Order of the Red Banner, two Red Stars, and the Order of the Patriotic War First and Second Class.

Their childhood was spent in the bleak landscape of wartime Polyarniy, headquarters of the Northern Fleet, which sits well above the Arctic Circle. They had memories of German bombers attacking the harbor at Ekaterina and of their mother Anna hustling her three sons to the bomb shelter. Boris, the eldest, remembers that she took up smoking in order to kill her appetite and leave every ounce of bread possible to her boys.

Like most families in a country that had always been vulnerable to invasion from its neighbors, there was a long and proud history of military service in the Sablin clan. Valery's maternal grandfather was a sailor, his paternal grandfather was a cavalryman, and, if further reassurance was needed, his great-grandfather went down with the cruiser *Pallada* in World War I. All had seen combat in at least one war.

In the early 1950s, Mikhail Sablin was transferred to Gorky, a city 250 miles east of Moscow, where he taught military science at a local school until his retirement. Afterward, he and Anna remained in Gorky, and Mikhail got a job teaching navigation to Volga River boat captains. They raised their boys in the relative peace of this provincial town. Valery was the middle child, two years younger than Boris and seven years older than Nikolai. He was the only one to follow in his father's footsteps, and he did so without any reservation. He had fond memories of the coastal towns in which he spent time as a boy. Not all of these memories were pleasant, of course, especially those from the war years, but they nevertheless gave him an appreciation of the navy and the sea that he held with him for the rest of his days.

He was bored with life in Gorky and wanted to avoid a future there at all costs. While he respected his father's service, Valery's decision to enter the navy was also made to spare him the dull routine that would be his fate if he remained there. Many Russians considered Gorky to be "in the sticks," and like so many other young people, Valery was drawn to the excitement of the big city. At the very least, life in the navy would give him a taste of the excitement he craved.

He set his eyes on enrolling in Leningrad's Frunze Military Academy, and it was taken for granted that with his pedigree and ability, he would one day command his own ship. Ironically, he was not to make a name for himself as a ship captain but as a *zampolit,* a political officer (see the glossary). The term was an acronym for "deputy chief for political indoctrination." A special position in the Soviet military, the *zampolit* descended from the pre–World War II Soviet commissar and was the political watchdog assigned to every unit of the Soviet armed forces to guard against subversion and educate servicemen in party doctrine. As a rule, they were deeply resented within the officer corps, not least of all because they held the same rank as the commander of the unit to which they were assigned, thus violating the military principle of unity of command. In the old days, when conflicts arose between military efficiency and political expedience, the latter would usually get the upper hand.

Nowhere was this more apparent than in the Stalinist purges of the 1930s. Like all other institutions of Russian life at the time, the military was decimated by this political terror. Stalin made sure his allies were promoted and his enemies, or potential enemies, were driven from service, imprisoned, or executed. By the time it was over, the armed forces had lost most of its ablest men, including 3 out of 5 marshals, 13 out of 15 army commanders, and 220 of 406 brigade commanders. Of the 80-man Supreme Military Council, 75 were purged, along with all 11 vice commissars of defense.[1] Officers who remained were thoroughly intimidated. Most abandoned their attempts to modernize the armed forces; such efforts would attract attention, and anonymity was a cherished status in those days.

The ultimate price of this terror was paid in the terrible months after 22 June 1941, when Nazi Germany invaded Soviet Russia. By the end of August, the Germans had advanced more than five hundred miles into the Soviet Union, killing or wounding seven hundred thousand Russian soldiers and taking nearly a million prisoners.[2] While much of this success was attributable to superior German tactics and equipment, the effect of Stalin's purges on the morale and effectiveness of the Red Army cannot be underestimated.

Since the Red Army's near defeat at the hands of the Germans, the commissar's role had changed. The *zampolit* was no longer equal in rank to the unit commander. In the Soviet Navy, or Voenno-Morskoi Flot (VMF) as it is known in Russian, this meant that he was now subordinate to the ship's captain. Although answering to a separate political chain of command, the *zampolit* did carry military responsibilities, which fell under the captain's jurisdiction aboard ship. On major combatant vessels, the political officer was third in command, following the captain and his *starpom* (short for *stariy pomoshnik,* or senior assistant), who was the equivalent of an executive officer in the U.S. Navy. The *zampolit* was required to qualify as an underway watch officer like any other officer on the ship and so had to have some operational competence.[3]

In contrast, the old political commissars were not required to have military qualifications. Consequently, they were drawn directly from the civilian populace and did not mesh well with other members of the ship's wardroom. In the mid-1970s, the *zampolit* was recruited from armed forces personnel who showed promise as Communist Party activists. At a special school in Kiev, Ukraine, the prospective political officer not only received extensive schooling for his primary mission of political enlightenment but also was trained to fulfill a military function in his unit.[4]

This and many other ideas were implemented to improve the traditional reputation of the *zampolit* as the shipboard informer. He subsequently functioned as a combined personnel officer, chaplain, and welfare and recreation officer, in addition to removing the majority of the burden of political education from the other officers.

The *zampolit* also ran the library and distributed the official propaganda literature; he was supposed to ensure that it was read by the troops, but this was easier said than done. He created the "Red corners," which were like altars throughout the base or ship and were decorated with symbols of the faith—busts of Lenin and diverse patriotic slogans and insignia. He promoted national campaigns aboard ship, such as energy and food conservation. The *zampolit* prepared group trips, including any shore visits in foreign countries, and organized "socialist competitions" either between ships or just within divisions and departments aboard his ship. These wide-ranging responsibilities were not supposed to detract from his most important function: to lead the political indoctrination to which each sailor had to devote at least five hours a week. In short, he was a very busy man.

The *zampolit* thus sat in the unique position of being the one person to whom all sailors were encouraged to take their welfare problems, similar to an ombudsman, but who could still command the ship and earn respect from the sailors. If he was sensitive to their problems and not just a party hack or informer, he was the one officer who was able to establish some sort of rapport with the crew.

Sablin was very successful at this and probably knew the enlisted men better than any other officer on the ship. Even if they did not come to him, Sablin would usually go to them, making his rounds and striking up conversations. He enjoyed hearing about their lives before the navy—where they came from, what they wanted to do when they got out. The sailors, recognizing his sincerity, returned his trust and told their *zampolit* what was really on their minds.

The relationship between officers and enlisted men in any military service is complicated. Although similar to the division between management and labor in the civilian world, the military version is much stricter and more bound by protocol. It is also much more subtle. In the U.S. military, enlisted men are required by oath to obey the orders of the officers appointed over them, provided they are lawful orders. Blind obedience is not a military virtue, and even the armies of totalitarian nations have at least paid lip service to the value of subordinate initiative and decision making. In practice, however, rewarding such initiative is difficult, especially if the subordinate's decision is the opposite of his commander's. Professionalism in this case dictates that the subordinate make his case honestly and completely. Once the commander has made his decision, however, the subordinate should follow and support it, even if he does not agree with it.

In the Soviet armed forces, the lack of a truly professional enlisted class meant that officers assumed more of the daily duties. Unlike his American counterpart, a Soviet sailor was not encouraged to go to the senior enlisted man aboard ship with a personal problem; this chief was not considered the senior representative of the enlisted men. Rather, he was thought of as a kind of "first among equals" who was free from performing the more unpopular duties aboard ship by virtue of his time in service. Nor, in a country that was officially atheist, could a sailor go see a chaplain about a personal matter, as he might aboard a U.S. warship.

Lacking these two channels, the enlisted men aboard *Storozhevoy* had little choice but to turn to Sablin. They did so willingly, however, because he was totally lacking in pretension and earned their trust for the very simple favor of listening to their problems. His approachability was in sharp contrast to the aloofness of *Storozhevoy*'s skipper, 2nd Rank Capt. Anatoly Vasilievich Potulniy, nicknamed the "Count" by the sailors.

Other junior officers may have had an interest in their subordinates but did not have time to develop this interest due to numerous responsibilities. Junior officers were not only the shipboard managers and leaders but also the main technical specialists in their departments. They had to supervise and often perform the major maintenance and repair functions. They still carried some burden of political work; they were the backbone of the political officer's "socialist competitions" and fulfilled their own responsibilities as candidate Communist Party members. Fully 80 percent of all

Soviet officers were party or KOMSOMOL (acronym for the All-Union Lenin Communist Youth League) members.[5] The Soviet Navy figure was 95 percent.[6]

While the army has always been the senior service in the Soviet Union, the navy holds a special place in Russian history. As the creation of the man many Russians consider to be their most farsighted leader, Peter the Great, the navy has always been viewed as the more glamorous branch of the armed forces. It has also been the more radical one. When revolt came to tsarist Russia, the navy was usually in the thick of it. Such was the case in 1905, when the Russian fleet's defeat in the Pacific at the hands of Japan nearly toppled the regime of Tsar Nicholas II. Several ships of the Black Sea Fleet mutinied, most famously the battleship *Potemkin*. Sailors on the battleship *Pamyat Azova* bayoneted their captain to death, killed their engineering officer with a sledgehammer, and shot a nineteen-year-old junior officer who had just reported aboard.

Only last-minute political concessions by Nicholas, such as the creation of an independent parliament, prevented a full-scale revolution throughout the country. Revolution would come in 1917, however, when the three-hundred-year Romanov dynasty came to an end after Nicholas II abdicated his throne. That winter, the flames of rebellion spread quickly through the armed forces. In St. Petersburg, the mutiny aboard the cruiser *Aurora* was immortalized in Communist folklore because it was this ship that fired the shot signaling the Bolsheviks to storm the Winter Palace in October 1917. By killing their captain and supporting the Bolsheviks, the crew had earned a place in Soviet history. Their portrait hung in the Naval Museum for seventy years, and *Aurora* is still moored on the Neva River in St. Petersburg—a floating museum to the revolution. If there was ever an indication of how mutiny was institutionalized in the newborn Soviet Navy, this was it.

As such, it was not long before the fleet proved its fickleness to Lenin's Communist government as well. The first garrison to abandon its loyalty to the hammer and sickle was the Kronstadt Naval Base in St. Petersburg. In March 1921, sailors stationed at Kronstadt joined with local workers to demand that the Communists release their tight-fisted control of the Soviet government. The mutineers who seized the base called not only for a sharing of power by the non-Communist political parties but also for dramatic political and economic reforms, including freedom of speech, the press, and assembly, and voting by secret ballot.

The Bolshevik leaders refused to negotiate with the Kronstadt sailors and demanded unconditional surrender. The Red Army launched full-scale attacks across the ice of the Gulf of Finland against the mutineers and their island base. Lenin had to suspend the Tenth Communist Party Congress and send three hundred of its members to help put down the rebellion. The two-week revolt ended, and the cries of "Free Soviets" and "Down with the Commissarocracy" were finally drowned out. Lenin's secret police, the dreaded Cheka, carried out immediate executions of the remaining five to six thousand sailors and workers who had participated in the revolt. After this, Lenin considered disbanding the Baltic Fleet altogether. Only when the Tenth Party Congress reconvened and assured Lenin that it would "strengthen the navy with political workers from the ranks of sailor-communists working in other fields" did he agree to keep it intact.

This was the legacy seventeen-year-old Valery Sablin inherited when he entered the prestigious Frunze Military Academy in 1956. Frunze was one of several college-level military academies around the Soviet Union that trained the country's future navy and army officers. Many of Sablin's classmates were, like himself, sons of naval officers and party officials. Since officers were essentially required to be Communist Party members, indoctrination began at a very early age. Most participated in the Little Octobrist group from ages six through nine, the All Union Pioneer Organization from ten through fourteen, and then the KOMSOMOL at fifteen. All this was preparation for official party membership, which came at age twenty-eight.

This political instruction was very intensive and did not just begin with the Little Octobrists. It began at the preschool level for all Soviet children, with cartoon comics depicting military heroes, and continued throughout the required ten years of secondary schooling. All children began indoctrination into the party teachings at an early age; the struggle between the Soviet Union and the Western world was particularly emphasized. Soviet educational literature contained statements such as "Schoolchildren must know the real danger which imperialism poses to mankind. The work done in a school by way of military-patriotic indoctrination must prepare students in practical ways to overcome difficulties during times of severe trial."[7]

The year 1956 was an auspicious time for Sablin to enter military service. On 25 February of that year, Nikita Khrushchev gave a speech to the Twentieth Communist Party Congress in Moscow that shocked his audience (for that reason the speech was kept secret). It denounced Josef Stalin and suggested that his political terror and forced collectivization of agriculture were mistakes.

Stalin had died three years earlier without leaving a chosen successor. He probably figured that once he was gone, the man who was ruthless enough to liquidate or marginalize his enemies and win a Kremlin power struggle deserved to rule the Soviet Union. This survival-of-the-fittest mentality pitted Khrushchev against some formidable foes, and for two years, Soviet experts in the West watched closely to see who would emerge as the front-runner. Would it be Georgi Malenkov, the consummate bureaucrat; Lavrenti Beria, the secret police chief; Nikolai Bulganin, the party philosopher; or Khrushchev, the former Ukrainian metal worker?

The 1956 speech gave them the answer. Any man who could comfortably criticize Stalin, even in a secret meeting with other Communists, had to be confident of his power base. A copy of his speech was eventually obtained by the Mossad, Israel's spy service, and passed on to the West. Radio Free Europe (RFE) duly broadcast the speech around the clock to Soviet citizens. Since RFE transmissions were routinely jammed, not everyone heard it, but enough did for word to get around that Khrushchev had a taste for reform. Thus began what was known as "the thaw," a term consistently associated with Khrushchev's time in power.

In March of the same year, Khrushchev gave another secret speech, this time to Polish Communists in Warsaw. The gist of his message was the same—Stalin's "cult of personality" had terrorized the Soviet Union—but it was a much more candid speech:

> Stalin had his own methods. He said that in order for the working class to succeed, in order to take power, many thousands and millions of workers had to die. Maybe it was a mistake. At such a moment of revolutionary struggle, it's possible that there are mistaken victims. But, he says, history will forgive me. Is it possible? Perhaps. The whole question concerns the scale of these mistakes.

A question of methods. Because his doses were incorrect, because an incorrect method of leadership was used. And we want to avoid this. Comrades, we ourselves aren't guaranteeing that mistakes won't be made. We also can't allow—we also arrested people, and will probably make arrests in the future. I think that you'll also have to do this. But, if you now become liberals, and look at everybody and pat everybody on the back, then these enemies will bite your hands off.[8]

It was a revealing look at the split personality of the Soviet regime—the need to fulfill Communism's stated aim of serving the people set against the practical necessity of keeping power in a totalitarian state.

It was at Frunze in the late 1950s that Valery Sablin's personality was forming in a way that was very different from his peers. All faiths are eventually challenged, and those who fervently believed in Communism and the ideals of Lenin would soon find that faith sorely tested outside the classroom. Most would see the yawning chasm between what Communism was supposed to be and what it really was and be disturbed by the experience. Others did not care and recognized their membership in the party as a ticket to a better life: a better apartment, better food, and better vacations. The cold resignation of lost faith would embitter some and be shrugged off by others.

Cadet Sablin would come to see this contradiction during his time in Leningrad and observe how often the needs of the people came second to the needs of the Communist regime. This political awareness was further inspired by a family member who was also at school in Leningrad at the time—his cousin, Tamara Sablina. Tamara was a student at the School of Journalism, just a few blocks from Frunze on Vasielevski Island. Unlike Valery and most of his classmates, Tamara's classmates were not party members; they were more skeptical of official Soviet history. Nevertheless, they were just as excited by what seemed to be loosening of the political shackles under Khrushchev. "The International Student and Youth Festival had just wrapped up, and had come as quite a shock to our unprepared minds," Tamara later recalled. "For the first time the Iron Curtain lifted, and we could see the world we had been cut off from for four decades. Khrushchev's 'thaw' had begun. Students in the university were getting their hands on prohibited writings and provocative poetry. I gave some of these to Valery to read. He was growing up before my very eyes and taking in everything he could, soaking up the spirit of the university's freedom."[9]

He was indeed, but he was not completely sold on the individualism this freedom inspired. As a military man and future officer, Sablin understood the need for unit cohesion and teamwork. He valued this quality in the navy most of all. Shortly after returning from his first deployment as a cadet, Sablin wrote his parents: "We just returned to port after being at sea for two weeks. We haven't yet gone ashore. These fifteen days passed quickly, one day into the next: we didn't know when it was day or night, when it was Sunday or Monday. The longer I stay here (on this new destroyer), the more I'm convinced that it was a good idea to go into the navy. Here you get the feeling that the captain, the ship, and the crew move as one. With a single word, the skipper can send the ship tearing ahead at flank speed, firing off all its weapons, with everyone responding as a team."[10]

Sea duty gives a person plenty of time to read, and Sablin did so voraciously. He became very well versed in Communist literature, especially the works of Lenin, and could quote from them at will. He showed an intensity that would have grated on his classmates had it not been balanced by a dry sense of humor and a robust enjoyment of nearly everything life had to offer. He was well liked by his fellow cadets, who called him the "class conscience" and appointed him to be the student liaison with the faculty committee. His superiors noted his dedication and rewarded him for it; he became a company commander and one of the first cadets to join the Communist Party.

Nikita Krushchev's efforts to reform the Soviet regime proved to be short lived. He was living on borrowed time. There was so much to do and so little time in which to do it. As the head of that regime, Krushchev spent half his time "riding the tiger"—making sure his Kremlin rivals did not best him in a power struggle. A series of bewildering economic decisions, including an attempt to cultivate thousands of acres of cotton (a very thirsty crop) in the middle of the Kazakhstan desert, were ruinous. His behavior abroad when meeting foreign dignitaries was often outrageous. In one famous incident at the United Nations General Assembly, Krushchev actually took off his shoe and used it to bang the desk in front of him to emphasize a point he was making. Russians have always demanded a certain amount of decorum from their heads of state, especially on official visits overseas, and Khrushchev's erratic nature began to wear their patience thin. After a very dangerous game of brinkmanship with John F. Kennedy during the Cuban Missile Crisis, the Politburo decided that enough was enough. In October 1964, Nikita Khrushchev was thrown out of office and replaced by Leonid Brezhnev.

Communist ideology, which had called for so much sacrifice in return for the future payment of a glorious workers' paradise, had run its course by then. Cynicism became an ingrained feature of Soviet life; no one believed what the press wrote or what the radio said. The two newspapers with the widest circulation were *Pravda* (truth) and *Izvestiya* (news), and an old Soviet-era joke went, "There's no truth in *Pravda* and no news in *Izvestiya*." What's more, no one felt the system could be fixed; the notion of civic responsibility had completely eroded.

But not to Valery. No, to a true believer, faith tested is faith strengthened. Like baseball fans who root for a team of perennial losers, there are always some left in the stands at the end of the season who pledge that "next year will be the one." This was the motivation the regime used to rally a weary population: just work a little harder and pull your belt a little tighter—paradise is right around the corner.

Valery believed this as much as any of his classmates. While his superiors just assumed they had done a good job of instilling Communist virtues in him, a few of Sablin's classmates saw something more. One of them later recalled:

> In general, he was very demanding of his comrades—this didn't come from the lockstep ideology of a KOMSOMOL careerist, but from a deep internal conviction. I'll give you an example. We discovered that there was a thief among us cadets. Money began to disappear from our jackets and lockers. We became more careful. But Sablin found a way to catch him, because we suspected it was another cadet. Valery was shocked. You've got to understand; he just couldn't comprehend that a future naval officer could be a thief (much less a head of state)! He considered it a disgrace to be in the same unit and live under the same roof with someone like that. Forgive me if I exaggerate, but I consider him the ideal Soviet man.[11]

So did many others. Upon graduating from Frunze in November 1960 and being commissioned as naval officers, the newly minted lieutenants gave pictures of themselves to each other with comments written on the back of them. Valery's comrades had this to say to him:

"To Valery, who was and always will be with us. Y. Mikhailov."
"To the most upstanding, most principled Valery. Kolenov."
"The things I admire most about you are your principles and your
    honesty. Don't ever change those. A Matyushin."
"I hope very much, Valery, that you'll always keep your bright opti-
    mism about life. G. Rodygin."
"To a fighter for justice. G. Kanevski."
"I hope that you'll be a hero in the world, and uphold the pride of the
    Russian Navy!"[12]

After he was commissioned, Sablin began his naval career as a lieutenant with the Northern Fleet in Severomorsk. He served aboard two destroyers, *Svedushiy* and, later, *Ozhestochenniy*. His first command was of an antiaircraft section (*otdeleniye*), then a division. Like the U.S. Navy, the Soviet Navy divided its shipboard commands into sections and divisions. A section contained roughly ten sailors, while a division had as many as thirty.

On American warships, an enlisted person normally leads a section, while a junior officer commands a division. Jobs that would usually be accomplished by senior enlisted personnel (chief, senior chief, and master chief petty officers) aboard U.S. vessels had to be undertaken by officers on Soviet ships. The Russian naval officer was therefore a specialist and technician foremost, whereas his American counterpart was a generalist and manager first. Some of this difference was driven by necessity, as the large uneducated conscript force of the Soviet Union required that the officers be more technically proficient.

As a result, a Soviet junior officer was paid twenty times as much as a second-year conscript.[13] The pay system was very complex; rank and time in service were the major determinants, and extra money was given for housing and travel. Pilots, submariners, and remotely assigned personnel received more pay due to the unique nature of their service (either very dangerous or very boring). The most important factor in extra pay was position—up to 100 percent more money if the officer was assigned to an important staff or job.[14] An officer's pay was approximately one-third more than that of a Soviet civilian of similar responsibilities.[15] Enlisted conscripts received a salary of three to five rubles per month (approximately four dollars at the official exchange rate in 1975). In addition to greater pay, the Soviet officer was likely to receive an apartment faster than his civilian counterpart. He also got a uniform allowance, and free clothing in the Soviet Union was no small benefit.

Because of this security, 95 percent of the Soviet officer corps stayed in the service until retirement (twenty-five years). This career progression usually included five years at the higher naval schools, the eleven college-level academies throughout the Soviet Union that graduated and commissioned most of the country's naval officers. Time spent on submarines or in remote areas like the Far East counted as double time in service. Since very few officers left the military prior to retirement, the shape of the Soviet officer corps was rectangular rather than triangular as in the U.S. military. In the Soviet Navy there were almost as many senior officers as there were junior officers. There was no "up-and-out" promotion system. Not being selected for command or passed over for promotion did not end a man's career.

Before Sablin could begin his officer-of-the-deck qualifications (allowing him to stand watch on the bridge) or become a division officer, he first had to qualify in his specialty as a third-class, second-class, first-class, and master specialist just like enlisted personnel. In his case, the specialty was navigation. Frunze was the most prestigious naval academy in the country, and the future captains of the Soviet Navy's capital ships learned their seamanship there. When Sablin graduated and eventually moved on to the fleet, his commanders had nothing but the highest praise for him. The skipper of *Ozhestochenniy* even took time out to write Valery's father this letter on 22 January 1965:

Dear Mikhail Petrovich!
On behalf of the wardroom of the ship on which your son, Senior Lieutenant Valery Sablin, serves, I want to thank you as his father for raising such a fine son for the Motherland and the Party. He is a devoted Communist and an exemplary naval officer.
    As a matter of fact, for this period of service, your son had eight commendations from the ship's captain and fleet commander.
    We're proud of Valery, and hold him up as an example to the entire ship's company. His stamina and youthful enthusiasm have

contributed greatly to the ship's combat readiness and strengthened the good order and discipline of the crew. . . .

THIRD RANK CAPTAIN MALAKHOVSKI,
Commander of the *Ozhestochenniy.*[16]

The crucial point in the shipboard officer's career was when he
became an assistant commander (department head), usually at the
rank of captain-lieutenant. A decision had to be made by the ship's
commanding officer to determine if the officer would remain in the
specialist career path or make the lateral move over to the *starpom*
(executive officer) position and the command path.[17] The specialist
would continue to be promoted and serve in staff and shore billets.
In some cases, he would remain aboard the same ship in his specialty
even when he came to outrank the captain. This rank inversion was
commonplace in many commands in the Soviet armed forces and
caused complications in the promotion system as well as lower
morale among some specialists. Engineering and communications/
electronics specialists were not often considered for command, which
left the officers in navigation, antisubmarine warfare, and weapons
divisions with the best chance of being selected. Normally, these officers were given a couple of chances for executive officer (XO) selection before becoming career specialists.

Captain-Lieutenant Sablin reached this point in 1968. During
his service aboard *Ozhestochenniy,* in September 1963, the ship was
transferred to the Black Sea Fleet. It was common for ships to transfer to different fleets depending on the naval command's threat
assessment. In the early 1960s, the Soviets began to build the
nucleus of a Mediterranean squadron, which fell under the responsibility of the Black Sea Fleet. After two years living in Sevastopol
on the Black Sea coast, Valery and his family went back to Severomorsk when *Ozhestochenniy* returned to the Northern Fleet. They
remained there until 1969. It was now time for shore duty, and the
captain of *Ozhestochenniy* reluctantly agreed to send Sablin to the
Lenin Military-Political Academy in Moscow, the training ground
for political officers. This was something Sablin himself had
requested four years earlier, before he had enough command time
or time in grade. By accepting a position at the academy, Sablin was
choosing the specialist path as a *zampolit* rather than the command
path that might eventually give him his own ship.

For all intents and purposes, he was killing his career by doing this, which was why his commander was so reluctant to agree to it. He saw great leadership potential in Valery and felt he would make a fine ship's captain. Normally, *zampolit*s were older officers who had been rejected for command or career political officers who had been chosen for this work early on because of their party credentials and loyalty. For someone to reject a promising command path and choose political work instead was practically unknown. This was especially true of an officer like Sablin, who was a Frunze graduate.[18]

Promotion as a specialist was faster, however, and he would attain the next rank of third rank captain sooner this way. Such considerations were unimportant to Valery, however. He had already demonstrated this in 1963, when his promotion from lieutenant to senior lieutenant was held up for almost a year. It seems that Lieutenant Sablin had decided to write a letter to Nikita Khrushchev himself, criticizing the Communist Party and suggesting that it "needed to rid itself of sycophants and corrupt officials on the take."[19] At the time, he was on temporary duty in Murmansk with the Northern Fleet. Shortly after he wrote the letter, he was called out on the carpet by the Murmansk Party Committee and reprimanded. There was no permanent damage to his career or party membership, but he was scolded for not seeing the big picture and told that the country's leaders were grappling with issues of great complexity. It was the typical condescending answer given by bureaucrats—critics needed to understand how things were at the top, but of course they never could from their lowly positions. The response was an improvement from the one they might have given him in Stalin's time, but the government's patience was not infinite. As it turned out, neither was Valery's.

As he entered the Lenin Military-Political Academy in the summer of 1969, Sablin looked forward to immersing himself in his studies. He needed a distraction, or at least some answers for what had happened the previous summer. In early 1968, Alexander Dubcek, the reform-minded Communist leader of Czechoslovakia, had been inspired by Khrushchev's thaw and modeled his own liberalization policies after it. He called it "socialism with a human face," but most would remember it as the "Prague Spring" after Czechoslovakia's capital city. Many writers and artists who would later achieve international recognition got their first inspiration from the Prague Spring.

Milan Kundera, author of *The Unbearable Lightness of Being,* playwright and future Czech president Vaclav Havel, and film director Milos Forman (*One Flew Over the Cuckoo's Nest*) were all in Prague in 1968. It was an intoxicating time for the Czechs after enduring twenty years of grim Communist rule. Dubcek had loosened the stifling restraints on free speech and commerce, finally giving Czechs the opportunity to speak their minds and do business the way they wanted.

This liberalization was too much for the Russians. On 21 August, Warsaw Pact forces invaded Czechoslovakia. Special KGB troops arrested Dubcek and his entire cabinet. The man who sent in the tanks, Leonid Brezhnev, had delivered a clear signal to everyone on both sides of the Iron Curtain that attempts to liberalize the Communist system would not be tolerated.

Like many Russians, Valery was disturbed by this turn of events. Why should Brezhnev care if Dubcek wanted to reform Czechoslovakia? It was the kind of question that only someone who had grown up believing his own government's propaganda could ask. Sablin's loyal opposition to the regime was beginning to fade, to be replaced by revolutionary fervor. He was even able to provide the date of this transformation—1971, when he was at the Lenin Military-Political Academy. Always a believer in constructive criticism, Sablin suggested a program of social reconstruction (which would be described fifteen years later as perestroika), as well as the professional reorganization of the armed forces. His instructors at the academy were quick to dismiss such idealism (these kinds of things are best left to the party, comrade, not to you). His fellow students in the *zampolit* course could only listen patiently to his musings and then give the traditional Russian shrug with the comment, "*Shto delat?*" "What can you do?"

Brezhnev's rule would have a profound effect on the life of Valery Sablin and, for that matter, on the lives of all Soviet citizens. The thaw Khrushchev had initiated was quickly reversed, and Soviet thought and speech returned to the deep freeze. If Khrushchev's rule would be forever associated with "the thaw," Brezhnev's reign would also be identified by one word: stagnation. Stories about his crudeness and vulgarity became legendary: the social gaffes he made on state visits abroad, the obscene jokes he would tell during official visits aboard warships, jokes that would make the sailors blush. For Sablin, the man who would rule the Soviet Union for eighteen years would become an obsession. All the waste, corruption, and sycophancy that he knew so well from his military service was personified in this one man. It would eventually propel the young naval officer to advocate his overthrow.

The fuel that stoked this fire continued to come from Sablin's political education. His time at the academy was like his time at Frunze—an opportunity to observe his country's development and the philosophical underpinnings of its government. Contrary to what he was seeing around him, Sablin became even more of a fervent Communist. Brezhnev's misrule only drove Sablin deeper into the arms of his revolutionary idols. He wrote down his favorite quotes from each, in something that would come to resemble an atheist's Bible:

From Karl Marx: "The moral state expects its people to be civic-minded, even if they oppose it; there is no law issued by the government that punishes citizens for what they think. Rather, this is the law of one party against another."

Feliks Dzerzhinsky: "We Communists must conduct ourselves in a manner that shows the mass of workers that we are servants of the people, and that we are using the victory of the revolution and the power of the government not for own aims but for the good and happiness of the people."

Alexander Blok: "So many things in life cry out to be done. . . . Don't think about what can't be done, but what should be done; even though it may not be done now or for a long time. This is what gives life meaning."

As the contrast between these socialist ideals and Brezhnev's Russia sharpened, Sablin felt himself betrayed. He felt the Motherland had been betrayed as well—not by Communism but by its custodians. He was certain that if only the true principles of socialism, as outlined by Marx, Dzerzhinsky, Blok, and Lenin, were followed, there would be no more Brezhnevs. That a corrupt totalitarian regime might be the unavoidable consequence of a one-party Communist state seems never to have occurred to him.

Valery's tenure in Moscow was also a time to get reacquainted with his family. In his second year at Frunze in 1958, he had met a young university student in Leningrad, Nina Mikhailovna Chumazova. They first laid eyes on each other at one of the frequent dances that threw young naval cadets together with local university girls.

Nina recalls that it was love at first sight; they danced, and then he walked her home. Before long they were spending every free minute they could together. Leningrad was known as the "Venice of the North" because of its canals, which Peter the Great insisted on building after visiting Amsterdam and admiring that city's use of canals as traffic channels. Strolling along these embankments was a part of life in Leningrad, and Nina and Valery took frequent walks past the Winter Palace, the statue of the Bronze Horseman, and the Peter and Paul Fortress. In winter they would skate at Kirov Stadium and watch movies at the theater on Rebellion Square.

They quickly fell in love and were married two years later. Their wedding picture shows them in one of the great ballrooms of the Frunze Military Academy. In a country that was officially atheist, all marriages had to be performed by the state, and in their case, a naval officer pronounced them man and wife. Valery stood handsome in his dark blue lieutenant's uniform, holding his officer's dagger in one hand and Nina's arm in the other. She wore a knee-length white dress, no veil, and held a bouquet of white carnations. She was a very pretty, petite woman with a beautiful smile. Both looked as young as they were; he was twenty-one and she was twenty-two. For their honeymoon, they took a cruise on the Black Sea.

In September 1962, their one and only son Mikhail (Misha) was born. Since Valery spent much of his time in the fleet at sea, he missed out on most of Misha's early life. In Severomorsk, Nina kept a calendar and crossed out every day that Valery was gone. By New Year's Eve 1966, nearly the entire calendar was marked with Xs.[20] His transfer to Moscow ensured that he would get to spend more time with his family.

He loved being a father and took note of the small details of his son's everyday life as all new parents do. He frequently wrote to his own mother and father, passing on news of their grandson's high temperatures or accidents he suffered. In one letter, Valery told them Misha was "a funny kid. He's always playing with his toys, and it's hard to keep him still because he's so curious about everything around him. That's why when we come to see you on vacation, it will be like another world for him."[21]

By all accounts, Valery and Nina's marriage was a good one. Even Nadezhda Potulnaya, the wife of *Storozhevoy*'s skipper, who had only met the couple once, remarked that "they were made for each other." Nina was as active as Valery and enjoyed the outdoors as much as he did. They hiked up Mount Elbrus in southern Russia, the highest peak in Europe, twice together. She was a native of Leningrad, and like so many others her age, she was marked by the blockade of the city during World War II. This famous siege, during which the Germans surrounded the city for nine hundred days in an effort to starve it to death, ranked high in the annals of Soviet heroism. Russians remain proud of the fact that the city never fell to the Germans, but every one of those nine hundred days was a grueling one for the inhabitants. The city could only be resupplied in the winter, when nearby Lake Ladoga froze over thick enough to support truck convoys. That was the only time the wounded could be evacuated, along with children. Nina was three when she and her mother escaped over the frozen lake to safety on the other side. After the war, with the city liberated, her family returned, and Nina eventually went to college to become a structural engineer.

Valery's parents adored Nina and always looked forward to seeing her when she visited Gorky. They did not meet her until after she and Valery were married; Nina's parents were the only ones at the ceremony. Mikhail and Anna recognized that Nina brought out the best in their son. Valery always had a dry sense of humor and laughter came easily to him; his mother once said, "You only have to listen to Valery's laugh. None of my sons has such a beautiful and happy laugh." Nina took some of the edge off his humor, however, and made it more lighthearted. She was his intellectual equal but had never been very interested in politics, thus providing a welcome distraction to his study of dense Marxist theory. As she later recalled, "Valery was born talking about politics. He spent so much time at the library digging through books." While other couples talked about movies and music, Valery would "enlighten" her about politics, she remembered with a touch of sarcasm.[22]

They had a zest for life that was common to youth, but in Valery's case it was also driven by a strong sense of romanticism, a quality that has always been ambiguous in meaning. Webster's defines "romantic" as that which is "marked by the imaginative or emotional appeal of what is heroic, adventurous, remote, mysterious, or idealized." It is also defined as "having no basis in fact" and "impractical in conception or plan." It is two sides of the same coin, and Sablin struggled to bridge the gap between the two. He was no technocrat, but he realized that he needed some of those skills to be an effective officer.

A romantic may persuade people to do the impossible, but that does not guarantee success. Sablin knew how socialism's martyrs had failed to take this fact into account throughout Russian history. It is probably why he admired Lenin. Here was a man who could both inspire revolution and put it into effect. In his use of Lenin as a role model, Sablin also displayed the romantic's casual disregard of consequences. Lenin's ruthless application of violence and contempt for political opponents left a dangerous legacy for the young Soviet state. If he was expected to lead by example, then the example he left was one of obsessive political intrigue and dangerous power struggles.

As much as Sablin came to despise these qualities in his own government, he would use the same argument they did in persuading the Russian people to put up with their conditions a bit longer—hardship toughened you up and built character. Russians have always had a romantic streak in them, and the call to bear one more burden for the Motherland can be found throughout their history and literature. When Valery's brother Boris (an engineer by profession who was less prone to this romanticism) was transferred to a duty station in Siberia's remote Komi Province, Valery wrote him: "Is it tough out there? If it's easy, that's bad. Hardship is more memorable, and allows you to better appreciate the good things. Then you really feel like you've accomplished something. That's why I wish you difficulty—not so your body will moan and your spirit will ache, but because under these conditions your spirit will keep its vigor, enthusiasm, romance, humor, and zest for life."[23]

Russians have also had a strong sense of antimaterialism, a curious attribute in a country that has suffered so much poverty. Anyone who has seen the breathtaking opulence of the Winter Palace in Petersburg or the Summer Palace at Peterhof has probably asked himself, "All this for one family?" These were built when the majority of Russians still lived in serfdom, a condition similar to slavery. It is not difficult to understand how the seeds of revolution were constantly sprouting throughout the country; the contrast between serfdom and royalty provided fertile ground. In the conviction that money is not everything, the Russians are hardly alone—Christianity and Judaism both make their case against materialism, and greed is one of the seven deadly sins. Russian literature is unique, however, in its sensitivity to the corrosive effects greed and avarice can have upon people.

This is also true of that other great theme in Russian literature, redemption. Writers from Gogol to Dostoyevski paid eloquent homage to a person's ability to redeem himself in the eyes of God and his fellow men. This was a core element of Valery Sablin's personality, the ability to forgive himself and others for past failures and in so doing renew their own virtue. In his classic nineteenth-century novel on the subject, *Dead Souls,* Nikolai Gogol explores the redemption of his main character Chichikov, a greedy and cynical businessman who defrauds his clients and his government to enrich himself. He is eventually caught and, as always too late, realizes his mistakes and begs forgiveness for them. The governor general of the province where the crimes have taken place sentences him to jail. In the course of his investigation, the governor uncovers a web of dishonesty and corruption in his administration. Moved by Chichikov's honesty, the governor assembles all of his officials together and admits to them that he bears as much responsibility as they do for this moral breakdown. He then asks them for their help in making things right:

> Now the man in whose hands the fate of many lies and whom no supplications were able to move, this very man now flings himself at your feet and entreats you all. Everything will be forgotten, erased, forgiven; I will myself be the intercessor for you all if you do as I ask. This is what I ask: I know that it is impossible to eradicate injustice by any means, by any threats, by any punishments: it is too deeply rooted. . . . But I must now—at a decisive and sacred moment when we all have to do our best to save our country, when every citizen bears everything and makes every sacrifice—I must now appeal to those at least who still have a Russian heart beating in their breasts and who still know the meaning of the word honor.[24]

This appeal to a mystical soul that could not be tainted by earthly possessions was the essence of Russian antimaterialism. Its patron saint was Leo Tolstoy, author of *War and Peace* and *Anna Karenina.* For the last two decades of his life, Tolstoy gave up his vast estate and lived as a penniless farmer. His writings influenced Gandhi's political philosophy and the Zionist movement in Palestine, both of which dismissed material comfort for higher spiritual goals. Valery Sablin was also a fan of Tolstoy, inspired by both his personal example and his call for social justice. Valery once told friends that "people's happiness cannot be found in palaces or fine crystal."

Communism was not necessarily antimaterialist in the sense that it rejected temporal pleasures, but it did equate capitalism with greed and decadence. There was an element of moral Puritanism in Communist Russia that the country's leaders used to set the Soviet Union apart from the West. By rejecting the capitalist world's corrupt material consumption, they boasted, they were further proving Communism's superiority. Sablin's faith in its stated aim of redistributing wealth for the common good never wavered. His problem was with the tyranny of one-party rule. He was confident that Communism would come out on top even in a pluralistic society. His analysis of Marx convinced him that this was inevitable.

Like her husband, Nina had a sharp analytical mind, but as an engineer she preferred to confine her analysis to problems of construction. She realized, probably better than her husband, that there was something unnatural about applying scientific laws to human behavior, as Marx had. People were not steel girders that could be bent and shaped to serve someone else's purpose; they had properties and qualities of their own that could not be measured in scientific terms. They were not always guided by logic and rational thought. In a word, they were human, and by their very nature unpredictable.

Nina had warned Valery on several occasions not to get too carried away by his politics. She saw a latent fanaticism in her husband that worried her. He would talk politics with anyone, even total strangers such as cab drivers. Nina understood how dangerous this was—she had no illusions about living in a totalitarian society—and begged him to be more discreet. In 1963, he had discussed his letter to Khrushchev with her beforehand. At the time, she had grudgingly given her support to the idea, but after the KGB visited both of them in Severomorsk afterward, she became even more apprehensive of his political appetites.[25]

Sablin's indiscretion caught up with him again in the summer of 1968. He was on leave visiting his parents in Gorky and ran into an old friend from Frunze, Sergei Rodionov. They met at a restaurant and talked for hours, about everything. They also argued over politics, and Sablin poured his heart out to him, revealing his true motivation for becoming a *zampolit:* to make a new revolution within the Soviet state. After their meeting, Rodionov went home and wrote a letter to the Northern Fleet political department, claiming Sablin wanted to overthrow the government.

The Russian word for "stool pigeon" is *stukach,* and even in a society that encouraged people to inform on one another it was an undesirable label. Twelve days before he was due to be transferred from the Northern Fleet to Moscow, Sablin was once again called onto the carpet. A member of the Fleet Special Branch asked him several detailed questions about his political views. Rodionov had a reputation in the KGB as a somewhat erratic informant, however, seeing counterrevolutionaries behind every tree, so his letter was not given great weight. After the interview, the Special Branch sent Rodionov's letter to Rear Admiral Sizov, the Northern Fleet chief of staff. Sizov filed it away in an archive, obviously unmoved by its contents and probably annoyed that a *stukach* had ratted on one of his officers. Nothing happened to Captain-Lieutenant Sablin and he was transferred to his new assignment.

Part of the course work at the Lenin Military-Political Academy consisted of visits to factories and shops around Moscow, where the aspiring *zampolits* would hone their public speaking and persuasion skills by lecturing to workers. Like soldiers and sailors in the armed forces, factory workers, the very proletariat for whom Lenin had launched his revolution, had to undergo political instruction. Party officials would go before them and read off the new Five Year Plan— quotas assigned by the central government to industry, telling factories how much of what they would produce. As he made his rounds to factories and shop floors across the city, Sablin saw how the party's rhetoric fell on deaf ears. He called for more sacrifice and more political zeal, but these men and women had no more to give. Communism had squeezed every drop of effort from them, and they did not have much to show for it.

In spite of these experiences, which could not have been very motivating for a budding political officer, the four years in Moscow were good ones for Valery, Nina, and Misha. They were only a short train ride away from Valery's parents in Gorky and made the trip often. The elder Sablins had retired there but often spent weekends and holidays at their country home (*dacha*) just outside of Gorky in the village of Belyn. They enjoyed one another's company. Valery, Nina, and Misha would all take turns writing notes that they would leave around the house for Valery's parents to find later on. Mikhail

Sablin would go out to his woodshed to get a shovel and find a note taped to it from his son that read "Take it easy, old-timer! Don't overdo it!" Anna would open up a book she was reading and see a note from her daughter-in-law and grandson: "Don't forget to put on your glasses!" It kept them laughing for the rest of the week, providing many of those poignant memories that enrich a family's time together.

Valery was especially close to his father, and he was not above chastising Mikhail Sablin as if he were one of his sailors, particularly when it came to his health. It had been deteriorating for several years, and in a letter to his parents, Valery implored his father to take better care of himself: "It's too bad that Papa has gone off his diet in anticipation of our arrival and aggravated his liver. It's even worse that I've picked up a general disregard for my own health from him, and Misha might pick this up from me, and so on and so forth. That's why Papa's got to set the example and really try to improve his health and take care of himself."[26]

Valery's older brother Boris was also living in Gorky at the time. He was serving as an engineering officer in the army and had just finished a course at the Polytechnic Institute there. Boris made frequent trips to Moscow to visit his brother and sister-in-law. He knew about Valery's voracious reading habits but was nonetheless shocked to find practically every square inch of their Moscow apartment covered with books, magazines, and newspapers—he subscribed to more than fifty a year.

Valery was also a talented artist, and like many amateur artists, he drew to take his mind off his job. Going through his sketches, one notices how his skill and eye for detail progressed over time. The first pen-and-ink drawings from his teenage years were good but somewhat awkward and crude. By the time he was at Frunze, however, his pencil sketches had improved remarkably; one of a Cuban girl, presumably from Castro's rebel army of the day, was superb. Always the political animal, he drew several profiles of Lenin and even an abstract pen-and-ink picture of Karl Marx with his wife, which he gave to Nina for her thirtieth birthday.

His thirst for knowledge was insatiable. Among his subscriptions were publications on politics, economics, science, technology, culture—no subject escaped his interest. He would talk with his brothers for hours about everything under the sun, offering up provocative questions such as "Why are we worse off in so many areas than China?" or "What good does it do to treat the people like one monolithic mass?"

Boris noticed that a special place in his brother's library had been set aside for literature on Lieutenant Schmidt, the mutinous officer of the old Russian Imperial Navy who was executed after leading a revolt against the tsarist regime in 1905. Valery collected newspaper articles, pictures, portraits—anything about the "Red Lieutenant" that he could get his hands on. He began to draw parallels between himself and the rebellious officer who had become a martyr to the socialist cause.

After eight years in the cultural isolation of Polyarniy on the Barents Sea and Sevastopol on the Black Sea, Nina and Valery soaked up the attractions of Moscow. Although they had small-town roots, both were big-city lovers at heart. They took long walks around Moscow, their favorite excursions being along Pirogovskaya Street and the Novodevichniy Monastery. They visited theaters and saw the symphony perform *Spartacus* at the Bolshoi. Misha remembers his father taking him on a visit to the Museum of Paleontology, sparking a lifelong interest in biology that has led him to his current job as a paleontologist with the Russian Academy of Sciences. Valery also took Misha to hockey games, and during the world championships in 1970, he somehow acquired three pucks with the championship emblem stamped on them for his son. "The navy uniform helped!" he told Nina when explaining how he got them.[27]

One thing the uniform could not help with was filling his mother's prescriptions. Anna Sablina was suffering from the early effects of Parkinson's disease, and Valery went from pharmacy to pharmacy in search of the necessary medicine, but it was usually an exercise in futility. It might have passed through his mind that these drugs were easily available to the *nomenklatura,* the senior officials of the Communist Party who shopped in separate stores and received special privileges in everything ranging from medicine to automobiles. As a midgrade Soviet naval officer, Sablin was making more than his civilian counterparts, so he could afford to send money to his parents, which he did from time to time. As a political officer and Communist Party member, he was considered to be part of the elite of Soviet society, in the upper middle class, so to speak. The *nomenklatura,* however, were the upper crust, the senior army officers, politicians, diplomats, and bureaucrats who ruled the country. They might as well have been royalty, Sablin thought. The new tsars.

Sablin was never one to go through the motions, but he did at the Lenin Military-Political Academy. He felt that if he pushed the envelope too much there, he would be thrown out. Rodionov's letter had made him more cautious. As with his previous run-in with the party over his letter to Nikita Khrushchev in 1963, Sablin knew when to hold back. It was probably at this point that his thinking took the turn that would lead him directly to the events of 8 November 1975. He had tried to do it the party's way and exercise loyal opposition, all to no avail. Like so many others, he had been inspired by Khrushchev's attempts to loosen the ideological straitjacket and breath some fresh air into the Communist Party. Now Khrushchev was gone. It might have occurred to Sablin in these years of stagnation that the system was not reformable because it tolerated no opposition that could do the reforming. But more and more fingers were being pointed in the direction of Leonid Brezhnev and his corrupt regime. Who else could be at fault?

His family began to notice his disillusionment. The gap between an idealist's dreams and what he eventually has to accept in adulthood varies from individual to individual. Sometimes the dreams become reality, but it can take years to achieve personal goals. Sablin wished little for himself. As a man who was pursuing a career he had always wanted, with a wife and son he loved, he had all he needed. What he wanted was something on the grand scale—a free society. It was the pot of gold at the end of the Communist rainbow that had eluded two generations of Soviet citizens. It was a lofty goal and probably never within reach.

Not surprisingly, when someone's reach exceeds their grasp, disillusionment is the result. His younger brother Nikolai recalled how upset Valery was when he saw the course material he would be studying at the academy. He had hoped to read some of the same contraband literature that he had come across during the Khrushchev era. Instead, it was the same old Communist propaganda. "He once complained bitterly to me that all his hopes had been dashed," Nikolai said. "He thought that students at the Academy would be given more privileged access to information and books. He was really upset that even there, students got an education based on the same stereotypes as everyone else."[28]

His classmates noticed this disillusionment as well, but there was a fair amount of it to go around at the academy. One of his old classmates from Frunze, Gennadi Kanevski, recalled of the Brezhnev era, "There was a lot of dissatisfaction at that time, especially among the military. Everyone was irritated by the government's love of self-indulgence, flattery, and high living. Military men looked upon this as an insult."[29]

No one took it more personally than Sablin. In those days, Soviet Russia celebrated New Year's Day rather than Christmas; that is when the "New Year's trees" went up and gifts were exchanged. For the new year of 1970, Valery received a copy of Karl Marx's book *Das Kapital* (Capital) from his classmates. This was Marx's two-volume, thousand-page explanation of the philosophy that would later bear his name. Its dense, long-winded prose is tough reading for anyone, even a Russian political officer, but Sablin read it cover to cover, underlining countless passages and making numerous notes along the margin. He knew it so well that he could quote passage and verse—his recall was amazing—and tell what page it came from. That is probably what set Sablin apart from everyone else—his genuine belief in Marx's vision of a perfectible society. Kanevski would remember this as the one point on which he and his old classmate could never agree: "People don't live like that—they don't do what pages seventeen to thirty-seven say they're going to do, or any other pages for that matter. They just live."[30]

Sablin was so confident in Communism as the wave of the future that he could see no reason why the Soviet government should suppress criticism of it. A country that really believed in its system should be confident and open about it, regardless of the flaws. He felt this was especially true of *zampolits*, the official cheerleaders of Communism. If they could not be trusted to keep their ideological faith in the face of anti-Communist literature, then who could in this society?

Sablin had come across some of this anti-Communist literature at Frunze, courtesy of his cousin Tamara. Far from seeing it as a threat, he felt it instrumental to let Russia's rich literary tradition flourish, especially under Soviet rule. One of his favorite writers was Yevgeniy Yevtushenko, a controversial poet of the time who was revered by Russian youth and referred to simply as "the Poet." He was one of Khrushchev's favorites, which is why he had been allowed to publish his poetry in spite of its occasional anti-Soviet tone. He was allowed to travel abroad, especially in the West, and received wide international acclaim. Yevtushenko was constantly walking a tightrope during the Brezhnev era, however, between criticism and support of the Soviet regime. He would publish something attacking the government one minute, then write a poem praising the party's leadership and glorifying the opening of a new hydroelectric dam the next.

Yevtushenko never suffered the same fate as his colleague Alexander Solzhenitsyn, who was arrested and exiled after winning the 1970 Nobel Prize for Literature with his landmark book *The Gulag Archipelago*. Valery actually acquired the poet's address and phone number and called him in Moscow, but Yevtushenko refused to meet with him. If he had, he might have learned a few things from his fan. As he was walking his literary tightrope, his countryman was putting his life on the line and making a statement no poem could ever match.

As he pored over the great works of Communist literature, Valery was struck by the fact that all his heroes were men of action. Had Lenin not returned to Russia in 1917 after the tsar was overthrown, to lead a Bolshevik Party that had been scattered and hounded to all corners of the country, their revolution would not have succeeded. Sablin was certain that Lenin would have been disappointed in the Soviet Union of the late 1960s. How could his ideals be resurrected and his legacy revitalized? All these thoughts were much on Valery's mind as he finished his four-year course at the Lenin Military-Political Academy in June 1973. He had been promoted to third rank captain in December 1971 and graduated from the academy with distinction. His name was even carved into the white marble roll of honor there.

Three years later, after he had matched his idealism with action, his name would be chiseled out of that marble, an attempt to forever relegate it and the man behind it to obscurity. In a letter to Nina, he recalled his transformation from a loyal party man to an instrument of its destruction:

> I have not always been a revolutionary. For a long time I was a liberal, satisfied that just a little change here and there was all that was necessary to fix our system; satisfied that just one or two articles exposing its deficiencies needed to be written; satisfied that

just one or two leaders needed to be replaced, and then justice and honesty would prevail in our society.

That was until 1971. My studies at the academy finally convinced me that the armor of the state and party machine is so thick that even direct hits on it won't make a dent and are ultimately futile.

This machine needs to be broken from within, using its own armor against it.[31]

Chapter 2

THE CAUSE

On 22 May 1972, Richard Nixon became the first serving American president to visit the Soviet Union. He went there to sign the Strategic Arms Limitation Treaty (SALT) with Leonid Brezhnev. Its name was accurate—it did limit American and Russian production of antiballistic missiles and missile launchers—but that was about it. By the end of the 1960s, the United States and the Soviet Union were, between them, spending $50 million a day on nuclear arms.[1] It was an intolerable burden for both sides, but especially for the Soviets, who did not have as efficient an industrial base. The SALT agreement did not mandate any cuts in nuclear arsenals, and, in fact, by the end of the 1970s, the United States and Russia would add another twelve thousand warheads to those arsenals.

Meager though SALT was, it was at least a first step. It ushered in the era of détente, the relaxation of tensions between the superpowers. Nixon and Brezhnev both recognized that their countries had enough firepower to destroy the world several times over. Even if neither side intended to launch a first strike, the more nuclear weapons they put into service, the greater the risk of an accident.

With the response time to a nuclear attack measured in minutes, there was not much time for American or Russian missile crews to launch their weapons. It became critical to ensure that some part of the nuclear strike force survive a first attack in order to preserve the capability to retaliate. Atomic missiles were put aboard submarines and aircraft that sailed and flew twenty-four hours a day, seven days a week, in constant vigilance. It was Mutually Assured Destruction

(MAD), and if both sides understood that neither could win with a massive first strike, it acted as a deterrent. Nevertheless, this deterrent was built on a hair trigger. It was a very dangerous time, and the need to relieve pressure on this hair-trigger was what inspired détente.

But the Cold War was not over—not by a long shot. In August 1975, the Soviet Union and thirty-four other nations met in Helsinki, Finland, for a Conference on Security and Cooperation in Europe. The final act of the conference was to sign the Helsinki Accords, which set forth basic human rights that all signatories were pledged to honor, including "the freedom of thought, conscience, religion or belief, for all without distinction as to race, sex, language, or religion."

When he affixed his signature to this document, Leonid Brezhnev probably had no idea how much trouble it would cause him. Over the next several years, the subject of human rights within the Soviet Union would receive international attention and shine a spotlight on the fate of Soviet dissidents who opposed Brezhnev's regime.

One of those dissidents, Anatoly Sharansky, would later credit the Helsinki Accords with focusing attention on the plight of "refuseniks"—Soviet citizens, often Jewish, who were attempting to leave the country but were refused exit visas by the government. Sharansky, himself a refusenik, was sentenced to thirteen years in prison in 1978 for espionage and treason. He said Brezhnev and the Soviet leadership regarded the accords as "just a piece of paper," but Sharansky and his colleagues viewed them as standards to which the West could hold the Soviet Union accountable.

This was easier said than done. Soviet foreign minister Andrei Gromyko convinced the Politburo to approve the Helsinki Accords only when he pointed out that no one could interfere in Soviet domestic policy, so they would not have to worry about honoring it. Thus the Russians agreed to it in principle but not in practice. Gromyko did indeed refer to the treaty as "just a piece of paper," a cynicism toward binding legal agreements that was common in the Politburo. In fact, any accountability of political leaders to the law was beyond the understanding of the men in the Kremlin. Anatoly Dobrynin, the longtime Soviet ambassador to Washington, recalled the reaction of the Soviet leadership to President Nixon's resignation from office in 1974 over the Watergate scandal. The Politburo could not believe that the most powerful man in the Western world had been removed from power by legal means. They simply could not understand how Nixon was forced to resign for stealing "some silly documents."[2]

In keeping with the old saying, "A fish rots from the head down," this cynicism made its way through Soviet society with a vengeance under Brezhnev. Communist ideology had overstayed its welcome; living standards were low, basic housing was in short supply, and consumer goods production was being sacrificed to higher spending on defense. Russians are famous for their endurance in the face of adversity, and this trait often manifested itself in their equally famous gallows humor. A popular joke of the Brezhnev era had a man calling an electrician to fix a malfunctioning circuit in his apartment. The electrician tells him the earliest possible date he can come to fix the man's circuit is exactly one year from today. "Will that be in the morning or the afternoon?" the man asks. "What difference does it make?" replies the electrician. The man responds, "Because the plumber is coming in the morning."

As the propaganda war continued unabated, Soviet techniques became ever more sophisticated. One émigré recalled that when reading domestic news reports, Soviet announcers spoke with confident, lighthearted voices. When it came time to read the international news, however, specifically from the United States, their tone of voice changed, becoming grimmer and more serious. News from the United States frequently included reports of natural disasters and social ills, painting the picture of a country "where all black people are beaten, all Indians are kept on reservations, and hurricanes are always raging."[3] When it came to promoting the cause, the Soviet government spared no effort.

The cause to which Third Rank Captain Sablin was so dedicated had a long and violent history. Its modern incarnation began in the early half of the nineteenth century, when a group of noblemen petitioned Tsar Nicholas I for some limits to his autocratic powers. Nicholas refused, and on 14 December 1825, the noblemen marched into Senate Square in St. Petersburg to protest his refusal. These "Decembrists" were arrested and immediately executed, earning a place on the long list of Russia's martyrs.

Russian history, like that of many countries, has been characterized by frequent struggles between a strong central authority wedded to the status quo and a small group of reformers interested in freeing their country from those authoritarian bonds. It routinely has been Russia's misfortune that by the time the authorities have recognized the need for change, the country was already in the grip of violent forces. In March 1881, revolutionaries assassinated Tsar Alexander II. Six years later, five university students tried to assassinate his son, Tsar Alexander III. They failed and were captured and executed in St. Petersburg. Among them was the older brother of Vladimir Ilyich Ulyanov. The younger Ulyanov would earn his own revolutionary pedigree and take on the pseudonym of Lenin. Oddly enough, one of the other pseudonyms Lenin would use over his career was Sablin.

In the years before World War I, Russia was an empire seething with political intrigue, especially after the 1905 revolution. Lenin was by then a committed Marxist. He did not style himself as a "man of the people" and, in fact, held most Russians in low regard. He was convinced they were apathetic, lazy, and would rather accept the status quo than actively change their condition. Marxism appealed to Lenin because Marx believed this as well, counting on a vanguard of revolutionaries to educate and radicalize the proletariat (urban factory workers). Lenin called this "democratic centralism" and believed he was perfectly suited to the role of revolutionary: "In times of revolution it is not enough to ascertain the 'will of the majority'— no, one must be stronger at the decisive moment in the decisive place and win. Beginning with the medieval 'peasant war' in Germany . . . until 1905, we see countless instances of how the better-organized, more conscious, better-armed minority imposed its will on the majority and conquered it."[4]

Lenin intended to do just that. He was joined by a dedicated band of followers, most of whom had spent time in prison or exile. There were Lev Bronstein, a.k.a. Leon Trotsky, and Josef Djugashvili, a.k.a. Josef Stalin, both of whom followed the underground tradition of adopting revolutionary names. The Social Democratic Party that Lenin joined in 1895 had split into two factions: the Bolsheviks ("those in the majority") and the Mensheviks ("those in the minority"). In truth, the two had the same number of members, but the Bolsheviks were far more committed to violence, both for the sake of the revolution and for keeping their movement solvent. They financed their bombing and assassination operations through bank robberies and counterfeiting.

Lenin's ruthless measures and contempt for the people would not bode well for Russia. Nonetheless, Sablin remained a great admirer. While anti-Communist eyes read with alarm about a better-armed minority imposing its will on the majority and conquering it, Sablin saw Lenin's pragmatism. While liberals looked with horror upon Lenin's belief in Communist one-party rule, Sablin viewed it as a necessary measure for the only party that really had the interests of the people in mind. While others were appalled by the Communists' bloodthirstiness, Sablin saw violence as an unsavory but necessary tool. Revolution was, after all, a dirty business.

There were actually two revolutions in Russia in 1917, the one in February that dethroned the tsar and the one in October that brought Lenin's Bolsheviks to power. In those days, Russia operated on the Gregorian calendar, while the rest of the world used the Julian calendar. The Gregorian was two weeks off the Julian, so February and October in Russia were March and November in the rest of the world. When the Soviet Union adopted the Julian calendar in 1921, the October Revolution came to be celebrated on 7 November.

This celebration, which had brought the crew of *Storozhevoy* to Riga, commemorated the day Lenin's Bolsheviks seized power in St. Petersburg. His ruthlessness had advantages, and in the Communist prism through which Valery Sablin saw the world, it was these advantages that he came to admire. One of them was speed. When Lenin moved, he moved fast. He judged most of his fellow socialists to be intellectuals who talked a lot but would not act because they were terrified of responsibility—"vegetarian tigers," as they were often called. It was this emphasis on action that so preoccupied *Storozhevoy*'s political officer. If you did not act on your beliefs, what good were you?

After seizing power in St. Petersburg (its name was changed to Petrograd) in October 1917, Vladimir Lenin and the Bolsheviks spent 1918 consolidating their power throughout the country. As more of their rivals discovered that the Bolsheviks intended to become the only political party in Russia, their opposition moved from parliamentary debate to armed resistance. If they doubted what Lenin and his colleagues had in store for them, Grigori Zinoviev, the Bolshevik leader in Petrograd, dropped a hint of it in a public speech in 1919 when he said, "We must carry along with us ninety million out of the one hundred million Soviet Russian population. As for the rest, we have nothing to say to them. They must be annihilated."[5]

Bad news if you were one of the ten million. But who would decide which people belonged in this group? By framing their position this way, the Bolsheviks were putting Russia and the world on notice that they were using different language now. Political opponents had become mortal enemies. Instead of debating them, they would destroy them, politically and physically.

It is difficult to re-create the terror the Russian Revolution caused in ruling circles around the world, especially in Europe. The rich and powerful had much to lose should the red flag fly over their capitals, and at the end of World War I, revolution stalked many of Europe's cities. German sailors in the port of Kiel mutinied and set up their own soviet (council) like their counterparts in Russia. Hungarian Communists under Bela Kun briefly established their own revolutionary government in Budapest.

The very fabric of the old order was unraveling. Centuries-old monarchies had fallen in Russia, Austria, and Germany, and the Ottoman Empire, the last vestige of the old Roman Empire, collapsed in 1918. The hardened veterans of disbanded armies were returning to civilian life and distorting postwar politics everywhere. In Germany, they joined private armies and took up arms against one other in Berlin and Munich, fighting for a return to monarchy or for a Soviet Germany or just because fighting was all they knew. In Britain, returning veterans were recruited to fight IRA gunmen, and the heavy-handed tactics of these "Tans" (so known for the color of their uniforms) stoked the fires of rebellion for generations of Irish Republicans.

In Russia, soldiers returned from four years of war with a foreign enemy only to face another three years of war among themselves. The odds were stacked heavily against Lenin and his Bolsheviks (who changed their name to Communists in 1918). Fortunately for them, they had a brilliant organizer in Leon Trotsky. Threatening to shoot any soldier who retreated, Trotsky rallied the Red Army to victory against its numerically superior but disorganized foes. One of his cavalrymen was Peter Sablin, grandfather to Valery and three-time recipient of the Order of the Red Banner. Valery's other grandfather, Vasily Buchnev, was at that time a sailor in the Baltic Fleet. He was stationed at the Kronstadt Naval Base in St. Petersburg when it rose up against Lenin's party in 1921.

The Communists eventually gained the upper hand in the civil war and controlled most of Russia by 1921. Their success came at a terrible price, however, not only in lives but also in the precedent set by the young Communist government. Revolution was nothing new in history, but the Bolshevik version was the most radical the world had ever seen. It combined the bloody anarchy of the French Revolution with a completely new ideology—one that was openly atheist, intolerant of opposition, and dependent on class warfare for its success. In its opinion that the state had the right to dictate the thoughts and beliefs of its citizenry, Soviet Russia qualified as a dictatorship. In its unrelenting efforts to influence these citizens in every sphere of their personal and professional lives, it also became the first modern totalitarian state. Its reliance on violence to achieve its public policy aims became addictive, and like any narcotic, to abandon it would lead to withdrawal syndrome. The Soviet state began to exhibit symptoms of an addict at an early stage: paranoia and a pathologic mistrust of opponents and supporters alike. Naturally, these were not the lessons any *zampolit* would teach his men, and Valery Sablin was no exception. He fervently believed in the official Soviet version of the revolution: "The victory of the Great October Socialist Revolution was a triumph of Marxism-Leninism and the defining event of the twentieth century that changed the course of human history. The revolution saved our Motherland from an impending national catastrophe and pulled it from the depths of a world imperialist war. It put the country on a path of independent development, ending political, national and class oppression, and securing genuine freedom and democracy for the working classes. It also created the conditions for comprehensive socioeconomic and cultural progress for the nation, thereby enhancing its power."[6]

The party line was that the civil war was a "war of the workers and peasants of Soviet Russia, under the leadership of the Communist Party, against the combined forces of international imperialism and internal counterrevolutionaries, with the goal of defending the world's first socialist state."[7] In a country that had been perpetually threatened with invasion from the Far East, Central Asia, and Europe, this "us-against-the-world" mentality was used to great effect by the Communists. If the Russian people were kept on constant watch for external and internal enemies, it would distract them from the party's failures. This also allowed the Soviet leadership a convenient excuse to blame those failures on a host of enemies bent on the destruction of the world's first socialist state.

For someone who had been born and raised among the Communist elite, Sablin was remarkably immune to xenophobia. His letters and statements barely mention the "imperialist West" or "counterrevolutionary enemies." This probably had more to do with Sablin's personality than anything else. Although a thoughtful and contemplative man, he was not prone to agonizing over decisions. He looked upon knowledge as a guide that took you wherever it led, not as a reinforcement to a predetermined conclusion. He also held a strong sense of personal responsibility, which is ultimately what separated him from his colleagues. If you wore the uniform of a Soviet officer and carried the card of a Communist Party member, those privileges meant you also shouldered more responsibility than your average countryman. It meant you could not bury your head in the sand and pretend you had no control over your life or actions.

Sablin's convictions had kept him from the jaded cynicism so common to his peers. He was also assisted by generous reserves of compassion, which allowed him to discount the cynicism of others as a reaction to a government that had been commandeered by corrupt party officials. This notion of a good system in the hands of bad people was probably his ideological life preserver. It was too much to condemn it all, to say that the system and the party made people worse than they should have been. His compassion was evident in a letter he sent to his parents about one of his sailors:

> My service is going well. I've grown accustomed to the ship and the crew. Morale is high—even their political officer can tell. I love talking to the men about their lives before the navy. They love recalling those times, and I already know a lot about them—details both small and large.
>
> Yesterday, I had a conversation with one of them, Smirnov. He's from a town in the Kalinin region, and as a boy he worked as a stable hand. When you listen to him, it's like reading a book on life as a peasant. . . . These sailors are very interesting! Cousin Tamara was wrong when she complained about the ignorance of the peasantry. It's true that the majority of them don't have more than a fourth-grade education and they don't know a lot of things, but pound-for-pound I think they're better people than the urban intelligentsia. Well, I'll tell you more about it when I get home. Exactly one month left.[8]

The fact that Lenin would most likely have viewed Seaman Smirnov as nothing more than a tool to use as the party saw fit was an alien concept to Sablin. Such depersonalization was common in totalitarian societies, but not to Sablin. His instincts were to treat the crewmen as individuals. He felt that as their leader, it was his duty to promote and protect their interests.

One of the most salient weaknesses of Soviet leadership was the unpredictable power struggle that resulted when a leader died. This first became apparent with Lenin's death in 1924. Winston Churchill would call Lenin's birth the Russian people's greatest misfortune, and his death, because of the turmoil it caused, their next greatest. There were no elections in Communist Russia, but Lenin had made it clear in a kind of political last will and testament that he did not trust Josef Stalin and wanted to remove him from the party leadership.

There were few checks and balances in the government Lenin had created, however, and shortly after he died, Stalin and Trotsky began to square off against each other in a fight to the death for leadership of the Soviet state. Stalin had not distinguished himself in matters of organization, like Trotsky, or in Marxist philosophy, like Nikolai Bukharin, but he was very shrewd when it came to acquiring and maintaining power. This may be why Lenin never completely trusted him. Stalin had great self-control that masked a very cruel temperament. His rivalry with Trotsky, which Lenin spoke of in his testament, became legendary because of the personal hatred that fueled it. Stalin was jealous of Trotsky's success, and Trotsky mocked Stalin's lack of education and mediocre party record.

Both of these men were extremely ruthless, but it was a telling indication of just how ruthless Stalin was when he outmaneuvered Trotsky for the leadership of the Communist Party, eventually hounding him into exile in 1929. Then, eleven years later, in a disturbing example of how he neither forgave nor forgot, Stalin had one of his agents assassinate Trotsky in Mexico City by smashing his head with an ice pick.

Throughout the 1920s, Stalin formed alliances with colleagues to destroy his political rivals and then turned on those colleagues by allying himself with others. After each purge, Stalin would replace key positions in the Politburo and government with his own men. Once securely in power, Stalin set the Soviet Union on a crash course of industrialization. Between 1929 and 1932, 12.5 million Soviet citizens entered the industrial sector. Two-thirds of them came from the countryside, however, and were driven to find work in the city by the horrible famine that afflicted the countryside between 1930 and 1933. Stalin had required all farmers to give up their personal landholdings and work on vast collective farms, which sold their crops to the government at a fixed price. All free enterprise, including private land ownership and the sale of grain surpluses on the open market, came to a halt.

This initiative was opened by a propaganda campaign against the *kulaks* (*kulak,* Russian for "fist," was at the time slang for a rich farmer). The term was thrown around indiscriminately in the early 1930s and could apply to anybody who owned some livestock or had a larger house than his neighbors. This class warfare was inspired and instigated by the Soviet secret police, the Cheka. Along with the forced collectivization of the nation's farms, it sent the countryside into chaos, and there was deep and bitter opposition among the rural population to these decrees coming from the central government in Moscow.

The greatest toll, of course, was the human one. In addition to famine, the Cheka's punitive war against the *kulaks,* or anyone they deemed "rich," "counterrevolutionary," or "bourgeois," sent millions to an early death or imprisonment in Siberia. For a time, there was active resistance to this collectivization, with farmers burning their crops rather than giving them up to the Soviet government. Contributing to the surreal nature of this landscape was Stalin's campaign in the mid-1930s to blame the failures of collectivization on foreign agents and domestic traitors. His purges of the late 1930s affected every walk of Soviet life. Stalin settled longstanding scores he had kept with the Bolshevik "Old Guard" from the revolution. His terror also led to a frenzy of false denunciations, show trials, and forced confessions that weakened Soviet society to a degree that no external enemy could have.

No full accounting of the death toll in the Soviet Union from this period will ever be known. The KGB destroyed many government records, and many documents are inaccurate because people simply could not keep track of so many dead. Historian Robert Conquest has probably carried out the most detailed count. He puts the death toll from famine between 1930 and 1937 at eleven million, along with three and a half million who were arrested in this period but later died in concentration camps.[9]

The Sablin family, as city dwellers and party members in good standing, were largely unaffected by this devastation in the countryside, as Stalin had made sure that the cities and the armed forces got enough to eat. Mikhail Sablin was commissioned as a naval officer in the late 1930s. In 1939, the family lived on the naval base at Vasielevski Island in Leningrad, where Valery was born that year. Mikhail was too junior in rank to be caught up in the maelstrom of political purges that cut through the ranks of the Soviet officer corps at the time. On the contrary, he and his peers benefited from the open command slots left by their executed and imprisoned superiors and were quickly promoted into them.

Then came the German invasion of 1941, and these young officers, faced with the gravest threat to their country in over a century, realized just how seriously their security had been imperiled by Stalin's purges. They fought bravely, but so many of them would die in the war that it would actually produce a sort of "lost generation." An example of this occurred when Mikhail Gorbachev came to power in 1985. He was born in 1931, but his three predecessors, Konstantin Chernenko, Yuri Andropov, and Leonid Brezhnev, had been born in 1911, 1914, and 1906, respectively. There were no Soviet leaders from the intervening generation because most of them had been killed. They suffered the full force of the triple tragedy—collectivization, the purges, and the war.

Mikhail Sablin was on duty with the Northern Fleet in 1941 and spent the war years on its staff in Polyarniy. By all accounts he was a model officer, admired for his competence, modesty, and high sense of personal honor. They would later say the same thing of his son. While the elder Sablin was organizing convoys that brought U.S. and British military aid to ports in northern Russia, a gargantuan struggle was raging far to the south of Polyarniy. Hitler's armies came within a hair's breadth of capturing Moscow; German officers on advance reconnaissance patrols could see the spires of the Kremlin in their binoculars. They were stopped at the outskirts of the capital in December 1941, and the best chance of a quick campaign to conquer the Soviet Union disappeared into the snows of a particularly brutal Russian winter.

The aura of the German Army's invincibility had faded, but they still held the momentum the following year, when Hitler launched a campaign to capture the oil fields of southern Russia. This offensive ended in Stalingrad, on the banks of the Volga River, when the entire German Sixth Army was surrounded by the Soviets. In February 1943, starved, frozen, and outgunned, the Sixth Army surrendered. The Germans lost 250,000 men at Stalingrad, and after 1943, it was only a matter of time before they were driven out of Russia and pushed back to Berlin.

The end of the war did not improve the lives of Soviet citizens a great deal. With the collapse of Nazi Germany in 1945, Soviet power now stretched into the heart of Europe. The four victorious Allied powers—the United States, the Soviet Union, Great Britain, and France—all shared in the occupation of defeated Germany. Whereas the Western powers demobilized and reverted to peacetime economies, Stalin refused to give his own people a taste of these fruits of victory. The Americans alone reduced their armed forces from a wartime high of twelve million men to one and a half million. The Russians kept their standing army at ten million.

The world now had two superpowers. After 1945, their wartime alliance quickly deteriorated. The Russians viewed Eastern Europe as a buffer between themselves and the Western powers. They wanted to put as much distance as possible between the Soviet Union and a potentially resurgent Germany. As Stalin's grip over the eastern half of the continent tightened, the West formed the North Atlantic Treaty Organization to counter Russia's perceived expansionism. When the Soviets exploded their own atomic bomb in August 1949, the American monopoly on nuclear weapons ended. For the next forty years, both sides would build up huge atomic arsenals that could be delivered by artillery, aircraft, submarines and intercontinental ballistic missiles.

Hitler had invaded the Soviet Union in order to destroy Communism and subjugate the Russian people. His war achieved exactly the opposite, ending with the Russians in his capital city, Hitler dead by his own hand, and Soviet influence expanded well beyond its own borders. It also reinvigorated Communist ideology at a time when Stalin's brutality was taking much of the luster off of it. His Non-Aggression Pact with Hitler in 1939, and the failed leadership that had preceded it, were all but forgotten when the first German tanks rolled across the Soviet border in 1941.

Once the war ended, however, the outside world was reminded of why it had opposed Communism. Inside the Soviet Union, the past was still unmentionable, except as the party wrote it. Khrushchev tried to loosen the reins after Stalin's death, and succeeded for a time, but there was so much darkness in the Soviet past that too much light might expose the whole structure as a rotting, corrupt enterprise. Surely all that sacrifice, all those lives, all those years of bone-weary work had not been in vain?

If nothing else, Russians could always point to their victory in World War II, which they referred to as the Great Patriotic War, as justification for this sacrifice. This was most certainly true, but now that the war was over, and those who had not taken part in it had reached adulthood, what then? They were indeed proud of what their parents had done in the war, but should they not benefit from it in other ways besides the endless monuments, patriotic songs, and party slogans?

Where was the better life? It was a tough question to answer. Valery Sablin frequently asked it of himself, and, once they trusted him, his men asked it of him as well. Soviet Navy recruits in 1975 had been born in the mid-1950s. Many of their fathers were World War II veterans who believed that any reduction of Soviet military strength was a display of weakness that the capitalist countries would exploit. Fear of invasion ran deep within the Russian psyche. On the other hand, some of their older brothers had taken part in the Warsaw Pact invasion of Czechoslovakia in 1968 and came back wondering why Russians should care about how Czechoslovakia ran its own affairs. They were not unlike their American counterparts during the Vietnam War. The generation of Americans who had fought in World War II usually pointed to the Munich agreement of 1938, when Britain and France had failed to stand up to Hitler's aggression, as an example of what happened when totalitarianism went unchecked. This was the justification they used to explain to their sons why Communism had to be stopped in Southeast Asia.

However they looked at the other side, Communist ideology was running on fumes with the young sailors on *Storozhevoy*. You could only blame so much on imperialists and counterrevolutionaries before people became fed up with it. Vladimir Semichastny, the KGB chief in the early 1960s, later admitted, "People forgave us a lot because of the Cold War. The West didn't only harm us. It also helped us. Because by frightening us it played into our hands. We could say to the people, 'Tighten up your belts, be patient, we have to wait for a better life and be prepared for the worst.' And we used that."[10]

By the mid-1970s, Leonid Brezhnev, his health rapidly deteriorating, was no longer controlling the day-to-day functions of the Soviet government. When he met President Jimmy Carter in Vienna in June 1979 to sign the second Strategic Arms Limitation Treaty (SALT II), Carter was shocked by Brezhnev's inability to discuss the basic framework of negotiations without referring continuously to his notes.[11] Nikolai Leonov, a KGB analyst who worked with Brezhnev, described the situation in the Kremlin at that time: "The doctors began to limit the time he [Brezhnev] was allowed to work. His eyesight was going. We had to change the font of his typewriter to the largest one possible. At that time the whole central running of the state was in disarray. Each member of the Politburo began to work in his own interests and in the interests of the section of the economy he represented."[12]

That economy was stagnating, for this and other reasons. Central authority meant that Moscow decided how resources in the Soviet Union would be allocated, not the market. Bureaucrats in the capital set quotas for the production of everything from fertilizer to shoes. The laws of supply and demand were ignored, and recessions were not acknowledged or tolerated. The only way for most farmers and workers to meet their quotas was by producing goods of inferior quality. When they did meet them, Moscow would raise their quotas for the next year. When they did not meet them, every level of the bureaucracy would lie and say they did. Distribution was a disaster because transportation was also regulated from the center. Grain piled up and rotted at rural train stations, and it took weeks for consumer goods to reach their intended destinations.

Priority was given to military production. Contrary to the Cold War perception that the Soviet government was an omniscient institution, controlling everything in its power, the right hand often did not know what the left hand was doing. This was especially so when it came to the procurement and production of military hardware. When the new Soviet medium-range SS-20 nuclear missiles were deployed in the late 1970s, the KGB did not even know about them. According to Nikolai Leonov, the decision to deploy them was made in total secrecy. "Even our intelligence didn't know about it," he recalled. "The military industrial complex was out of control, including the army. We in intelligence learned about it from American sources."[13]

Both the KGB and the Soviet Army had fearsome reputations inside and outside the Soviet Union, but they probably feared each other more than anything else. These were the two most secretive institutions in the country, and as Leonov's comment indicates, they deeply mistrusted each other. Another example of this took place at the beginning of the SALT I talks in Vienna in 1970, when Soviet negotiators showed up without even knowing the size of their own nuclear arsenal. They had to rely on the estimates American negotiators gave them, because the Soviet Army refused to release these details to their own diplomats.

Without a firm hand at the rudder, the country was not so much slipping into anarchy as sliding into indifference. It was not long before the every-man-for-himself attitude that infected the Politburo percolated into the rest of the Communist Party and society as a whole.

Valery Sablin watched all this with growing alarm. The schism that separated the Communist Party and the Soviet state was much like the conflict that was tearing at him—the responsibilities of the loyal party man were making war on the duties of the Soviet officer. His fight was not only with the conditions that created such a situation but also with the very Russian inclination to put up with it, accept it, and do what you could elsewhere. The difference was that Sablin took it personally—all the corruption and cynicism. He knew he could motivate others to follow him because he knew his crew was willing to rise above the pettiness, selfishness, and fear that kept so many others in check. All they needed was a little leadership, and that is where he came in. After all, he was a Soviet officer, and in his mind Soviet officers put everything on the line for their country. What was his life when so many others might be changed by its sacrifice? In a letter to Nina, he quoted the poet Inessa Armand: "Whatever you do, don't be one of those people who condemn everything around them, who constantly complain about their surroundings, don't abide by their ideals in life and continue to live like those they curse. Those people are hypocritical, weak and insignificant; they are people who don't have the courage to align their lives with their convictions."[14]

It was a rather uncharitable view coming from a man who was otherwise so generous to his men, his family, and his country. But it would probably be more accurate to describe Sablin as uncompromising rather than uncharitable; he held himself to very high standards and expected the same of others. He was convinced that Communism could rise above the weaknesses of the state, just as the human mind could rise above the body's physical weaknesses. In 1975, the trick would be to cure the Brezhnev disease without killing the Soviet patient.

Behind the propaganda, the Soviet bogeyman was very human. Ethnic tension and drug abuse, the same problems that affected the U.S. military during and after the Vietnam War, would later plague the Russians in Afghanistan. Alcoholism, poor living conditions, the strain of continued deployments on their families—the Soviet serviceman could relate to them all.

Conscription in a multiethnic country like the Soviet Union meant that young men of every heritage served together in close quarters. It also meant that the racial tensions present in the civilian world were magnified in the military. There were over ninety different nationalities in the Soviet Union and 130 different languages and dialects. In the military, minorities served in many different assignments, but in small numbers and usually in the lower ranks. The non-Slavic populations of the Baltic regions and Central Asia were considered the minorities. The majority population consisted of ethnic Russians, Ukrainians, and Byelorussians. Not all of the minorities spoke fluent Russian, so recruits from Central Asia, for example, found that their most common assignments were in the army construction battalions (*stroibati*).

Few minorities were given advanced assignments and even fewer became officers.[15] One sailor said that he never saw an officer of any nationality other than Russian, Ukrainian, or Byelorussian.[16] In all the services, 95 percent of the senior officers and 85 percent of the junior officers were Russian.[17]

The policy of "extraterritoriality" prevented minority conscripts from being stationed in their homeland.[18] One reason for this was that the farther a soldier or sailor was from his home, the more difficult it was for him to desert his unit or ship. Additionally, the Soviet government evidently did not wish to foster any links between the military and the local civilians. A Soviet soldier described "extraterritoriality" this way: "A great deal of translocation is going on all the time. For example, Russians would go to the Ukraine. Ukrainians could serve in Georgia, Georgians somewhere in the Baltic area, and the Baltic people might end up in Russia. . . . The government is trying all the time to make sure that military personnel will not have ties to the local population."[19]

This was confirmed by a 1980 Rand Corporation study, which noted that "if you keep minorities away from their home areas, it will be easier to maintain control in times of crisis. You have to keep minority soldiers from assisting their own people against the Russians."[20] Fear of its own citizens, and the calculating efforts the government took to plan for armed uprising, kept the military on edge. It would be the equivalent in the United States of allowing Hispanic servicemen to be stationed only in New England and white servicemen to be stationed only in southern California out of fear that neither could be trusted to live in their home states.

In any case, most minorities would not have been much assistance because they seldom served in combat units. The exception was the 250,000 security troops of the Ministry of Internal Affairs (MVD), who were essentially soldiers working for the national police. Besides them, minorities very seldom handled weapons. They became unarmed construction troops or were assigned jobs as drivers or cooks or in railroad units. Even during their oath-taking ceremony at the end of their period of basic training, they were given only dummy wooden rifles to hold.[21]

Many Baltic people (Latvians, Lithuanians, and Estonians) regarded the Russian military as an occupying force, and there were frequent fights between them and Russian servicemen stationed in the Baltic states.[22] For a time, the Russians were successful in their attempts to "colonize" the non-Russian republics. Russian migration throughout the country ensured their domination of leadership positions. This "Russification" caused considerable resentment among many minorities, particularly among the Baltic peoples. They were often regarded as security risks, and on one occasion the Estonians on the crew of a *Kresta I*–class cruiser were removed prior to a cruise to the Mediterranean so they would not be tempted to desert in a foreign port.[23]

It's interesting to note that after the *Storozhevoy* mutiny, the final investigation report that went to Marshal Grechko, the defense minister, included an ethnic breakdown of the ship's crew. Of the 194 officers and sailors, 49 were members of ethnic minorities. If the investigators were trying to find a connection between sedition and ethnicity, it was not there; the man responsible for the mutiny was a third-generation Russian naval officer and, on top of that, a political commissar.

The year 1975 was a good one for Soviet foreign policy. On 1 May, Saigon fell to the North Vietnamese, ending South Vietnam's existence as an independent nation, and with it America's twenty-year patronage. Soon, warships from the Soviet Pacific Fleet would be making port visits to Cam Ranh Bay, which until 1973 had been one of the largest American naval bases in the Far East. In 1975, it was now in the hands of Vietnamese Communists. Laos and Cambodia would also fall to Communism in 1975, although they would be the only two dominoes to drop in Southeast Asia.

Soviet influence was extending into Africa as well. In Ethiopia, Emperor Haile Selassie was overthrown and replaced by a pro-Soviet dictatorship in 1974. The Portuguese were withdrawing from their colonies of Angola and Mozambique, both of which were now leaning toward the Soviet bloc. In fact, when Angola slipped into civil war in 1975, Russian aid was immediate and decisive; their warships even provided naval gunfire support to Angolan government soldiers ashore.

The Communist world would not reach flood tide for a few more years. That would happen in 1979, with Afghanistan in Russian hands and Sandinistas taking power in Nicaragua. Yet American thinking had not changed considerably for thirty years; it still regarded that world as monolithic, with plans hatched in Moscow taking root in Latin America, Asia, and Africa. American foreign policy never could quite come to grips with the fact that Ho Chi Minh regarded himself as a Vietnamese nationalist first and a Communist second. It took a dozen years for American policy makers to take advantage of the huge rift that opened between China and the Soviet Union in the late 1950s. What started as a disagreement over nuclear weapons eventually degenerated into border skirmishes between the two countries in the late 1960s.

All this, of course, is with the benefit of hindsight. But it may go some way in explaining why the West was so surprised at how quickly Communism collapsed between 1989 and 1991. The writing was on the wall much earlier, and one of the men doing the writing picked up his pen in November 1975 to make his statement in blood. When he did, most in the West once more allowed their thinking to be shaped by Cold War blinkers and assumed he was defecting. In an ironic twist, while Moscow was chalking up successes in Third World countries far from its own borders, a true believer was trying to put a stake into the very heart of the Communist center. In fact, he was en route to Leningrad—the very cradle of the Revolution. Valery Sablin would save Communism from itself if it was the last thing he ever did.

Chapter 3

THE SERVICE

Storozhevoy was a *Krivak I*–class large antisubmarine ship, one of thirteen the Soviet Navy had in service in 1975 (see Appendix B for more details on the *Krivak I*). The Russian acronym for its type was BPK (*bolshoi protivolodochniy korabl*), while the Americans referred to it as an FFG, a guided-missile fast frigate. This difference had to do with the fact that while the Russians classified it as an antisubmarine vessel, the Americans did not think that was its only intended purpose. They assumed that the Soviets built ships the same way they did, with multipurpose functions, so the U.S. Navy used one of its own designations. The North Atlantic Treaty Organization also gave this class of ship the designation *Krivak,* which was completely arbitrary and means nothing in Russian, because the Soviets kept their own designation for it, Project 1135 *Burevestnik,* classified.

Regardless of the name, the ship was fast and had antisubmarine weapons on board, so essentially it was a destroyer. As surface ships go, destroyers are ideal submarine hunters because of their speed. *Storozhevoy* could sail at thirty knots (about as fast as a car traveling thirty-five miles per hour, quick for a ship) and run down a sub with its active sonar. Once it got a good fix on the sub, it could then use its weapons to sink the boat or force it to surface.

The *Krivak I* class was loaded with antisubmarine warfare (ASW) weapons. They had two launchers on the stern that could each drop twelve depth charges, along with two RBU-6000 launchers that could fire rocket-propelled depth charges. They were also armed with an SS-N-14 quad rocket-assisted torpedo launcher and eight torpedo tubes amidships, which could be used for ASW or against surface targets. The *Krivak I*s had two 76.2-mm guns mounted on the stern and two surface-to-air missile launchers for close-in air defense.

There was little difference between this ship and other BPKs in the Soviet Navy, other than the officers and sailors who manned her. *Storozhevoy* had a crew of 194 men, 29 officers and 165 sailors. It was 403 feet long, weighed four thousand tons, and had a draft of fifteen feet. Third Rank Captain Sablin reported aboard on 9 August 1973. He was part of the first crew to man the ship, and therefore *Storozhevoy*'s very first *zampolit*. He would certainly be the most memorable.

Storozhevoy was built in the Kaliningrad shipyard in 1972. It was commissioned in early 1974 and spent much of its time at sea. In October 1974, it accompanied a cruiser and another destroyer to East Germany to celebrate that country's twenty-fifth independence anniversary. At sea the entire following spring, it participated in the *Vesna* naval exercises from 16 to 27 April. For those two weeks, 220 ships and submarines of all four Soviet fleets, plus aircraft, merchant vessels, and two newly deployed *Cosmos* reconnaissance satellites, performed a simultaneous and centrally controlled strike against simulated hostile shipping. *Storozhevoy* played a role in the anticarrier portion of this massive Atlantic Ocean exercise—so vast that it had never been achieved before and has not been matched since.[1] Afterward, *Storozhevoy* went to Cuba and made a port call in Havana, much to the pleasure of the crew, who regarded Castro's island as a mysterious paradise, the Hawaii of the Communist world. In October 1975, the ship participated in some live missile exercises in the Baltic Sea, along with seven cruisers, two other destroyers, and a number of *Osa*-class patrol boats.

That same fall, the navy took the unprecedented step of extending the service of senior conscripts who were due to be discharged in anticipation of their deployment to Angola should the United States intervene on behalf of rebels fighting the Communist government in Luanda.[2] This order was lifted only when it became clear that the U.S. Congress, mired in its post-Vietnam hangover, had no interest in sending troops or tax dollars to Angola. It was a busy time for Brezhnev's navy, and *Storozhevoy* was in the thick of it.

The ship's Baltic deployment in 1974 was actually mentioned in *Krasnaya Zvezda* (Red Star), the official military newspaper. On 24 December, an article appeared at the top of page two that criticized *Storozhevoy* by name (see Appendix D for the complete article). Citing a visit by Defense Minister Grechko, who went aboard *Storozhevoy* to observe the missile-firing exercises, *Krasnaya Zvezda* claimed that the ship had finished the training year very poorly. The story criticized the lack of discipline aboard the vessel, accusing some "comrades" of lapses on the "ethical front" and "taking up the liberal position in the fight for purity of the heart."[3] Translated, this jargon meant that the officers were not very good at maintaining discipline and were not particularly interested in being good party members.

Comparing the two gun batteries of Senior Lieutenants Dubov and Kolomnikov, the article said that the former's subdivision was always successful in competition while the latter's continuously lagged behind. Kolomnikov was then excused due to his youth and inexperience, and especially due to the lack of guidance by the Communist Party organization on board ship. The article further criticized this organization when it condemned party members Firsov, Sazhin, Potulniy, and Sablin by name for their inability to explain the ship's problems. The news account ended with the standard lecture to do better, recommending that the Communists aboard ship "carry their party cards next to their hearts."[4] It is notable that these four officers were not referred to by their ranks or titles, only by their party affiliation. It was almost as if their military responsibilities were irrelevant or, at the very least, subordinate to their duties as Communist Party members.

This public criticism was all the more startling since Marshal Grechko had said after his visit to the ship that *Storozhevoy* "had all the requirements necessary to win first place in the socialist competition among outstanding ships."[5] Grechko's inspection was no doubt carefully planned in advance, like all "dog-and-pony" shows for visiting dignitaries. Still, if a unit or ship performed below expectations, protocol demanded that this news be kept within the chain of command. To "drop dime" (criticize publicly) on a specific ship was a major breach of military etiquette, equivalent to the *Navy Times* calling the officers on a U.S. warship derelict in their duty. This was even truer of a closed society like the Soviet Union, which took pains to present an ideal image of itself, and especially its armed forces, to the outside world. The editors of *Krasnaya Zvezda* had to know that their open-source publication would be translated and read in the West. All the more unusual, then, that they would subject one of their own crews to such blatant scolding.

For officers like Senior Lieutenant Kolomnikov, who was identified in the article by name as someone whose "service has not always been successful," one can imagine the effect this had on their morale. An officer who was not even part of the ship's crew (Second Rank Captain Lysenko, the article's author) had observed Kolomnikov and his section in one gunnery exercise and then announced their shortcomings to the entire armed forces. Kolomnikov may very well have supported the mutiny because of this incident; in his mind, a system that was unwilling to show loyalty to its officers was not worthy of receiving loyalty.

In a confusing bit of reporting, two more articles covering *Storozhevoy*'s operations were written in *Krasnaya Zvezda* around the same time period. One had appeared only six days prior to the critical article and discussed *Storozhevoy* in a positive light after it had participated in a coordinated ASW exercise with aircraft and submarines. The story praised the tactical competence of the commanding officer and the sections led by Captain-Lieutenant Ivanov and Senior Lieutenant Vinogradov for "seizing the combat initiative." They were given an outstanding grade.[6] It is unknown if this was the same exercise that was discussed six days later. Another article published in early 1975 related *Storozhevoy* to another successful ASW exercise. This later report gave no indications that the ship had overcome its problems or that it would be rated "outstanding."[7]

Behind the scenes, however, and beyond the official evaluations of readiness, there was an atmosphere aboard *Storozhevoy* that Russian naval historian Nikolai Cherkashin would come to describe as "revolutionary." The above-mentioned accounts were only the symptoms of a serious illness. While the navy received the best recruits, the submarine service, specifically the crews of atomic subs, received the best of the best. The surface fleet got the remainder. This is not to say that some very fine crews did not man Soviet surface ships, but much of this quality had to do with how well the men were trained and led. That was the responsibility of their officers. Mediocre sailors can be turned into outstanding crews provided they are led by men who care about them and their performance.

Capt. Anatoly Potulniy was a competent commander, but his leadership style was definitely "hands off" when it came to his men. Like Sablin, he had graduated from the Frunze Military Academy and been put on the fast track to command. Unlike Sablin, however, he had remained there, essentially becoming what Valery could have been if he had not chosen a career as a *zampolit*—captain of his own vessel. By dint of hard work and faithful service, he had climbed the ladder, first as the skipper of a small antisubmarine ship, then a minelayer, and now *Storozhevoy*. Potulniy was only thirty-seven when he was given command of *Storozhevoy* in 1973, and he had just been promoted to second rank captain. A colleague who had served with him aboard another ship remembered him this way:

> To look at the crewmen as people was beyond Potulniy's comprehension. The coldness, the callousness, the rudeness did not diminish in the least over the course of his career. He once caught a sailor at his post reading a book. Fine, give him a reprimand, impose a penalty on him, whatever. But Potulniy took the book and threw it overboard. Colors [raising the flag on the ship's stern mast in the morning] was a mandatory ceremony for all the crew—no one was allowed to miss a moment of this pageantry. The crew responded to his greetings sluggishly, scarcely opening their lips. There was no *esprit de corps* at all, but he didn't see this. Or he preferred not to see it. I asked him once: "Does your wife make love to you as roughly as you treat the men?" His face turned red, but he didn't say anything.[8]

Sablin surely noticed that *Storozhevoy*'s crewmen responded more positively to him than to Potulniy. As far as is known, he did not exploit this advantage until the night of the mutiny. He got along well with his captain. Although they rarely saw each other socially at home, they often spent time with one another on liberty when they were deployed, going to the beach in Cuba and wandering the streets of Havana together. Potulniy trusted his *zampolit* and came to rely on Sablin as his second in command as much as he did his executive officer, Third Rank Captain Novozhilov.

As distant as Potulniy was, he probably needed another officer to confide in and felt most comfortable doing so with Sablin, a fellow Frunze graduate and a peer. Potulniy's rapport with the junior officers

under his command was not much better than what he had with the
enlisted men. Roughly half of *Storozhevoy*'s wardroom (ship's officers) were warrant officers, *michman* in Russian. Like their American counterparts, Russian warrant officers were enlisted specialists
who were appointed as officers after applying for selection, although
they were not considered commissioned officers like Potulniy and
Sablin because they had not been to college. Unlike their American
counterparts, sailors in the Soviet Navy could apply for a position
as a warrant officer after only two or three years' service. As such,
most of the *michman* aboard *Storozhevoy* were still in their early
twenties and every bit as receptive to Sablin's powers of persuasion
as the enlisted men. One of them who would play a key role in
supporting the mutiny was Viktor Borodai. His relationship with
Potulniy was also strained, and he vividly recalled the difference
between the skipper and Sablin: "The first six months for every new
officer and *michman* were pure hell, thanks to the captain. I went
through it, too. The alternative to Potulniy, for the officers and men
alike, was his *zampolit,* Third Rank Captain Valery Mikhailovich
Sablin."[9]

Had Potulniy not trusted Sablin implicitly, he may have viewed
his *zampolit*'s popularity among the crew as a threat to his command. Given his stated inability, or unwillingness, to view his
sailors as anything more than tools, it is unlikely that Potulniy ever
regarded them as men whose respect he needed to earn. In fact, he
may have been glad that Sablin had such a good rapport with the
crew, since it relieved him of the need to develop these personal
contacts himself. All he had to do was tell Sablin what he wanted,
and the *zampolit* would ensure that the crew did exactly as they
were told.

The difference in style between Potulniy and Sablin poses some
fundamental questions about leadership. In essence, leadership is
the application of personal power and authority that makes people
do things they ordinarily would not. Aside from questions of tactical
execution, an officer also sets a tone for his unit that is subtle in its
application. This tone is very much determined by the officer's personality. If he is comfortable in his own skin, confident of his position and how he got there, the enlisted men will recognize this at
once and breathe a little easier because of it. "The Old Man's a hard
ass, but he's fair" may be one of the things they say about him, and
it is not an uncharitable description. It means the commander is

respected not only for sticking to rules of conduct but also for being flexible enough to know that most rules are not written in stone.

Correctly determining this balance is the most complicated aspect of military leadership. Some officers spend their entire careers trying to find it and never do. At one end of this spectrum are the by-the-book officers for whom rules and regulations are sacrosanct; bend one, they say, and soon you will be bending them all, undermining the very concept of standards. Potulniy fit into this category. At the other end are those officers who want their men to like them rather than respect them, preferring to seek the favor of their subordinates rather than enforce policy. Sablin was somewhere in between. While he had respect and compassion for his sailors, he did not tolerate any undue familiarity. He needed their help, but he also knew that they needed his direction. Valery's confidence, force of personality, and skills of persuasion were powerful motivators for the officers and men of *Storozhevoy* and would prove to be indispensable when the time came to use them. Subtly and slowly, he was gathering these strands of power, which he would come to exercise in a way that was totally beyond the imagination of Capt. Anatoly Potulniy.

Most sailors enjoy going to sea. It is the reason they joined the navy or, in the case of Soviet conscripts, the reason they chose the navy over the army. But life at sea can be crowded and miserable. There is very little privacy, a lot of noise, and, depending on what part of the ship you're in, the stench of body odor, fuel, and trash from the mess decks. In such close quarters, illness spreads like wildfire, and even on the most modern ships, toilets back up, air conditioners break, and the power goes out.

Yet sea duty has its advantages. There is nothing quite like watching the sun drop slowly into the vast emptiness of the Pacific, or drinking in the cool scent of rain just before the monsoons unleash their thunderstorms over the Indian Ocean. Most people arrive in Hong Kong by plane, but there is something spellbinding about approaching the city from the sea, especially at night when this citadel of light rises so effortlessly from the water.

Of course, warships are not cruise liners, and their sailors are not tourists. Their purpose is to serve their country's interests by sinking other warships and killing other sailors. A ship is a self-contained community, trained and equipped to act as a single unit.

A captain at sea has enormous power; on ballistic missile submarines, he and his officers have the ability to launch a nuclear
arsenal capable of laying waste to a dozen cities. In the U.S. Navy,
he can still send any member of his crew to the brig on bread and
water rations, and in the event of a mutiny, especially in wartime,
he literally has the power of life or death over them. Few shore commanders would dispute whatever reasonable measures he took to
put down a revolt at sea, and in all times, in all navies, such measures have included the penalty of death.

When examining the everyday life of *Storozhevoy* and the Soviet
Navy, it is important to look at the quality of that life at sea and
ashore. Mutiny is serious business, and any officer who asks it of
himself and his men must know that he is crossing a bridge over
which he can never return. It is critical to paint the right picture and
set the right context in order to understand just what made these
men say yes to rebellion. Youthful indiscretion can only go so far in
explaining their motives. A fuller picture of what life was like for the
officers and men of *Storozhevoy* helps to answer the question, Why
did they do it?

Like everyone else, they were concerned about their families and
how they would provide for them. Seeing their wives and children
housed in inadequate hovels with poor food, shabby clothing, and no
prospects of improvement must have eaten at the self-esteem of the
crewmen and tugged at their sense of injustice. Symptoms of this
dissatisfaction were evident in the country's high rate of alcoholism,
and binge drinking occasionally took place aboard *Storozhevoy*.
There are many components to morale, and many things that con-
tribute to it or erode it, but they all add up to Napoleon's old rule of
thumb: the spiritual is to the physical as three is to one. When soldiers and sailors have their basic needs met—adequate pay, housing, clothing, and food—their minds will be more focused on the
mission in front of them than the homes they left behind.

Morale problems associated with harsh living conditions can be
particularly significant for naval personnel both afloat and ashore.
The habitat provided by Soviet ships was substantially worse than
that of corresponding Western vessels, a fact Westerners who visited Soviet ships during this time substantiated. They noted that
living space was limited because Soviet ships, at the expense of the
crew's comfort, were much more heavily armed than Western ones
of similar tonnage.

Ships built in the 1960s and 1970s were much improved, however. The greatest change between the newer and older vessels was the addition of air conditioning to the crew's quarters, since more and more cruises were going to tropical climates. Special "air showers" (cool air jets at hot spots in the ship) were installed, mainly for cooling the more sophisticated shipboard electronics, but also for the comfort of the crew. The Soviets realized that living conditions, especially on the increasingly common longer voyages, had a great effect on morale, although overcrowding was still a problem.

On a mid-1960s vintage *Kresta I*–class guided missile cruiser, for example, fifteen sailors were billeted in a twelve-by-fifteen-foot bunk room.[10] Showers were not readily available, and fresh water was a particular problem on Soviet diesel submarines, where the crews were described as filthy and odorous. Soviet shipboard regulations only called for conscripts to bathe and change underwear once every week, unless their work was particularly dirty.[11] Evidence indicated that baths were no more common on ships where fresh water was available (i.e., on nuclear-powered vessels). As a result, skin diseases such as athlete's foot, boils, and carbuncles were common. Soviet officers lived two to four to a stateroom and had the use of communal showers.[12]

The overall impression one received when visiting a Soviet ship was that it was cramped and drab but clean. On the older *Kotlin*-class ships, the berthing spaces were dimly lit and crowded, although one sailor said that "crowded conditions make for better cooperation."[13] Bunks were three-tiered with a two-by-two-foot non-lockable box for each sailor. These spaces were not air conditioned, but portable air-conditioning units were available for voyages to tropical climates.[14] There were no drinking-water fountains in the living areas. Drinking water was available from a portable metal barrel with a community drinking cup.[15] On older ships, food was carried from the central galley and consumed in berthing spaces because there was no crew dining area.[16]

In contrast to the older ships, *Smolny,* a Soviet midshipman training vessel that was put into service in 1976, was centrally air conditioned. It had a comfortably furnished officers' mess and three dining rooms for the enlisted men. In addition, *Smolny* had a "Lenin room" for political instruction that accommodated forty men, a movie theater (only for movies with political messages), and a six-thousand-book library.[17]

Visitors aboard the helicopter carrier *Moskva* described their impressions of the vessel: limited space, spartan living conditions, rudimentary equipment, nauseating odors, and one unusual condition—the presence of Russian women (nurses) in white uniforms. It seems that nurses were not uncommon on the largest ships. The all-pervasive smell aboard *Moskva* was described as "a mixture of cabbage soup, bacon fat, and that black, slightly rancid, typical Russian tobacco."[18]

The fleet's smaller ships had their own problems, because they were designed with the thought that the crews would actually live ashore. They were supposed to remain on board only during training exercises or combat, but due to the scarcity of adequate housing ashore, most sailors actually lived on the patrol vessel. A former officer recalled that service on motor torpedo boats was especially arduous due to the cramped conditions and constant vibration resulting from the ship's high speed. As a consequence, this officer developed high blood pressure and was discharged at the age of thirty. Seamen on torpedo boats were compensated with special rations, including luxury items like chocolate, but these did not eliminate the special hardships of their service.[19]

A navy exists ashore as well as afloat, and accommodations on land both in enlisted barracks and in family housing were often times worse than at sea. Each naval conscript reported to a training unit prior to joining his ship or shore station. When a conscript in the mid-1970s reported to a Northern Fleet training platoon, he found the buildings unheated in the winter, even though the temperature often fell to twenty below zero. His *kazarma* (barracks) slept close to a hundred men packed in two rows of three-tiered bunks. The beds were so close together that any infectious disease spread rapidly throughout the whole unit. Even sailors used to crowded conditions at home found life in the *kazarma* intolerable.

The latrines and washstands were outdoors, the former housed in a long shed with many holes in the floor. The mid-1970s conscript reported having to clean the latrines in the winter when urine had frozen to the floor and many of his drunken comrades had vomited there after a night on the town.[20] He held no fond memories of this experience, though he did report that conditions improved when he got to his shore-based technical unit.

Of all the Soviet domestic problems, the housing shortage remained one of the most persistent. The situation under the tsars was dismal, and early Soviet leadership did nothing to alter the housing shortfall. In fact, Stalin made it worse. He invested significantly in heavy industry but failed to provide housing for the millions of peasants who left the farms to work in the new factories. Soviet citizens lived in communal squalor, and it was commonplace for several families to crowd into a single apartment. In 1950, it was estimated that each person had less than fifteen square feet of living space.[21]

After 1957, Stalin's successors built 2.2 million housing units per year. The results of this achievement were visible in every city. By 1982, per capita living space had increased to twenty-seven square feet.[22] This improvement, however, only dramatized the shortfall for the millions still waiting for their own apartment. The tremendous quantity of construction did not keep pace with rising expectations. Soviet citizens continued to suffer the poorest housing conditions of any industrialized nation, and in the late 1980s an estimated 20 percent of all urban dwellers still lived communally. The waiting period for an apartment was indefinite; it could take anywhere from a decade to a lifetime if you lacked connections.

The Soviet authorities appeared to make no better effort to improve housing for service families, either in quantity or quality, particularly in such inhospitable areas as Polyarniy in the Arctic and Vladivostok in the Far East. Viktor Belenko, who would defect to Japan in his MiG-25 fighter only ten months after the *Storozhevoy* mutiny, was stationed at an airbase in the maritime provinces of the Russian Far East. Just prior to his defection, he and his wife shared a two-room apartment with another officer's family. They considered themselves lucky; other apartments were packed with three or even four families.[23]

Most dependent housing was built by Soviet naval construction personnel and was extremely poor in quality. Letters in the "Letters to the Editor" section in *Krasnaya Zvezda* often complained of leaking roofs, poor insulation, use of inferior quality building materials, the absence of bathing or laundry facilities, and inadequate ventilation, water, and electrical systems. Often these shortcomings were only remedied by *subbotniki,* the supposedly volunteer weekend work details made up of military personnel. More often than not, servicemen's complaints elicited no response at all from housing authorities.

It seems that the military hierarchy was aware of these problems and acknowledged them, but according to Belenko and others, it did not give them the priority they deserved. In *Krasnaya Zvezda* in 1974, Rear Admiral Sidorchuk (chief of the fleet rear services) discussed the housing situation for naval personnel in the Pacific Fleet in fairly frank terms: "The party and the government are showing consistent concern with regard to improving the housing and living conditions for service families. . . . In the Pacific Fleet in the last three years alone, thousands of families have received new living quarters. There is a problem of maintenance, however. In isolated far-off garrisons there is often a lack of trained maintenance specialists. . . . In some areas housing maintenance committees exist solely on paper and actually do nothing. This has resulted in problems which can affect the serviceman in the performance of his regular duties."[24]

Housing for servicemen in other areas of the Soviet Union was better but not without problems. Members of the military, particularly officers, were given priority on the list to receive new housing in urban areas where a shortage existed. When he reported to a new duty station in the western Soviet Union, Viktor Belenko expressed his excitement over getting a new apartment in a building only one month old:

> To be promised an apartment was one thing, but to be given an apartment as promised, quite another. Eagerly and expectantly, I unlocked the door and smelled dampness. The floor, built with green lumber, already was warped and wavy. Plaster was peeling off the walls. The windowpane in the kitchen was broken and no water poured from the faucet. The bathtub leaked; the toilet did not flush. None of the electrical outlets worked. . . . Another lieutenant and I confronted the first party representative we could find, a young political officer in the same building. He was cynical yet truthful. The building had not been inspected as they had been told. The military builders sold substantial quantities of allotted materials on the black market, then bribed the chairman of the acceptance commission and took the whole commission to dinner. There the acceptance papers were drunkenly signed without any commission member ever having been inside the building.[25]

Valery Sablin was a graduate of the most prestigious naval academy and a promising junior officer on a front line Soviet warship, yet the litany of his housing problems must be more than indicative of what tribulations all crewmembers of *Storozhevoy* faced with their families.

After they were married, Nina met Valery's family and the couple spent a month with them in Gorky before Valery reported to his first duty station in Severomorsk in 1961. They were not given an apartment, but they added their names to the never-ending waiting list for one. Moving up the list was more a function of military or party connections than time spent waiting. Valery's father still had many connections around the navy, despite being retired for a number of years, and he was able to find a place for them to rent. For the beginning of their married life, they shared a one-room apartment with another woman, three of them in only 150 square feet. After one month, they moved to the one-room apartment of an officer who lived upstairs but was deployed at sea. Eventually, they got one room in a barracks-like building for navy families. They shared a kitchen with two other families, had no hot water, and despite the presence of a wood-burning stove, they were always cold. The tin-roofed building was, according to Nina, not insulated at all against the Arctic winds of Severomorsk.

When Nina went home to Leningrad to give birth to Misha in 1962, Valery gave up their apartment and moved aboard his ship, at least in part to help other families waiting for housing. When his ship moved to Sevastopol on the Black Sea in 1963, the young couple again only found housing through connections of Valery's father. They were able to temporarily share a three-room apartment with another couple while they searched for their own place. Ultimately they found a two-room apartment with water and a bathroom outside, but no gas. Nina cooked on a kerosene stove.

Their never-ending housing problems continued when Sablin's ship returned to the Northern Fleet. Valery went ahead to find accommodations, while Nina and Misha waited with her family in Leningrad. From 1966 to 1968, they found a good apartment, with hot water for the first time, but still shared a kitchen with two other families. In 1968, they moved into their first apartment with their own kitchen and bathroom.

Even in the big city of Moscow, Valery and Nina started out in a one-room place of only twelve square meters (120 square feet). They moved again, and for the rest of their time in Moscow, they lived in an apartment of eighteen square meters (160 square feet). When Valery reported aboard *Storozhevoy* after living in Kaliningrad for three months in a hotel and another six in a small room of a communal house, his family finally got a three-room apartment in a Khrushchev building (Russians refer to the large apartment blocks by the name of whoever was in power during their construction). Their good fortune was only a result of Valery's promotion to third rank captain and the relative abundance of housing in Kaliningrad.[26]

If there is one thing Russians can remember with crystal clarity, it is the housing they lived in and how long it took them to get it. Privacy was a scarce commodity in the Soviet Union, almost as scarce as decent housing. With the state involved in nearly every aspect of their lives, it is hardly surprising that a married couple with a child would do all they could to find a little place to call their own. Finding their own apartment with hot water, a kitchen, and a bathroom was a major victory for Nina and Valery.

As for *Storozhevoy,* it had the same shipboard habitability problems as other Soviet vessels: it was crowded and met only the basic needs of the crew. Those crewmembers living ashore in barracks or with their families were not faced with the grim conditions that existed in the Far East ports. Living standards in the Baltic region were much higher, and cities like Riga were large and relatively modern. Housing was still scarce, however, and newer housing had quality problems due to corruption in the construction industry.

In the Soviet Union, where military power was so important, one might expect the consumers to suffer somewhat so that the soldier and sailor might eat well, but this was not the case. Food certainly could be the cause of low morale, but how bad could it be? Sailors in every navy complain about the food. In the Soviet Union, food consumption doubled between 1950 and 1974, but there were still numerous problems in getting adequate food to the soldiers and sailors.[27] Victor Suverov illustrated the Soviet attitude toward supplying food to troops in the field in his book *Inside the Soviet Army:* "The Soviet Army has a completely different approach to the problems of supply from that adopted in the West—one which avoids many headaches. Let us start from the fact that a Soviet soldier is not issued with a sleeping bag, and does not need one. He can be left unfed for several days. All that he needs is ammunition and this solves many problems."[28]

The Soviets, however, at least in their regulations, appeared to be very concerned that the troops be well fed. There was even a Central Food Directorate within the Ministry of Defense. Rations were provided free of charge to all soldiers, sailors, cadets and reserves when on active duty, while officers had to pay for theirs. Soviet authorities often boasted about their ability to provide the troops with adequate rations, setting a goal of twenty kilograms (forty-four pounds) of meat and vegetables per man per year.[29] It was also official policy to see that elite forces received better food than regular line forces. Every new Five Year Plan called for more dining halls, cafés, and tearooms in military garrisons.

Soviet regulations did not specify anything concerning the quality of the food, however, and the daily menu actually painted a somewhat more dismal picture than the regulations led one to believe. Soldiers were usually fed breakfast from 0730 to 0800. The morning meal generally consisted of a bowl of *kasha* (a barley or oat mush cooked with flour) with 150 grams of bread, 10 grams of butter, 20 grams of sugar, and a mug of tea.[30]

Lunch, the main meal, consisted of a thin potato or cabbage soup, sometimes thickened with buckwheat groats. If the crew got any meat at all during the day it was included in this soup: either a piece of cod, herring, or a hunk of pork fatback. On special occasions, a mug of *kissel* (a kind of starchy gelatin) was added along with more bread. Soldiers and sailors were given forty minutes to eat followed by thirty minutes to rest.[31]

In the thirty minutes allotted for supper, servicemen were often served the same meal of *kasha* and bread they had for breakfast. If they got any fresh vegetables, it was at this meal in the form of cooked cabbage or mashed potatoes.[32] Finally, they received more bread. A Soviet serviceman consumed an average of one and a half pounds of bread per day.[33] Primarily due to this excess starch, he managed to gain six to eight pounds during his conscripted service. In the West, the average weight gain for young men in the same age range (eighteen to twenty years) was almost double that.

In terms of caloric intake, it appeared that their diet was sufficient but dull and lacking certain essential vitamins. "It filled you up but made you feel sluggish all day," a former sailor recalled.[34] That lack of energy could be attributed to low simple sugar intake, which was most commonly found in fruits, since fresh fruit was unheard of in the Soviet armed forces. A sailor who served on a cruiser out of Murmansk in the Northern Fleet said that he never saw fresh fruit in his three years of service.

The navy had the advantage of being able to fish to supplement the shipboard diet. Fishing even became part of the "socialist competitions" and pledges for deployed units. One ship promised to augment the diet of its crew with ten kilos (twenty-two pounds) of fish per man.[35] It was reported that some diligent cooks aboard large combatants were rewarded for making sausages out of scraps and leftovers during an extended cruise.[36] The Central Food Directorate allowed naval personnel living in military housing to keep garden plots on base, where they could produce their own staples of cabbage, potatoes, and small amounts of other vegetables. They could also keep pigs or goats for their own use.

There was no general crew's mess aboard the older Soviet ships. The food prepared in the galley was carried to the crew's quarters in buckets to be consumed there. When the heat below deck became intolerable, sailors ate on deck on oilcloths with no tables or chairs. Eating utensils were not washed but wiped clean with damp newspaper, since cleaning brushes were kept spotless for daily inspections. These practices were not only unsanitary but dangerous; grease fires were common.[37]

Even submarines, which were supposed to get the best food of all, often put to sea with inadequate supplies of the common staples like potatoes and cabbage. After expending their fresh provisions during the first few weeks of a cruise, they resorted to *kasha* and canned bread. Larger ships did have bakeries for fresh bread. Since Soviet ships spent more time at anchor than their American counterparts, they consequently did not get to replenish fresh stores during calls at foreign ports.

Servicemen's feelings about their food were very strong. A former private, who was quartered for some time in the 1970s near a military installation where servicemen from other Warsaw Pact countries were training, said in reference to the Warsaw Pact allies, "They had an excellent mess. Soldiers from our battalion were twice sent on kitchen duty to their messes. They came back bringing pancakes! They brought sour cream! My friends were among them, so they brought some to me. It seemed like a miracle. We remembered it to the end of our service."[38]

Dissatisfaction with their food sometimes led to open protest, usually a refusal to eat. A former paratrooper told how, after a year with a particularly bad harvest, each soldier's ration of butter, bread, and sugar was reduced. The soldiers, after a brief organizational meeting, refused to eat. Half an hour later the division political officer appeared and ordered rations to be increased to their old levels. They were never reduced again, and no one was punished for his disobedience.

In interviews with former soldiers conducted as part of a study by Texas A&M, Robert Bathurst reported that a majority felt that their food situation was worsened by dishonesty on the part of those noncommissioned officers (NCOs; sergeants and above in the enlisted ranks) responsible for the galley. In addition, senior conscripts often extorted food from junior conscripts as part of a general policy of hazing, which was overlooked by senior personnel and officers. The fact that everyone stole food, particularly meat, was widely recognized and accepted.

The Soviet soldier was probably justified when he complained about the quality of food available to him. Even with the low standards of Soviet society, the majority of soldiers in the regular units believed their food was worse than that found in civilian life. Military rations were monotonous, poorly prepared, and inadequate in terms of vitamin content. Although the number of calories appeared sufficient due to the high starch content, it still was not enough to sustain a young man through the rigors of military life.

When looking at how this impacted the combat ability of Soviet soldiers and sailors, one must be careful to look at it from the Russian perspective. Certainly, if volunteer American soldiers had been fed in the same fashion as conscripted Soviet troops, their dissatisfaction would have been much deeper. However, many Russians had eaten boring, tasteless food all their lives, and their short stay in the military was little different. Instead, Russian servicemen fed on the sarcasm so common to Soviet-era humor when they joked, "Why do we have so little meat in the Soviet Union? Because we're moving toward Communism so fast the cattle can't keep up!" Another joke went, "What's a hundred meters long and eats cabbage? The line in front of the Soviet meat store!"

It is natural for servicemen to complain about their food, but the Soviet Union might have been the place where the serviceman had a real reason to do so. It is said that an army moves on its stomach, and if so, the Soviet military was not going very far. By the time of Gorbachev and glasnost, the Soviet draftee was less willing to accept the material hardships of military life. Moreover, none of the conscripts had firsthand experience of the trying years of World War II, an event that was viewed by the leadership as an important source of Soviet patriotism.

All Soviet men were required to serve at least three years in the navy or two years in the army. Normally, they were drafted right out of high school at age eighteen, but student deferments were available for those who went to college, with the provision that they would fulfill their service after they graduated. The conscription process provided for call-ups twice a year, in May/June and November/December. Consequently, they drafted almost 450,000 men per call-up for all of the armed services combined, plus the KGB border guards and Ministry of the Interior security forces. This steady supply of manpower was one of the reasons the Soviets were able to keep the largest standing army in the world, numbering five million men in the 1970s.

The number of men required for every call-up was determined by the Council of Ministers and the Ministry of Defense and was then divided among the Soviet Union's sixteen military districts based upon the number of draft-age males residing in each.[39] For simplicity, men whose birthdays fell between 1 January and 1 July were drafted in May and June, while the rest were conscripted in November and December.

Even with the extra year of service required, some conscripts (*prizovniki*) still chose to do their military service in the navy rather than the army. Many felt that since their tour of duty was unavoidable, they would prefer to serve in the more appealing branch of the Soviet armed forces. They were drawn by the romantic and macho image of the sailor and the appeal of the much more prestigious naval uniform. Another factor that made this service more attractive to at least some draftees was the possibility of travel to foreign ports, particularly Western ones.

In the supposedly classless society of the Soviet Union, there was harsh stratification between the haves, who were usually Community Party members, and the have-nots—essentially everyone else. This distinction carried over into the military. Russians subordinated themselves, at least on the surface, to those above them in the hierarchy. They also tended to distrust and abuse those below them on that same ladder. In the Soviet military this was translated into hazing, *dedovshchina* in Russian. Second- and third-year conscripts long enjoyed seniority over younger draftees, claiming special privileges within the unit and channeling the undesirable duties to the new men. Émigré sources indicated that moderate hazing was accepted by the conscripts and tolerated by officers and petty officers because it provided a convenient way of maintaining unit control. Excessive hazing, however, led to low morale among the younger draftees and less solidarity in the unit as a whole.

Depending on their intelligence and level of education, the inductees were assigned to various branches of the service by the *pokupateli* (literally, "buyers"), selection officers from each branch of the armed forces. The best conscripts normally went into the navy and the strategic rocket forces. After basic training, the soldiers and sailors were generally divided into the *Molodye* and the *Stariki,* the "young ones" and the "old men," respectively. The former were the conscripts in their first year of service, and the latter were those in their second or, in the navy, final year of service. Before the 1967 Law of Universal Military Service reduced the length of time served in all Soviet land forces from three to two years, there had been an intermediate group in their second year of military service. This group was still present in the navy, where sailors had the three-year obligation.

The *Stariki* rated a number of privileges at the expense of the *Salaga* (a derisive nickname for first-year sailors). When new conscripts arrived at their unit, one of the first orders of business was the uniform exchange. The *Stariki* exchanged their worn-out uniforms for the *Salaga*'s new ones, since the *Stariki* generally wanted to return home after they were discharged in brand-new uniforms. For instance, a sailor who had served on minesweepers in the Baltic Fleet sold his new uniforms to Central Asian army troops who found it more prestigious to go home in a navy uniform.

All of the heavy work and menial chores such as cleaning and kitchen work were done by the *Molodye.* A sailor in a Riga signal battalion had to shine boots for the second-year men. First-year sailors in his unit had to give up parts of their ration of sugar and butter to the *Stariki.* The "old men" also demanded a share of each food parcel or money gift received from home by the "young ones."

This system did not appear to meet with a great deal of resistance. The conscripts were probably away from home for the first time at age eighteen and giving one "old man" what he wanted without any fuss seemed to provide the new conscripts with protection from the other *Stariki*. Author Herbert Goldhammer suggested this reason for the lack of resistance: "When a young inductee arrives at his regiment, a traditional billeting ceremony takes place in the barracks. Sometimes the new soldier is placed next to the cot of a second-year soldier, often one of his own ethnic group or geographical area. He will thus be able to learn from his senior comrade."[40]

Another explanation for the passive acceptance of this hazing was that in their two or three years of arduous military life, most of the conscripts became considerably stronger, particularly in the army. The threat of physical harm was often used to induce compliance. All accounts of this phenomenon confirmed that physical force was occasionally used—in the form of ruthless beatings in the barracks after lights out when the men were alone. In his 1981 study, Robert Bathurst emphasized that attempts were being made to reduce physical violence used by the older men against the new recruits. This informal rite of passage continued despite its unpleasantness. It succeeded in building cohesiveness among newcomers, but not always among the entire unit. Andrew Cockburn came to the conclusion that the "unofficial organization of Soviet units in which at any time half the strength is being brutalized and exploited by the other half, is hardly likely to foster the trust and mutual confidence that makes for cohesion. . . . If combat action began, one half of the company might shoot the other, and even if this is extreme, it is quite evident that a lot of the soldiers would have severe doubts about whether their 'buddies' were worth taking a hill for."[41]

An émigré who moved to West Germany corresponded that when he became a *Stariki,* he and a few of his comrades were determined to treat the first-year men with dignity. This worked satisfactorily for a few weeks, until a senior enlisted man discovered that he and his comrades were being too easy on the *Molodye.* The lenient *Stariki* were ordered to dump thirty buckets of water in their barracks and clean it up with small rags. While these *Stariki* were cleaning up the mess, the *Molodye* were given free time. After this incident, the senior NCO had a meeting with the *Stariki* and told them to put more pressure on the first-year sailors or the incident would repeat itself.

Fistfights broke out often between junior and senior conscripts, particularly over the uniform exchange. Most of these fights went unreported or were overlooked by senior enlisted personnel and officers in all the services. The *Stariki* jealously guarded their privileges. A former private in the Air Defense described one episode: "During dinner an 'old man' received a slightly yellowish enameled cup (usually the *Stariki* receive only the new white cups). The 'old man,' without looking back, threw the cup with all his strength into the open kitchen door and hit a young Kirghiz soldier who was on kitchen duty directly on the forehead. The 'young one' was in great pain, but he did not dare to complain or seek revenge. The onlookers took the whole episode as no more than part of the army life. They all said, 'That's the way things are.'"[42]

It was apparent that the officers not only knew about the privileged position of the "old men" but also readily encouraged it. An army NCO stated that the officers for whom he worked did not find it unreasonable when a *Stariki* complained about having to do too much work. Officers said that the *Stariki* deserved some privileges because they already knew their jobs and, besides, eventually everybody got to be an "old man."

A sailor who served on a cruiser out of Murmansk said this conflict between junior and senior conscripts was the worst single cause of problems aboard his ship. The authorities, he noted, were attempting to deal with the ethnic problem, but the disruption caused by hazing was being overlooked. Hazing was a navy-wide problem and most likely present on *Storozhevoy* as well.

In the tenth century, Prince Vladimir of Kiev is said to have made Russia Christian rather than Muslim because, as he put it, "it is impossible to be happy in Russia without strong drink." Alcoholism is still a national malady that permeates the armed forces. In the late 1970s, alcohol sales among Soviet citizens accounted for over a third of all consumer spending in food stores.[43] Alcohol was the one consumer item that was never in short supply, even in the most remote areas.

The Soviet government under Mikhail Gorbachev and his two immediate predecessors took steps to combat the alarming increase of alcoholism. Yuri Andropov raised the price of liquor in state stores, reduced the strength of vodka, and substituted wine and beer for vodka in many production plans. Gorbachev, in turn, increased media campaigns about the problems of alcoholism and attempted to reduce on-the-job drinking due to the negative effects it had on worker productivity. For his efforts, the Soviet people gave him the nickname *Gensok,* a tongue-in-cheek reference to his official title of *gensek,* or general secretary (of the Communist Party). The word *sok* means juice, which is evidently what Gorbachev preferred they drink. Most of these efforts, particularly price increases, went nowhere, however, and only forced the public toward greater use of alcohol surrogates. It also cut government revenues, since approximately 10 percent of state income came from the sale of alcoholic beverages.

The situation in the armed forces showed that servicemen were not exempt from this disease that afflicted society as a whole. Alcoholism was both a cause and an effect of low morale. Liquor represented an easy escape from the pressures and hardships of military service in the USSR; conscripts, senior enlisted men, and officers used it extensively for this purpose. The scope of the problem created by alcoholism was evident in the press reports reflecting high-level concern with the extent and impact of excessive drinking within the armed forces. One 1974 article in *Krasnaya Zvezda* pointed out that more than one-third of all military infractions were caused by personnel under the influence of alcohol.[44] In the same journal, an article announced that the Officers' Club of the Baltic Fleet had made a training film to strengthen military discipline and combat drunkenness. Alcohol was a recognized problem in all the armed services. For example, Alex Alexiev of the Rand Corporation estimated that alcohol dependence in the Soviet military was well over 33 percent. By comparison, in the U.S. military that figure stood at about 18 percent.[45]

Soviet regulations permitted officers and NCOs to drink in their off-duty hours. The conscripts, in theory, were not allowed to drink at all, but the famous ingenuity of the Russian soldier, which was lauded in Soviet propaganda, proved itself when it came to getting a drink.[46] Strict discipline did not appear to be an effective deterrent, and the cost of alcohol (the price of half a liter of common vodka exceeded a conscript's monthly pay) led servicemen to other alternatives. Sailors generally obtained alcohol in three ways: from home through the mail, off base with pay or by barter of military equipment, or through various bad tasting or even deadly home brews.

The problem was apparently more widespread in the army than the navy. Since alcohol was not officially allowed aboard Soviet naval vessels for officers and conscripts alike, anybody who wanted a drink had to smuggle a bottle on board, which was difficult to hide. Sailors who served at sea said alcohol abuse was rare but occurred whenever it became available. Senior petty officers and warrant officers seemed to have been the greatest abusers. One émigré reported that before they were allowed to go on leave, a conscript had to promise his chief petty officer a bottle of vodka upon his return from home.[47]

The Soviet version of moonshine was called *samogan,* and it was often produced on farms in family-run stills. The military was a great consumer of this "home brew." In the Naval Signal Battalion outside Riga, the *samogan* supply came from a collective-farm woman who visited the mess hall once a week to pick up leftovers for her pigs.[48]

When vodka or *samogan* was unavailable, soldiers and sailors resorted to drinking just about anything in their quest for oblivion. Shoe polish was filtered through black bread and consumed for its alcohol content. Cologne, when it appeared in a ship's store, was completely sold out within fifteen minutes. It was often confiscated by the unit *zampolit* and its distribution rationed.

Alcohol-based fluid was frequently used to clean highly sophisticated equipment in the Soviet arsenal, and it often was drunk in one way or another by soldiers, which affected the equipment's overall maintenance. Victor Sokolov, as quoted in *The Threat,* spent his conscripted time serving in the air defense forces around Moscow. He remembered how the alcohol used for cleaning the moving parts of their radars was considered far too precious for that purpose. The men used gasoline instead, which made the metal clean and shiny but led to excessive corrosion.[49]

Lt. Victor Belenko told tales of the drinking and black market sale of the grain alcohol used in hydraulics and deicers for the MiG-25 fighter jet. He said fuel was often dumped to ensure that statistics sent to Moscow would show that the proper fuel-to-alcohol ratio was used.[50] The MiG-25 needed fourteen tons of fuel and half a ton of alcohol for the seventy minutes it could stay aloft. Much of that alcohol was consumed by the ground crew, which inspired the plane's nickname of "the flying restaurant."

The list of alcohol surrogates went on and on: antiaircraft gun coolant, vehicle antifreeze, and vinegar concentrate to name just a few. These were often not only intoxicating but also poisonous, although even Soviet commercial vodka could be impure and toxic.

In the early 1960s, the Soviet government switched the base of all internally marketed vodka from grain to a petroleum derivative due to continued failing harvests and the need to use the grain to feed livestock. Though alcohol-poisoning deaths were not published, they were said to be one hundred times that of the United States.[51]

A sailor who served on *K-8*-class minesweepers from 1968 to 1971 told this author that on two different occasions he could remember that sailors standing guard duty on these vessels were drunk. One fired his AK-47 into the air saying he thought there was an air raid. Another lost his rifle and himself overboard in a drunken stupor. The interviewed sailor was the diver who pulled the body and the weapon out of the water.[52] Both of these incidents were hushed up by local commanders.

Outside of alcohol, drug use was rare in the Soviet military in the mid-1970s. Then came Afghanistan, which made *anasha* (hashish) and *plan* (an opium derivative) a big problem in the Soviet Army. *Anasha* had long been the drug of choice for many soldiers from Central Asia, but it became popular among all ethnic groups serving in Afghanistan. The navy remained unaffected by this drug use due to fewer Central Asians in its ranks and very little contact between naval personnel and *Afgantsi* (veterans of the Afghanistan war). In addition, the lack of privacy aboard ship prevented surreptitious use of most drugs.

One former lieutenant said that "the time for Americans to attack would be New Year's Eve, because everybody was drunk and there was no one on duty." He then paused and added, "New Year's Eve wasn't much different from any other time."[53]

As the political officer aboard *Storozhevoy*, what exactly was Third Rank Captain Sablin teaching his sailors? Political education was a source of some dissatisfaction among both officers and enlisted personnel. More often, the whole process of political indoctrination was characterized by a remarkable lack of interest on the part of the officers, who were supposed to indoctrinate, and the sailors, who were supposed to be indoctrinated.

Each sailor, according to most interviewed, had two sessions per week for three hours each, usually on Monday and Thursday mornings.[54] The *zampolit* or other officers conducted these obligatory lectures or sometimes showed films on Marxist-Leninist themes. They emphasized the "leading role of the party" in the "military collective" and were designed to educate servicemen on Marxist-Leninist ideology.

On the surface, the quantity of ideological material that each man was subjected to seemed intense. The Navy Political Directorate outlined the curriculum of indoctrination, handing down which topics and guidelines were to be taught in each session. A 1972 *Krasnaya Zvezda* article describing the political material being prepared for a Baltic Fleet submarine getting ready to go on patrol noted that one day's activities included "a political-information session on the theme 'Sailor, protect and add to the heroic traditions of the Baltic submariners,' radio newscasts on 'Talks by advanced production workers in the socialist competitions in honor of the 50th Anniversary of the USSR,' a seminar with warrant officers on how to 'Help subordinates to fulfill socialist pledges,' a radio meeting on a 'Roll call of outstanding combat posts,' an evening meeting on 'Unabating hatred for the enemies of the socialist motherland,' and at the evening's end verses and songs about the motherland."[55]

Not exactly knee-slapping entertainment. One former conscript described the twice-weekly political sessions as boring and monotonously repetitive, with the same contents week after week.[56] Coinciding information came from another study, which reported that émigrés who had a sharp memory for details of their service times could not recall details of the indoctrination process.[57] They contended the experience was unimportant and insignificant: "Anything said could be found in a *Pravda* editorial."[58] Some sailors had mixed feelings about indoctrination. They found the sessions not entirely unwelcome, since they allowed a much-needed release from work and an opportunity to either write letters home or sleep. Others resented the large amount of time consumed by tedious classes that could have been better spent elsewhere. New enlistees who had not been KOMSOMOL members found that they now had to join and pay dues as part of their political training.[59]

Officers were not particularly happy about political indoctrination, either. Most sailors recognized the dispute between the *zampolit*'s political chain of command and the ship's command structure. Officers disliked having to give political lectures and resented the demands it made on their precious time. Those who led the training sessions seldom allowed discussions or questions because, as one former officer explained, any "provocative" question could put an officer in an awkward spot. To not answer at all made him appear stupid, but the riskier alternative was to offer an answer that might not have followed the party line, thus committing the "sin of ideological deviation." In either case, he could be reported to the *zampolit* or, worse, to the *Spetsotdel*, the ship's special KGB department, possibly harming his career.[60] One former officer who served for twenty years said few questions were asked anyway since most of the seamen were equally fearful of seeming politically unreliable and spent the sessions "picking their noses."[61]

The Soviets emphasized the importance of political indoctrination in the combat readiness of their forces. Based upon all available evidence, the utility of these training sessions in making the conscripts better sailors or soldiers was quite suspect, since it appeared that very few took it seriously. The repetitive, almost hypnotic character of political training, without other sources of information to balance it, may not have turned all Soviet conscripts into ardent Marxist-Leninists. However, as one sailor noted, "If every day for years a person is told that black is white and white is black, he starts to believe it."[62] Consequently, the leadership remained convinced that political training and military training had to continue hand-in-hand.

Sablin had his own ideas about what his men should be taught in these lessons. He could be very territorial when it came to protecting this autonomy. Most of the advice he received from his fellow *zampolit*s went in one ear and out the other. He felt very confident not only of his political credentials but also of his tactical proficiency. He believed he was a commander in everything but name. Although Potulniy was his immediate superior, Sablin also had a boss in the Baltic Fleet's political department, 2nd Rank Capt. Ivan Medvedyev. Medvedyev remembered how difficult it was to rein in his strong-willed subordinate: "My colleagues and I gave him advice about how to deal with the men; advice on how to motivate them as individuals and how to organize the Party and KOMSOMOL activities on board. But he didn't always go out of his way to carry out to the fullest orders given to him by his superiors. He had a character all his own, with several idiosyncrasies. He liked to do things on his own terms."[63]

As far as Valery Sablin was concerned, there were few officers who could give him advice on how to lead his sailors, because there were few officers who knew their men better than he did. While his colleagues were kept busy with their shipboard duties, Sablin roamed the vessel talking to the men, catching up on their personal lives and seeing how they were coming along with their various specialty certifications. Since he had only one sailor working directly for him, and being the energetic extrovert that he was, Sablin craved the personal relationships that these contacts fostered. It was one reason he enjoyed being a political officer so much; you got as much out of that job as you put into it.

One particular attitude that was commonly held by *Storozhevoy*'s crew toward political indoctrination was apathy. Most of the sailors believed that the vague and boring material discussed was totally irrelevant to their everyday lives. The power to influence political decisions was light years removed from their level. Sailors went along with memorizing basic political texts, paying no attention to what was being memorized.

Sablin recognized this indifference in his own men and sympathized with it. One of the duties that Seaman Alexander Shein had been assigned when he reported aboard *Storozhevoy* in October 1974 was the post of official ship's artist. Sablin, himself an aspiring artist, got to know Shein through this mutual interest. Once he came to trust him, he made Shein his assistant in preparing political lectures for the men. Once Shein came to trust Sablin, he confessed to him his disgust with these lectures: "Those political classes were a complete joke. People only went to them to take a nap. We realized that it was all for show, that it was completely insincere. I said to Sablin, 'what good is this window dressing? When there's a war, how are we going to defend anybody with this meaningless rhetoric?'"[64]

To his great surprise and relief, Sablin told him that he could not agree more. On the long deployment to Cuba the previous spring, he and his colleagues had plenty of time to discuss the dismal state of the Soviet Union under Brezhnev. Evidently, at some point these heart-to-heart talks convinced Valery that he had the support of the ship's officers for a radical break with the past. Now the time for talk was over; the time to act had arrived. He was past the point of no return. As he himself confessed, "This machine needs to be broken from within." On the Comet tape recorder in his stateroom, this architect of revolution had drawn up his blueprint for the overthrow of the Soviet regime.

Chapter 4

THE MUTINY

The place Valery Sablin called home in November 1975 was the city of Kaliningrad, about 250 miles southwest of Riga. The naval base at nearby Baltiysk was *Storozhevoy*'s home port and headquarters of the Soviet Baltic Fleet. Kaliningrad was its Russian name, but before it was captured by the Russians in World War II, it had been the German city of Königsberg, the ancient capital of East Prussia. Many of the old airfields in and around the city, which had been used by the Germans during their 1941 invasion of the Soviet Union, were now Soviet Air Force bases. In fact, much of the old German infrastructure was still visible in Kaliningrad; brick buildings still outnumbered the drab palaces of Soviet concrete on the skyline. When Sablin moved there with his wife and son in September 1973, they lived in an old German brick house for the first few months before housing closer to base became available.

A month before the mutiny, Sablin bought six padlocks at the Kaliningrad post exchange (*voentorg*). Any other customer would have put the padlocks to normal use on gardening sheds or gym lockers. The tall officer in the dark blue navy coat had other ideas. Instead of clothes or tools, he intended to lock up opponents of his mutiny in their cabins aboard ship.

Sablin probably knew the enlisted men better than any officer on the ship since he was the one man the sailors were encouraged to see if they had a problem. He prided himself on being able to feel the pulse of the crew, and that pulse was quickening. The sailors were drawn from a population that was wounded by fear, displaying the weary mistrust that was a hallmark of their society. Now, finally, they had a fearless man who was ready to lead them beyond that and take them further than they had ever gone. For almost two years, with countless heart-to-heart talks and simple acts of decency, he had cultivated their trust. He respected the men and their abilities, and he had faith in their devotion to duty.

When that devotion was not there, Sablin, unlike most officers, wanted to know why. What had let the men down? And unlike almost every officer, he asked them if the system had done it—Communism, the state, the party, Brezhnev. This was unprecedented. Complaints may have been tolerated, but the real taboo was questioning the Communist Party's ability to address them. Sablin broke this taboo, although he was quick to point out that he felt the party was the country's best hope. He tried to convince the sailors that Marxism-Leninism, properly applied, best met the people's needs.

Although most of the men were unresponsive to the dense philosophical underpinnings of Marxist theory, they appreciated the fact that Sablin cared about what they thought. They were probably more comfortable when the topic of conversation turned from politics to their families and homes and what they did before the navy. In this, Sablin was happy to oblige. It presented him with an opportunity to find out which of his men he could trust, because at some point during the fall of 1975 he had to choose his co-conspirators in rebellion. He could not carry it out alone, and even if most of the officers threw in their lot with him, they could not sail the ship by themselves. He needed the crew.

Enlisted personnel run the gamut of personality types. There are the high-strung worriers for whom nothing is satisfactory, the quiet ones who take what comes and move on, the "lifers" who love the navy and want to make it a career, the armchair warriors who talk a lot but do little else, and then there are the rebels. Sablin certainly fit into this category, and thus he found common cause with another rebel, his assistant, Alexander Shein.

Shein was a twenty-year-old sailor from the remote Soviet region of Altai, near the Chinese border. He was the Russian version of the kid who ditched class to hot-wire Chevy Novas in the high school parking lot. Shein had dropped out of school after finishing the tenth grade in order to go to work at a local factory in his hometown of Togliatti. One day, after his boss's car broke down, the man told Shein to find a transmission belt and fix it; Shein was good with his hands. Doing as he was told, he did indeed find a transmission belt—in another car. He was caught while removing it and charged with stealing state property. As punishment, 25 percent of his wages were to be garnished for one year. Since he was so near his military induction date, however, the sentence was commuted, and he entered the navy in the spring of 1973. He reported for duty aboard *Storozhevoy* the following October. Like Sablin, he was a "plank owner," meaning he was a member of the first crew to man the ship after it was formally brought into service.

Sablin's influence on the young sailor was profound from the start. Normally, the enlisted men cast a wary eye on their political officer; the *zampolit* had the reputation as the Communist Party watchdog and informer. Any sailor who grew too close to him was liable to earn the same label. But everyone recognized that Sablin was different, and Shein was too. Like a priest who offered absolution to a sinner, Sablin offered Shein the chance to redeem himself by supporting a new cause—and a new revolution. A few months before *Storozhevoy* left for Riga, Shein took some leave and returned to his hometown. His mother recalled that she had never seen him so elated. He kept talking about how great *Storozhevoy* and its *zampolit* were and how he could not wait to get back.[1] Sablin had not yet confided to him the details of his plan, but he thought he might have an ally in Shein. The problem was convincing him and the rest of the crew to cross that invisible threshold between talk and action. Sablin knew how difficult the struggle had been for himself; he could only imagine how tough it would be for the others.

On the morning of 5 November, just after *Storozhevoy* left Baltiysk for Riga, Sablin summoned Shein to his stateroom. The young seaman had grown to respect Sablin; he had noticed some time ago that Valery was on a "different wavelength" than the other officers. Sablin told the sailor that he wanted to talk about something very serious. He began to recite all the problems afflicting the Soviet Union and the deep unhappiness they were causing among the people. At first, Shein could not figure out where he was going with all this:

I asked Sablin how he planned to deal with this dissatisfaction throughout the country. He said that he wanted to take the ship out of Soviet territory and into international waters and send a telegram to Navy Headquarters making specific demands. Then, when he had accomplished this, he'd go on radio and television with an appeal to create a new party and social order. I didn't ask Sablin, and he didn't say, what kind of party he wanted to create. I didn't think there should be another party other than the Communist Party of the Soviet Union. Then Sablin said he needed my help. I told him I had to think about it. I went out on to the quarterdeck. I felt badly because I wasn't going straight to the captain and telling him everything Sablin was plotting. Maybe if I'd done something then, no one would have gotten hurt.[2]

Shein was shaken. He was most worried about the possibility that Sablin was a foreign spy, and he went back to Sablin's cabin later on to ask him point-blank. Sablin assured him that he was no spy and only wanted what was best for the Soviet people. With that, Shein relented and agreed to support his *zampolit*. Still, he was tormented by what they were contemplating. His best friend, Seaman Mikhail Burov, noticed something was wrong and asked Shein why he was so troubled. Shein told him everything and asked Burov what he thought. His friend replied that he loved a good fight but would wait to see what the rest of the crew thought. Neither of them could shake the fear that Sablin might doom them all by taking the ship to Sweden.

That same evening of 5 November, while the ship was en route to Riga from Baltiysk, Sablin played for Shein the speech he intended to give the officers, which he had recorded nearly seven months earlier on his tape player. Sablin gave him the tape and told him that when the time came, he wanted Shein to play it for his fellow sailors. Shein began to sound out his shipmates and approached another friend of his, Seaman Vladimir Averin, who worked in the torpedo section. Before he brought Averin into this intrigue, Shein decided, he would test the waters by posing Sablin's takeover of the ship as a KGB exercise designed to see how the crew would react to a mutiny. He told Averin the KGB wanted him to act as if he supported Sablin, then revealed more details of the plan. Averin agreed to participate, unaware that the "exercise" was very real indeed.

Shein then widened the circle of conspirators to include two more of his friends, Seamen Salivonchik and Manko. He told Salivonchik that something big would happen on 8 November and to stick close to him. Salivonchik agreed, and while Manko was initially dead set against a mutiny, Shein finally managed to win him over. Shein was taking a huge risk, because there was no guarantee that one of these men would not turn them all in, but he had to sound out some of the crew to find out how they might react once Sablin threw down the gauntlet. Over the next few days, Shein, Burov, Averin, Salivonchik, and Manko began to make their own preparations for rebellion. This included the critical task of acquiring all the keys to the various armories and compartments that they would be using as bases of operation once Sablin gave the word to move.

Storozhevoy arrived in Riga on the afternoon of Friday, 7 November, at its assigned buoy in the middle of the Daugava River. The next morning it took part in the naval parade that sailed down the Daugava, passing the Baltic Fleet flagship and rendering honors to it. Afterward, a detachment of sailors from *Storozhevoy* marched in a workers' parade down the wide riverside promenade past V. Alberg's sculpted memorial to the Red Rifleman. This statue, erected in 1972, visibly symbolized Soviet domination of the once sovereign Latvian state.

Shortly after lunch, liberty was sounded. About one-third of the crew went ashore, including Shein, who posted letters to his sister and best friend back home outlining what he was going to do that night. Sablin had made his confession in a letter to Nina, which he had mailed from Baltiysk four days earlier. The ship was quiet that afternoon. Seaman Oleg Maximenko later recalled, "I had to stay on board since I was on duty. It was such a strange feeling, a sort of tension in the air. There was this eerie silence on board."[3]

Dinner was served at 1800. Shortly afterward, once he had met in final consultation with his friends, Shein went to Sablin's stateroom and told him he could count on the assistance of his four friends. Upset at Shein for not keeping the plot secret, Sablin scolded him at first. Then, coming to terms with the inevitable, he gave his chastened conspirator his first assignment. He told Shein to prepare one of the ship's forward compartments so they could use it to detain the captain; he wanted the phone removed from it and a letter and some books placed there. Sablin also gave the seaman the unloaded Makarov pistol, referring to it as "Comrade Mauser." If things did not go his way, he told Shein, Comrade Mauser would have to do the talking. Sablin had a magazine full of 9-mm rounds for the weapon; he told Shein he would give it to him just before he convened the officers' meeting.

Shein complied, but he was worried about taking Potulniy prisoner. Originally Sablin had told him that the captain supported their plan. It would not be the last time he lied to the crew to enlist their support. In reality, Sablin got along well with *Storozhevoy's* skipper; they were comfortable working with one another and had an exceptionally good relationship for a commander and a *zampolit*. In order to avoid a confrontation, Sablin had tried to talk Potulniy into going ashore with him on liberty. Presumably, he would then ditch the captain in town and return to the ship alone, taking command of it and exercising his authority as third in command. Potulniy refused, citing other commitments. Ironically, he had approved leave for several of the officers, including the executive officer, Captain Novozhilov, before the ship left Baltiysk. Had the full complement of ship's officers been present that day, Sablin's task would have been much tougher.

At 1900, Anatoly Potulniy was sitting in his cabin aboard ship when Sablin burst in without knocking, pale and disturbed. "Comrade Commander, we have a CP!" CP was the Russian acronym for *chrezvychainoe polozhenie,* an extraordinary situation, the call word for an emergency aboard ship. Potulniy jumped up out of his chair. "What happened? Where?"

Sablin told him that some of the sailors were drinking in the Second RTC post, a forward sonar compartment below the main deck. The lack of a truly professional enlisted class in the Soviet military meant that the officer corps assumed many duties which would have fallen to senior enlisted men and women in the U.S. armed forces. This apparently was one of those moments. (The captain of a U.S. Navy vessel would not personally collar one of his sailors drinking, and no one would ask him to. Rather, a chief or leading petty officer would do the honors, so as to avoid a possible confrontation between an officer and some drunken enlisted men.) As he would do many times that night, Sablin was using the system's weaknesses against it.

So below decks they went, Potulniy leading the way and Sablin dutifully following him. They went to the lowest deck, fifteen feet below the waterline, with Potulniy calling back to him, "Here?" and Sablin answering, "No, lower." Finally, the captain entered the foremost compartment on the ship's lowest level, the second sonar post.

The compartment was empty.

Before he could gather his thoughts, the hatch above him slammed shut. He heard the latch close and looked around the

compartment, bewildered. In the corner he saw an envelope with
"Potulniy, A. V." written on it, along with several books from the
ship's library. His first thought was to call someone, but then he
noticed that the phone had been ripped off the wall. Potulniy's
jaw dropped as he read the letter addressed to him. It was from
Sablin. It explained why the captain was now locked in this room,
as well as what Sablin was going to do with his ship. Seeing his life
and career flash before his eyes, Potulniy immediately looked for a
way out.

At 1920, the ship's public address system announced that the
second film of the evening would be shown on the mess deck for
the enlisted men and that all officers must attend a meeting in the
warrant officers' stateroom. Over the next three and a half hours,
Valery Sablin and his enlisted converts would fight for the soul of
Storozhevoy.

Not all the officers could make the meeting. Five were on leave
and hadn't even made the journey to Riga and six others did not hear
the announcement, but the remaining sixteen gathered in the stateroom at 1930. Once everyone had settled in, Sablin gave them the
speech of his life. He began by pointing out the inequalities of the
Soviet system, and how, as the son of privileged parents, he had seen
the immoral use of these privileges first hand.

Next to the stateroom was the projector room, which had just
begun to show the movie to the crew. Sablin had summoned Shein
from his post guarding the incarcerated captain and told him to
operate the projector so he could also eavesdrop on the conversation
next door. Should the opposition to Sablin turn violent, Shein was
supposed to burst into the room and keep them at bay with the pistol, which was now loaded with a full magazine of 9-mm rounds.

Sablin continued his address to the officers for the next fifteen
minutes, emphasizing their duty to put a stop to the tyranny that
now had their countrymen by the throat. They had abandoned all
faith in the party because most Communists were manipulative,
opportunistic bureaucrats who put their own interests before those
of the people.

Coming from a political officer and Communist Party member in
good standing, this was heresy. Then he dropped the real bombshell.
He told them that he had detained the captain and would take
Storozhevoy to Leningrad to start a new Russian Revolution.
According to the medical officer, Third Rank Captain Oleg Sadkov,

that made everyone nervous: "On a ship, the commander is untouchable." Warrant Officer Viktor Borodai described the scene:

> Sablin arrived and turned to everyone with a speech. It was clear, prepared, reasonable and candid. He spoke of how the current leadership had put the country and its people on a path to disaster. To endure further suffering was impossible—his speech was not only about the navy. Specifically, he told us that the *Storozhevoy* would go to Leningrad, where it would make an appeal to the factory workers in the City of Three Revolutions.
> "Like the Kronstadt sailors?" someone asked calmly. "Will the Leningrad base support us?"[4]

Sablin replied that it would. He pointed to several chess pieces on the table in front of them. Take a white piece if you support this mutiny, he told them, and a black piece if you do not. Far from any active opposition, the officers did as they were told, laughing and joking as they chose their pieces. The vote was made, and it split right down the middle; eight officers supported him, eight did not (A roster listing the ship's officers and how they voted is in Appendix A.) For those who were against him, Sablin said no harm would come to them. Rather, he led them to Posts Number 3 and 4 on the deck below and locked them up. Not only did Sablin want them out of the way, but should the mutiny go awry, he also wanted these men to be able to deny any responsibility for what happened.

In 1992, after the fall of the Soviet Union, a public trial was held in Moscow to decide whether Valery Sablin should be rehabilitated. This was a process the new Russian government had implemented to address the status of victims of political persecution from the Soviet era. An official rehabilitation essentially was an admission by the government that the individual in question had been wrongly persecuted. One of those who testified was the ship's communications officer, Captain-Lieutenant Proshutinski, who chose a black chess piece on the night of 8 November. The prosecutor who argued the government's case against rehabilitation called Proshutinski to the witness stand and asked him why he and seven other officers had allowed themselves to be locked up. This exchange followed:

PROSECUTOR: You weren't alone. Yet the whole group allowed itself to be led away and locked up. Why?

PROSHUTINSKI: Because deep down they supported it and thought Sablin was doing the right thing. They didn't want to oppose it.

PROSECUTOR: So if I understand you correctly, you regarded this silence as passive consent?

PROSHUTINSKI: In principle, yes.[5]

Later, he described what the captive officers heard as the ship cast off: "We could hear the ship preparing to get underway. We could hear Sablin's voice over the ship's PA system instead of the captain's. Sitting in the compartment with me were most of the department heads—engineering, mechanical, etc. Without them, we figured the ship couldn't get underway, especially because of the conditions on the Daugava—the ship had to turn around in a very tight space. Then we began to move, and the ship started going faster and faster, and we just couldn't believe what was happening."[6]

As Proshutinski came to realize, he was wrong about one thing: Sablin could run the ship with eight officers, but he could only do so as long as the enlisted men cooperated. Would they? He planned to address them as he had the officers and called a formation on the quarterdeck after the movie ended.

The word "mutiny" is unambiguous in its meaning. There are no nuances to it. It strikes at the very heart of military discipline and order and is not tolerated under any circumstances other than those in which a commander clearly gives an illegal order. It is the most severe military crime short of treason, and many nations equate the two. Mutiny is a threat not only to military authority but also to civil authority, because if an officer has no qualms about disobeying his military chain of command, he probably would not abide by his civilian one either. For that reason, it is punishable by death everywhere.

In spite of this ultimate penalty, more than half of the ship's officers sided with Sablin, and the remainder let it happen. The tricky thing about rebellion is that it is only justified if you win. With that in mind, these officers must have been moved by Sablin's words and his confidence. Seventeen years later, during Sablin's rehabilitation trial, Viktor Borodai recalled his motivation for going along with his *zampolit*:

DEFENSE ATTORNEY: What kind of chance did Sablin's plan have to succeed?

BORODAI: It's very difficult to say. We had maybe a 10 percent chance of reaching Leningrad.

DEFENSE ATTORNEY: Nevertheless, you supported him?

BORODAI: Yes. After all, a 10 percent chance is still a chance.

DEFENSE ATTORNEY: But what did you think personally?

BORODAI: Well, I was a young and uneducated man back then and it was all pretty frightening.

DEFENSE ATTORNEY: Why then did you follow Sablin into this extraordinary situation?

BORODAI: Because in general I agreed with the aims outlined in his speech. It was the first time in my life that I heard somebody speak the truth about these matters.[7]

Contributing to the surreal nature aboard *Storozhevoy* that night was the movie the crew was watching while the officers were casting their fates. Films shown aboard Soviet warships were chosen by the political officer and were usually some form of propaganda praising the virtues of the party line. The movie Sablin chose that night was appropriate: *The Battleship Potemkin*. Fifteen minutes after Sablin locked up his opponents, the film started to roll.

Directed by Sergei Eisenstein, it was one of the first motion pictures to be produced in Soviet Russia. Like the Leni Riefenstahl film *Triumph of the Will*, which documented the 1934 Nazi Party rally in Nuremberg, *The Battleship Potemkin* is recognized by most critics as a propaganda piece, but nonetheless a fine work of cinematography. It was about a real mutiny that took place in the tsarist navy in 1905, one that held a special place in Valery Sablin's heart. One of his heroes was a naval officer who participated in it, Lt. Peter Schmidt, who was also a graduate of the Frunze Military Academy. In the Black Sea port of Sevastopol, Schmidt led the battleship *Pamyat Azova*, along with four destroyers and a naval garrison ashore, against forces loyal to the tsar. A portrait of the rebellious lieutenant, drawn by Sablin himself, hung in his stateroom.

The 1905 revolution was a watershed in Russian history because it exposed the weakness and corruption of the tsarist regime. The poor performance of the Russian Army and Navy in a war with the Japanese the year before was the real catalyst for this unrest.

The Russian officer corps, poisoned by nepotism and incompetence, was duly trounced by superior Japanese leadership and tactics. The country's outrage over the Russian defeat at Port Arthur in the Far East was profound and immediate. A protest in St. Petersburg on 9 January was met by gunfire at the gates of the tsar's Winter Palace, killing hundreds (among Sablin's collection of sketches was one he drew of this incident, known as Bloody Sunday). Revolt quickly spread to the rest of the country, seriously threatening the reign of Tsar Nicholas II.

Potemkin was a battleship attached to the Black Sea Fleet, and the mutiny that erupted aboard it in the summer of 1905 was less a political statement than the act of a crew apparently enraged at having to eat bad borsch soup. Made from red beets, borsch has long been a staple of the Russian diet and is often prepared with meat. The previous day, several sides of beef had been delivered to the battleship, which was at anchor in Odessa harbor. At some point, the beef had spoiled, and on the morning of 27 June, as it hung on hooks outside the ship's galley, it was crawling with maggots. The ship's surgeon declared the meat fit for human consumption, insisting that it need only be doused with vinegar and water to wash off the maggots.

The cooks did so and used the beef in the borsch they were making for lunch that afternoon. The men refused to eat it. Like their counterparts on *Storozhevoy* seventy years later, the crew of the *Potemkin* was dissatisfied with its leadership. The month before, many of their comrades had perished against the Japanese in the Battle of Tsushima Strait. The entire Baltic Fleet had sailed out to the Pacific to retake Port Arthur from the Japanese, and almost all of it had been sent to the bottom of the sea.

The total defeat of the Russian fleet in the Far East, combined with the ruthless suppression of the demonstrations in St. Petersburg that January, caused deep unrest throughout the Russian empire. Revolutionaries such as Lenin's Bolsheviks took advantage of this unrest, tapping into it and agitating for fundamental and violent change in the country. The people were becoming more receptive to this message in 1905, especially within the navy. In the eyes of the men, their officers' judgment had not been vindicated in battle, nor, apparently, was it any better when it came to inspecting the quality of food they ate.

Disaster wears many masks, and on the afternoon of 27 June aboard the *Potemkin,* it was worn by Comdr. Ipplolit Giliarovsky, the ship's executive officer. Giliarovsky had sensed that the mood of the men bordered on violence. He convinced the captain, Yevgeni Golikov, to call a formation of the ship's crew to put an end to any sedition at once. Captain Golikov spoke to his sailors and asked all those who would eat the borsch to step forward. Some did; most did not. Golikov then said he would send a sample of the meat ashore and have it analyzed. If it was determined that the beef was not contaminated, then he told them he would refer to the fleet commander for disciplinary action against all those who had refused to eat it.

An officer who faces disgruntled subordinates has two choices open to him. He can make concessions to them, which has its own risks since his men might then view him as weak and lose respect for his authority, or he can ignore their complaints and reassert this authority with force. The trick is knowing which option to choose and how much of it to exercise.

Shocked by the leniency of his commanding officer and convinced that it would only invite future dissent, Commander Giliarovsky impulsively re-formed the crew. He then "called for the tarpaulin," an old Russian Navy term that meant covering condemned men with a canvas sheet just before they were shot in order to make the executions as impersonal as possible. Giliarovsky was clearly hoping that the threat of a firing squad would bring the men back into line. When a majority of the crew again refused to eat the tainted soup, Giliarovsky, no doubt egged on by a desperate attempt to save face, raised the stakes and ordered the armed guard to round up several of the dissenters. About a dozen of them were gathered before a firing squad and covered with the tarpaulin.

In a matter of seconds, Giliarovsky had passed the point of no return and sealed his own death. Several of the dissatisfied crewmen rushed to the armory to get weapons, while others approached the firing squad and begged them not to shoot their shipmates. These appeals fell on sympathetic ears. Giliarovsky ordered the would-be executioners to fire, but they refused, turning their guns on him instead.

Within half an hour, most of the officers had been killed or thrown overboard; a handful joined the mutineers. When *Potemkin* reached the port of Odessa, the crew received support from the local Social Democratic Party committee, which called for a general strike that quickly spread throughout the city. The military governor of Odessa imposed martial law and sent his Cossacks, the infamous

horsemen who acted as the tsar's enforcers, to quell the rebellion.
The famous scene in Eisenstein's movie in which Cossacks attack an
advancing column of workers and sailors took place on the Richelieu
Steps in Odessa.

Word of the mutiny reached every port on the Black Sea coast,
igniting uprisings in several other cities, including Sevastopol, the
headquarters of the Black Sea Fleet, where Lieutenant Schmidt led
his rebellious garrison. After sailing around for several weeks,
Potemkin ran out of coal and food and eventually made its way to
the Romanian port of Constanza, where the crew was granted political asylum.

The mutiny aboard *Potemkin* was revered in Soviet literature
and sanctified in propaganda works like Eisenstein's film. It provided inspiration to Valery Sablin for two reasons. First, the mutineers of 1905 had declared their revolution to be a socialist one and
sailed *Potemkin* under a red flag. Second, their mutiny, touched off
by an argument over borsch, lit a tinderbox of unrest in southern
Russia that almost turned into full-scale revolution. Sablin hoped to
have a similar impact, but in trying to do so, he was risking a repeat
of the consequences; the fighting that broke out in 1905 claimed the
lives of nearly seven thousand people.[8] Among them was Lieutenant
Schmidt, who was found guilty of treason and shot by firing squad.

In another of the many ironies that surround the *Storozhevoy*
mutiny, Seaman Shein recalled a similar situation: "We all remembered, on our way back from Cuba in May of 1975, how they served
us lunch with bread that was infested with worms. We were outraged, but the supply officer assured us that the worms were harm-
less and the bread was of the highest quality. But no one would eat
it. Six months had passed and now—8 November—we remembered
that bread."[9]

Sablin called the formation for 2210; all hands were to meet on
the quarterdeck. Of the ship's crew of 194 officers and men, nearly
all had returned to *Storozhevoy* from liberty that night. In spite of
Sablin's attempts at secrecy, word of what had happened, including
the captain's arrest, spread throughout the ship. After the officers'
meeting, Shein had returned to his post guarding the captain. He
tried to stop two sailors who were walking down the passageway toward him, but they refused to pay attention. When Potulniy
heard their voices, he called out for help, shouting, "Sablin and
Shein are traitors to the Motherland!" The two sailors confronted

Shein and tried to free the captain. He pulled out the pistol Sablin had given him, but his assailants knocked it out of his hand. Shein would have been overpowered and the mutiny might have ended right there if four warrant officers—Borodai, Gomenchuk, Velichko, and Kalinichev—had not come to his assistance. They sent the two would-be rescuers on their way but did not detain them.

After this, the cat was out of the bag, and rumors were rampant. Sablin knew he had to make his appeal to the crew quickly. Of the 165 enlisted men aboard, 150 were present at the formation. The deck lights were on, bathing the quarterdeck in a bright white cone. There was a very bright, nearly full moon. The lights from the customs pier were visible, but the late evening fog obscured the rest of Riga. The sailors stood in rank and file, bundled up in their pea coats, the formation punctuated by their breaths condensing in the cold November air.

Sablin walked to the head of the formation. He was wearing his dark blue officer's overcoat with a pistol strapped to his shoulder holster. The men were surprised that he was the only officer who showed up. He was by himself, and what he said was unforgettable. In fact, it was unbelievable coming from a political officer. He told the men that they could not go on like this any longer; the country was moving toward the abyss. He said that while the nation's leadership constantly talked about equality, it used its position to get rich off the people. He did not criticize the Communist Party itself, or the October Revolution. He only considered certain people guilty of bringing the country to ruin. At the end of his speech, Sablin called upon the crew to follow him and go to Leningrad, where they would make the same announcement on television.

He had been planning this moment for many years and had undoubtedly gone over what he was going to say many times in his mind. He recorded several of his speeches on a tape recorder he kept in his stateroom, and the tapes were locked up in his safe, ready to be played over the radio. He had a flair for the dramatic and knew that these words, coming as they did from the *zampolit,* would have a profound impact on this group of eighteen to twenty year olds. It was probably the first time anyone in authority had spoken the truth to them and told them what they already knew: the system was broken and needed to be fixed.

His speech had an electrifying effect upon the young sailors. Sablin assured them that they would get the support of dozens of military units because there were honest officers in the USSR who also did not agree with the course the country's leaders were taking. The people did not have any kind of rights, the country was going to hell, the population was half-starved, and all the while they were supposed to be obeying a higher authority that was squandering Russia's national treasure. Brezhnev and his ilk were making fools of them all, Sablin challenged, and were exploiting the people. It is up to us as members of the armed forces, he said, to protect our people, and we must announce this on television. Great Russia must become a democratic and just nation in the world, not a meager and backward country led by the Central Committee and Brezhnev. To lead the country, they needed people who were democratically elected—honest, faithful patriots, not protégés of a political and family dynasty. He strode between the ranks of the formation, facing each of his men. As one of them later recalled, "Sablin asked: 'Do you agree with me?' We understood that what he was asking was dangerous, but it was for a worthy goal. . . . He made his way through the formation, stopping in front of each of us and asking: 'And you?' In reply you heard 'Yes' or 'I agree.'"[10]

Every sailor present at that formation supported mutiny. As he had with Seaman Shein and the officers, Sablin lied to gain their loyalty. He told the crew that officers in the Northern and Pacific Fleets were waiting for word from *Storozhevoy* and then they would join the revolt. It was a huge and very dangerous gamble. He was hoping that their mutiny would spark a larger revolution in the tradition of their predecessors on *Potemkin*.

Sablin was rolling the dice. In the process, he was betting not only his own life but also the lives of nearly two hundred men. Nevertheless, he had asked for and received the support of the crew. How much of this support stemmed from genuine outrage at the Communist Party and how much was the result of teenage boredom is unclear. Their motives were probably fueled by a little of both. Although they had very little with which to compare their young lives, they had a finely tuned sense of inequality. Contrary to conventional wisdom, the conformity of the military actually sharpens personality differences. If everyone has the same haircut, wears the same uniform, and acts according to the same rules, variations from these norms are all the more obvious. In their everyday lives, they certainly noticed the poverty of their own living conditions and those of their families when compared to the comforts enjoyed by high Communist Party officials. Why did they all seem to have their own cars and houses in the country? Why did they look healthier and cleaner than everyone else? In another time and place, these young sailors might not have begrudged such privileges, as long as they saw an opportunity to earn a few of their own. In the Soviet Union of 1975, however, the only way to do so was to embrace a conformity that demanded surrender to the thoughts and ambitions of the Communist Party.

For this and many unspoken reasons, the enlisted men threw in with their *zampolit*. They set up posts around the ship to guard the detained officers, the armory, Sablin's stateroom, and the bridge. They obtained keys to one of the ship's armories, getting pistols and ammunition. There were several machine guns and some rounds for them, but the heavy weaponry—missiles, depth charges, and 76.2-mm rounds—had been offloaded in Baltiysk. *Storozhevoy* was supposed to sail to Liepae for repairs on its way back to Baltiysk, and it was common practice for a vessel to offload all its weapons before entering dry dock. Armed and ready, Shein recalled the mood of the crew in those first few hours: "After his speech on the quarterdeck, there was general enthusiasm. We talked about it amongst ourselves in groups, with everyone speaking up. On the record and in front of the formation. It was like a holiday. We really felt like human beings for the first time!"[11]

Some of the officers who had not attended the vote in the warrant officers' stateroom had gotten wind of what was going on, however, and they were far from enthusiastic. One of the sailors, Seaman Sakhnevich, came to Sablin and informed him that several of them were meeting in one of their cabins and plotting against him. Sablin and Sakhnevich went there to confront them. Three officers, Saitov, Stepanov, and Kovalchenkov, had pistols, and they squared off against Sablin in their stateroom. They grabbed the *zampolit* and tried to disarm him, but Sakhnevich called for help. Several sailors came to his defense and pulled Sablin, who was brandishing his pistol at his four colleagues, from the cabin. Then they locked the door.

Why no one pulled the trigger is anyone's guess. It was most likely the simple fear of being killed if they did. Four pistols going off in a ten-by-ten-foot room did not leave good odds on survival. A gunfight was narrowly avoided, but that was not the worst news.

Just before the struggle, one of the officers told Sablin that the mutiny was over because Senior Lieutenant Firsov had jumped ship and swam ashore to warn the authorities. Sablin could not believe it. In the officers' meeting, Firsov had supported the mutiny, so he had not been detained. Whether out of conviction or calculation, Firsov now opposed Sablin. At around 2230, he crawled down the mooring line to the buoy that kept the ship anchored in the middle of the river and crawled up the bowline of *S-263*, a submarine moored next to *Storozhevoy*. He shouted for help at the conning tower, and the sailors on watch sent him to see the captain. Once inside the sub, Firsov stammered out an explanation of why he had jumped ship. The skipper, 2nd Rank Capt. L. V. Svetlovski, did not believe him at first. Mutiny in the Soviet Navy? Never! This fool must be another drunk on liberty. Nonetheless, he sent Firsov ashore in a launch so he could warn the duty officer.

This changed everything, and Sablin knew it. Had they been able to maintain the element of surprise, they might have had enough of a head start to make it to Leningrad. Now he had to assume that the harbor master and the Riga duty officer both knew what he was up to. *Storozhevoy* had to get underway immediately; they had to get out into open water as soon as possible. It was now 2300. Sablin went to the bridge and ordered the crew to weigh anchor. Potulniy heard the engines come to life from his confines below decks and knew what it meant. He became even more desperate to escape:

> I found several pieces of iron in the compartment and tried to pry the hatch open with them. Suddenly, I heard the engines rumble and I knew we were underway. Despair, anger, resentment; I felt everything that a man feels when he is suddenly powerless. I forced open the hatch and made it to a higher compartment, but it too was sealed. I faced yet another hatch, and began to hit it. Seaman Shein, who was guarding me, had a heavy shoring beam lodged against the door, but I continued to hit it. Shein cried out to me, "Comrade Commander please don't! Comrade Commander, I will be forced to shoot!" But I shook the beam loose and it fell. Then they put another beam against the hatch. It was clear that it wasn't going to open. There was no way out.[12]

Maneuvering a ship in port can be difficult. If a captain is unfamiliar with the waters, he will rely on a harbor pilot who knows them better to guide his vessel. Sablin did not have that luxury. When the mooring lines were cut, *Storozhevoy*'s gas turbine engines accelerated. It had to avoid the submarine in front of it, the submarine next to it, and the frigate behind it while turning around.

The man at the helm was Petty Officer First Class Soloviev. Nicknamed the "Master" by his shipmates, Soloviev was the best helmsman aboard. Even he could not make a clean getaway, however, and while turning the ship around to go downriver, the bow of the *Storozhevoy* hit the stern of the submarine in front of it. Once the Master had successfully turned the ship around and pointed it downstream, it was all ahead full. Carried by the tide and traveling at top speed, *Storozhevoy* was now sailing north along the Daugava River at well over thirty knots, at one point nearly colliding with a tanker that was also leaving port. The warship would continue on this course for another ten miles until the freshwater Daugava emptied into the saltwater Gulf of Riga. At the far northern end of the gulf were the islands of Saaremaa and Hiiumaa. The stretch of water that separated Saaremaa from the Latvian mainland was called the Irben Channel. If they wanted to reach the open waters of the Baltic, they would have to pass through this channel, which left them vulnerable to coastal artillery or even tanks on the Latvian side of this gauntlet.

Sablin originally intended to set a course straight for Leningrad, but now he knew that he did not have time to reach the city before patrol boats and aircraft caught up with him. He therefore contemplated taking the ship into international waters once they transited the Irben Channel. If all else failed, he would broadcast an appeal he had written to Kurt Waldheim, the secretary general of the United Nations, and broadcast their message to the entire world. He told his nervous sailors that they would only cross that bridge once they came to it.

Sablin kept the ship's radar off; he did not want to put out any signal that could be detected by pursuers. The only instrument activated was the fathometer, which kept track of water depth. He was careful to avoid leaving any footprint of *Storozhevoy*'s activity because he knew they would be coming after him. He was right.

It took approximately four hours for news of the *Storozhevoy* mutiny to reach Moscow. KGB Headquarters got wind of it around four in the morning of 9 November. They called Navy Headquarters, but the duty officer there had not yet heard about it. He had to call Baltic Fleet HQ to find out the details. Soon he was barraged by telephone calls, the most urgent of which came from the top man himself, Admiral of the Fleet Sergei Gorshkov. Gorshkov called from his *dacha* and wanted to know what was going on. He apparently had to brief Brezhnev about it, along with Marshal Grechko, the minister of defense.

Vice Admiral Kosov, the Baltic Fleet chief of staff, was the first high-ranking officer to get word of *Storozhevoy*'s flight. He was alerted by the duty officer in Riga, who got the story straight from the runaway Firsov. Kosov issued orders at 0400 for all vessels at anchor in Riga to get underway immediately. The captains were told to stop *Storozhevoy* and bring it back to port. Kosov did not yet give the "at all costs" amendment to this order; that decision was above his pay grade. He was trying to keep Gorshkov updated in Moscow, but military commanders in the capital were so gripped by panic they were issuing orders to whomever they could to stop this ship, convinced it was heading to Sweden.

Kosov got on the radio and demanded to speak with the captain. Sablin replied that the captain was no longer in command. Alexander Shein, who was also on the bridge, remembers hearing Sablin announce to his superior officers that *Storozhevoy* was now "free and independent territory from the Soviet Union."[13] Kosov ordered Sablin to stop the ship and drop anchor immediately. As the admiral recalled later, he did not meet with a warm response: "Comrade Sablin then announced that he had no interest in speaking with me, would not give me a report on the situation, and no longer felt himself accountable to me. I was in direct communication with the Commander of the Navy [Gorshkov], who was listening to Sablin very attentively. Sablin said he would speak to the commander, but would not take any orders from him. Gorshkov informed the Minister of Defense, Marshal Grechko, who woke Brezhnev up. At around 6:00 AM, Grechko told Gorshkov that Brezhnev had personally given the order—'Bomb the ship and sink it!'"[14]

Meanwhile, Swedish military surveillance posts were watching these developments with growing alarm. The first event that piqued the interest of a Swedish radar operator on Götland Island was the takeoff of two planes he detected while monitoring his screen, which was linked to an air search radar. He wondered why two Il-38 May reconnaissance aircraft had left their airfield in Latvia at 0400 on a Sunday morning and were flying over the Irben Channel. His colleague, who was monitoring the surface radar, had yet to see anything out of the ordinary.

That soon changed. Also on Götland Island was a secret National Defense Radio Institute (FRA) station near the city of Ostergarn. The FRA, the Swedish equivalent of the National Security Agency, is responsible for collecting signals intelligence on foreign nations. The Götland station suddenly received a signal from a transmitting Soviet shipborne radar in the Irben Channel. Within twenty minutes, the experienced operator had pinpointed the location and identity of the vessel. (Each ship has a radar crystal that makes the signal it gives off unique and, therefore, identifiable from other ships with the same radar type.) The Swedes identified the vessel as the *Krivak I–*class *Storozhevoy;* Sablin had switched on the ship's radar, probably due to fog in the Irben Channel. It was heading into the Baltic toward Sweden. The operator picked up the telephone and notified the FRA main headquarters at Lovon near Stockholm. Within thirty minutes, the pursuing vessels' radars were also detected.

The duty officers on the Defense Ministry intelligence staff were now very awake and trying to piece together the information coming in from both the radar site and the FRA station. It initially appeared that some sort of special training exercise had begun. The FRA communication center at Lovon, which functioned as the central reporting station for all the FRA intercepting stations, sent the alarm to the other posts to cover the entire area as soon as possible.

The operators were secretly hoping that this was indeed an unscheduled training activity; the alternative was too frightening to contemplate. That hope soon disintegrated, however, when the FRA eavesdroppers began to hear excited Russian voices broadcasting on tactical networks. These transmissions were almost always encrypted; when they were "in the clear" (unencrypted), it was only to pass on routine and insignificant information.

What they were hearing now was far from routine. The Soviets were in such a panic that they were not even bothering to code their messages. There were several FRA operators at Ostergarn who were Russian linguists (they were sent to a special language school for the sole purpose of listening in on Russian radio traffic), and while they normally had time to tape and transcribe the conversations they heard over the airwaves, checking and rechecking them for accuracy, now they were overwhelmed by a dozen shouting Russian voices. What they could piece together was disturbing. It was becoming clear that something was very, very wrong on the other side of the Baltic. For all they knew, the multitude of aircraft and warships the Soviets were launching was the prelude to World War III. Only the Russians knew that it was a desperate hunt for a mutinous vessel.

At 0700, the Swedes detected the arrival of ten Tu-16 Badger bombers in the region. Radar surveillance registered the planes flying at all sorts of different altitudes, at one point as low as fifty feet. What were they doing? Everyone was watching the blips on the radar scope. All the signals and voices were being taped and saved for subsequent analysis. The Emergency Defense Staff members who had been roused from their beds and called into work did not know what to think. At 0730, twenty new radar blips showed up on the screen. The FRA operators identified them as Yak-28 Brewer attack planes, and they could hear some pilots refusing orders to drop their bomb loads. According to FRA officials, these fliers were persuaded to carry out their mission only by the use of some "pretty bloody tough language" from their ground control.[15]

Others simply ignored their orders. Sergei Guliayev, the commander of the Baltic Fleet Air Wing, recalls the instructions he gave to a Yak-28 squadron leader: "So I said, 'Prepare to destroy the target.' The squadron leader acknowledged. Then there was a pause as if he'd been knocked unconscious. He couldn't understand how it was possible to sink one of our own ships. Several long, hard minutes passed. I should have heard the order to fire. Then I realized that they had flown over without doing so."[16]

For a few very tense moments, it appeared as if Sablin's mutiny was spreading to the rest of the navy. Grechko and Gorshkov were nervously monitoring the events from a command post in Moscow. They were beside themselves with rage when they found out the *Storozhevoy* had not yet been stopped. "Carry out your orders immediately!" they yelled to Guliayev over the phone.[17] If ever there was a moment when Valery Sablin's revolt caused the Soviet system to buckle, this was it.

In order to gain a comprehensive picture of what was going on, the Swedes had ordered their own reconnaissance planes to take off, but the order was rescinded after Russian air activity and communications ceased. Radar showed that several *Stenka* patrol boats had caught up with *Storozhevoy*. It was 0900.

If the Swedes were confused about what was going on, so were the Russians. The Il-38 May submarine hunters were indeed the first aircraft sent up to look for *Storozhevoy*. The alarm came just before 0500, which surprised everyone on duty since their training sorties the previous week had always taken place between six and seven. Then came the real shock: the pilots were given a "war alarm" as opposed to the "training alarm" that was normally used to scramble the crews. It was not welcomed with enthusiasm, as a combat sortie meant only one thing: World War III. The chief medical officer at Mogilevshina Airfield near Kaliningrad, Yevgeniy Tsukanov, overheard his divisional commander issuing the order to subordinates: load your aircraft with live ordnance and fuses and be prepared to arm them on my command. In seven years of service, Tsukanov said, he had never heard this order given. When the army commander arrived from Kaliningrad, all he told his officers was, "It's probably war."[18]

Word soon spread that it was not full-scale war. Rumor now had it that a West German frigate had violated Soviet territorial waters. According to Tsukanov, practically all the ship commanders at the nearby naval base were still drunk from the holiday festivities, and at his base he had to feed pure oxygen to one of the air crews to sober them up. Somehow they managed to get aboard their plane and take off, convinced that they were chasing after a West German warship. Soon afterward, the story changed again, and the officers at Tsukanov's base were told that the target was one of their own ships, led by a "Zionist political officer and like-minded sailors."[19] In the political vocabulary of the time, Zionist was the official derogatory term for a Jew. In a matter of hours, the identity of the enemy had changed from the Americans to the Germans and now, finally, the Jews.

Once Sablin turned on his surface search radar in the Irben Channel, the Il-38s picked it up and sent back the ship's location to ground control at Skirotava Airfield just outside Riga. The first pursuit aircraft, a flight of Tu-16 strategic bombers, had taken off from Skirotava shortly after the Il-38s did, waiting for the Mays to find their target. They were outfitted with AS-2 Kipper and AS-5 Kelt antiship missiles that could be used against aircraft carriers at long range but were unsuitable for attacking a runaway destroyer in heavy merchant traffic. They were halfway to *Storozhevoy* when ground control at the airbase realized they were the wrong planes for the mission and recalled them. They were replaced by Yak-28 bombers from Mamonovo Airfield outside Kaliningrad. Mamonovo had once been a German airfield, and in 1941 planes took off from there en route to the Irben Channel. Their mission then had also been to attack a Soviet warship.

The Yak-28s were armed with the right ordnance, conventional bombs and 30-mm cannon, and joined the hunt. Morning fog choked the Irben Channel and made visibility difficult for the pilots. While the Il-38s continued to track *Storozhevoy,* several patrol boats had already found it. By 0800, it was passing between Saaremaa Island and the Latvian coast. In less than an hour, it would be in international waters. The patrol craft, one of many small cutters the KGB used for their border patrols, employed every conceivable means of communication to order *Storozhevoy* back to port—semaphore, signal lamps, flares, voice commands over a bullhorn—all to no avail. Messages to *Storozhevoy* to stop engines immediately were coming in over the radio from Kaliningrad and Moscow. The sailors on the bridge were already nervous, and these warnings did nothing to ease their condition. Since they were broadcast in the clear, anyone could hear them, including Alexander Shein. According to him, Sablin had no intention of firing at the pursuing ships and aircraft. He got a megaphone and shouted at the KGB cutter alongside them that *Storozhevoy* had no hostile intent. The vessel backed off to take a firing position behind them, increasing the distance so it could use its deck guns. In response, Sablin ordered the two 76.2-mm guns aft pointed in the direction of the cutter. They had no ammunition for the guns even if they had intended to use them, but the warning was enough to keep their pursuers at bay.

Reveille was not sounded for the crew that morning, but breakfast was served at the normal time, 0800. As the watch came off the bridge, they would go to the galley and tell the other sailors what they heard the rest of the fleet saying about them. When they went topside, they could clearly see the patrol vessel off their port stern, signaling frantically for them to stop.

By 0900, *Storozhevoy* was being tailed by a dozen ships, including a destroyer and another BPK. Two more patrol craft came alongside her, port and starboard, with shot lines at the ready and armed boarding parties assembled on the main decks. Shortly before 1000, these ships suddenly backed off and took positions far behind *Storozhevoy*. At the same time, a flight of fighter-bombers arrived on station, circling overhead. When they saw the planes, the mood of the crew changed dramatically. According to Shein, "By morning we had made it into the Irben Channel. Ahead of us was the open Baltic. . . . Suddenly, aircraft appeared—fighter-bombers. They began to circle us, forming up for attack. A little earlier, the radiomen had received a warning that if we didn't stop, the *Storozhevoy* would be sunk. This word immediately spread through the ship, and all the previous enthusiasm was squelched for good."[20]

The first planes to reach the ship, at about 0800, were the Yak-28s. They were the first to open fire on *Storozhevoy,* but they were completely ineffective in their attack runs; many had simply ignored their orders to fire on their own ship. Grechko decided that naval aviators could not be trusted, so he turned to the air force. He jumped several levels in the chain of command and personally ordered an aviation regiment based at Tukums, thirty miles west of Riga, to send its new Su-24 Fencer fighter-bombers to stop the renegade vessel. Grechko told the regimental commander that if the ship crossed the twentieth meridian, his planes were to sink it regardless of where it was going.[21]

This ultimatum was also passed on to the bridge of *Storozhevoy.* Sablin heard it but ignored it, ordering the helm to continue on a course of 290 degrees, all ahead full. He had ordered his radioman, Seaman Nikolai Vinogradov, to broadcast the tape recording he had made of his speech. Vinogradov, however, had been trained to broadcast everything that came across his desk in code, so in the confusion he fell back on his training and played the following recording only on encrypted military networks (a full transcript can be found in Appendix E):

TO ALL! TO ALL! TO ALL!

This is the BPK *Storozhevoy!*

We are neither traitors to the Motherland nor adventurers seeking recognition for its own sake. An extreme but necessary opportunity has come for us to openly address a range of questions about the political, social and economic development of our country. The future of our people should be discussed by everyone without pressure from the state or Party. We decided to make this announcement with a clear understanding of the responsibility we have for the fate of the Motherland, and with a sincere desire to achieve genuine Communist relations in our society. But we also recognize the danger of physical and moral destruction at the hands of state institutions or hired guns. . . . Therefore, we are turning for help to all the honest people in our country and abroad. If at 2130 Moscow time tonight you don't see a representative from our ship on your television screens, we ask you not to go to work tomorrow, and to continue this strike until the government ceases its harsh repression of free speech and you hear from us again.

Support us comrades! Goodbye.

V SABLIN[22]

The ship's radios had a range of several hundred miles; Vinogradov broadcast this and other messages on VHF (very high frequency) and HF (high frequency) channels in code. He also used a command channel that went straight to naval headquarters in Moscow to broadcast his statement that *Storozhevoy* had "hoisted the flag of the new Communist revolution" and that the ship was now "free and independent from state and party institutions."

Since ordinary Soviet citizens were not allowed to buy shortwave radios, and in any case could not listen in on encrypted military channels, they never heard a word of Sablin's broadcasts. Even if they had, it might not have made much of an impact. The full text of his statement goes on for ten pages and contains such comments as "This dissatisfaction manifests itself in the passivity of the generation now reaching middle age, who dream of their upcoming pensions."[23] At a time when every minute counted, and a mutinous crew could have used every ounce of support from their fellow servicemen, one thinks Sablin would have been on the radio trying to convince his pursuers on the ground and in the air to join him. Instead, he was addressing them as if he was giving another long-winded political lecture to his crew.

His pursuers were in fact listening to him. A skipper of one of the patrol craft shadowing *Storozhevoy*, 1st Rank Capt. Yuri Mozhar, could hear everything. At Sablin's rehabilitation trial, he described his reaction to the speech: "I listened to what he was broadcasting with mixed emotions. You see at that time, I too understood that not everything in our country was going as well as the government and the party said it was. But I also understood that the actions of this one political officer amounted to suicide, and such actions could not possibly bring about the desired result."[24]

Not everyone was as understanding as Mozhar. Another patrol boat commander, 2nd Rank Capt. Alexander Bobrakov, regarded the flight of *Storozhevoy* as nothing less than a direct attack on Mother Russia. Bobrakov was not as circumspect in his analysis as Mozhar was. He was convinced the ship was heading to Sweden and taking with it a whole store of state secrets:

> I never had any doubt about carrying out my orders. It's the primary duty of an officer. I also judged that the damage which would be inflicted on my Motherland by the defection of that ship with all the classified documents, weapons systems and communications equipment it had on board—would be catastrophic. Most secret of all were the guidance systems on our missiles. To compromise this information was a crime, pure and simple. We're talking about billions of rubles in damage, because we would have been forced to change equipment identification numbers and encryption codes for the entire armed forces due to all the classified material on that ship. I considered it too heavy a price to pay—that ship couldn't be allowed to escape. If people died at the hands of the enemy and our ships were sunk because this information got out, then I'd have to answer for it. So I had no reservations about opening fire.[25]

It was a very persuasive argument. It was also true, or would have been if Sweden had been Sablin's ultimate destination. Americans might recall the outrage they felt at the revelation in 1985 that Warrant Officer John Walker of the U.S. Navy had compromised seventeen years of military communications by selling these secret codes to the Russians. The resulting scramble to assess the damage of this security leak, as well as the immediate supercession of all classified keying material worldwide, caused havoc in the U.S. armed forces. Furthermore, had war broken out, Soviet submarine captains would have been able to track the precise locations of their American counterparts underwater, thanks to Walker's treachery.

So Bobrakov cannot be faulted for his position. It was one of the possibilities that Sablin should have accounted for when he weighed the odds of taking off with one of his country's newest warships; not everyone would believe him when he told them he was only taking the ship to Leningrad.

By now, *Storozhevoy* was in international waters. It is possible that Sablin had abandoned his attempt to go to Leningrad because he kept the ship on a course of 290 degrees, almost due west. However, he had not yet reached that point where the shipping lanes split and fanned out across the Baltic. One led to Stockholm, one to Copenhagen, one to Helsinki, and still another to Leningrad. Would *Storozhevoy* run the gauntlet to the city, or would Sablin adopt his backup plan? If it was the latter, then he would sail the ship around the Baltic, like his predecessors aboard *Potemkin* had done seventy years earlier in the Black Sea, and create an international incident by appealing to the United Nations for help.

The pursuit force had now been joined by several patrol craft from the naval base at Liepae on the Latvian coast. Second Rank Capt. Alexei Neipert led a flotilla of three ships from the base and caught up with *Storozhevoy* by midmorning. He was in communication with his headquarters at Liepae and had a direct line to Naval Headquarters in Moscow. He described the near panic and confusion as the military leadership tried to decide what to do: "The situation was extraordinary and extremely tense. Over one telephone, they would tell me, 'Make a decision!' Over another, 'Here is a situation analysis for you.' Over a third, 'Take control. Try to think of something that can be done to stop it.' And I rushed between all these receivers. You can imagine how many commands I received. Sometimes they were simply incompatible."[26]

With such contradictory instructions, Neipert put off making a decision, and when a final order came to open fire with the intent of sinking the runaway ship, he ignored it. A message *Storozhevoy*'s bridge had flashed to him stuck in his mind: "Friend, we are not traitors to our Motherland. We are headed to Leningrad."[27] Even the normally self-assured Bobrakov was uncertain of *Storozhevoy*'s destination. "I calculated that the ship had approximately ten minutes before she reached that point in the Irben Channel where the shipping lanes split," he recalled. "One led north to Leningrad, but if she maintained her course of 290 degrees, it was a direct course for Stockholm. I had no idea where she was going. She never reached the point where I could know for certain that the ship was heading for Sweden, because at that very moment, planes from the Baltic Fleet Air Wing appeared."[28]

In fact, they were Soviet Air Force planes. Grechko's instruments of retribution, the brand-new Sukhoi-24 fighter-bombers (which the navy had not yet received), had arrived on station. The pilots had no idea what their mission was until the last minute. Brezhnev's order had been transmitted to the squadrons so quickly, and with such urgency, that the pilots were simply ordered to get up in the air; further instructions would be given later. It was probably because of this frantic departure that the pilots did not even have time to activate their cryptographic equipment, and since all the stations on their network needed to be encrypted to talk to one another, the only option left was for everyone to talk in the clear.

The pursuing ships, meanwhile, were ordered to back off and make room for the planes to drop their payloads. The Su-24s were the newest aircraft in the Soviet military and had just been deployed to the Pribaltiysk Military Region. Several squadrons of them took off from the airfield at Tukums at around 0800, loaded with live ammunition and 500-pound bombs. Once they found *Storozhevoy,* the pilots were ordered to fly at an altitude of thirteen hundred feet and a speed of 450 to 500 miles per hour for their attack runs. This was a fast and high approach, but the intentions of the renegade destroyer were unclear. For all they knew, Sablin was defecting and would shoot down any Soviet plane that tried to stop him. The pilots might have been told by ground control that the ship had offloaded her surface-to-air missiles before going to Riga, but that was a chance they could not take.

The plan was to disable *Storozhevoy's* rudder so it would have to stop engines, then board the ship and tow it back to Riga. Visibility in the Irben Channel was not cooperating, however. Although the sun was out, it had not yet burned off the morning fog, so pilots could only see the tops of the ships. As usual, there was a lot of traffic in the channel that day—it was a busy waterway—so the pilots in the attack force had to descend to a very low altitude and read the hull numbers off the ships. This is what the Tu-16 bombers were doing when the confused Swedes first picked up their radar signatures at 0700.

Due to the fog (of nature and of war), they had already shot up another *Krivak*-class destroyer by mistake. That ship was part of the squadron pursuing *Storozhevoy.* A rear admiral had impulsively boarded the ship in Riga once the order went out to hunt down *Storozhevoy,* and he took command of the vessel from its captain. He ordered it to weigh anchor and put to sea at its maximum speed of twenty-eight knots. The crew was told the political officer on the ship they were chasing had "lost his mind and wanted to raid Kronstadt." After nearly three hours of sailing at flank speed, it had almost reached its prey. Unused to going this fast for this long, the crew had to spray the ship's smokestack with a fire hose to keep it from getting too hot. The signalman remembers the rear admiral on the radio, ordering the approaching pilots to use whatever means necessary to stop *Storozhevoy,* when suddenly "they began to attack *us!* We stopped what we were doing and panic broke out. I was ordered to get on the radio and identify us as friendly, but I couldn't find the codebook, I don't remember what happened to it. Finally somebody told the pilot that he was bombing the wrong ship, and by that time the [*Storozhevoy*] had come into sight."[29]

The misidentified ship was so badly damaged it had to be towed back to Riga. Afterward, the crew all had to sign nondisclosure agreements about what they had seen and were sworn to secrecy over it. As far as officialdom was concerned, this "friendly fire" incident had never happened.

It was ten o'clock when they finally found *Storozhevoy.* It was now in international waters, about forty miles past Soviet territorial waters. When the aircraft arrived on station, they radioed their command post at Tukums. The air regiment's commander there had a direct phone line to Grechko in Moscow. At this point, Admiral Gorshkov himself got on the radio and ordered *Storozhevoy* to stop. There was no response. Marshal Grechko personally issued one final order for *Storozhevoy* to stop engines. It too went unheeded.

Grechko then gave the air commander approval to make his attack. At 1025, a combination of Yak-28 and Su-24 fighter-bombers got into assault formation. The first wave flew perpendicular to the ship, shooting up the port side and the main deck. The second wave flew parallel to *Storozhevoy,* dropping its payload on the stern and fantail, aiming for the rudder. Seaman Maximenko was below decks in the galley when the attack came:

> It was quiet and then there was a strike on the port side! We fell on the shelves and out came the dishes. The planes were hitting us with their cannon—they were trying to damage the rudder and the turbine. They hit us on the main deck, the fo'c'sle, the sides, amidships. . . .
>
> It took me a few minutes to regain my senses—I couldn't tell which way was up and which way was down. Anton was shaken. I tried to calm him down by saying "And you thought we'd never see combat!"[30]

The ship took several hits from 500-pound bombs and 30-mm cannon. One of the attack flights succeeded in disabling the rudder, and *Storozhevoy* began to turn in a circle. Smoke poured out of its damaged stern and a thick black cloud spread toward the horizon. The pursuing surface craft then moved in to board the ship. Before the boarding parties arrived, however, several of the crew had decided that enough was enough. Petty Officer Second Class Kopilov, together with Seamen Borisov and Lykov, unlocked the detained officers from their compartment. Then they joined Captain-Lieutenants Kuzmin and Proshutinski, along with Senior Lieutenant Vinogradov, in freeing Captain Potulniy, who got a pistol from one of the armories and insisted upon going to the bridge himself. As *Storozhevoy*'s captain, he felt that he should be the one to regain control of the ship. He ordered one armed group to cover him from the fantail and another from the bow.

Potulniy was burning with rage at what Sablin had done and had made up his mind to kill him. As he climbed the ladder leading to the bridge, he knew that his naval career was over; what he did to Sablin in the next few seconds would be his last act as a ship's captain. At the last minute, however, just as he reached the top of the ladder, he changed his mind and decided to spare Sablin's life. Viktor Borodai thinks it was because he still regarded Sablin as a fellow officer rather than a criminal. Potulniy knew Nina and Misha, and as a husband and father himself, he did not want the responsibility of making her a widow and the boy fatherless. Besides, Borodai pointed out, "It's always easier to kill a man in your head than in reality."[31]

Potulniy ran onto the bridge, where Sablin was still at the radio broadcasting. After a moment's hesitation, he raised his pistol at the man who had once been his trusted advisor and maybe the closest thing he had to a friend. He pulled the trigger. Sablin fell into the corner, grasping his leg in pain. Potulniy then disarmed him and sent him to his stateroom under guard. Then he got on the radio and shouted in a hoarse voice, "Cease fire, I have regained command of the ship!"

The mutiny was over. It ended at 1032 local time on the morning of 9 November 1975. *Storozhevoy* was stopped and boarded in the middle of the Baltic Sea, at approximately 57° 58' 6" N latitude, 21° 02' 9" E longitude. The ship was twenty-one nautical miles from Soviet waters and fifty nautical miles from Swedish waters. Miraculously, other than Sablin, no one was hurt. The pilots, who had been so reluctant to fire on one of their own ships, had done their job and disabled *Storozhevoy* without killing anyone. It was cold comfort to them. Most thought Sablin was defecting, and while they had little sympathy for him, they were disturbed at the prospect of killing sailors on board who were just following orders. One of the officers at Tukums, Lieutenant Colonel Prozhogin, described the attack as well as the pilots' reaction upon their return: "I don't remember moving so quickly on anything in my entire military career. It was a feverish hustle. For the last attack run we used our best pilot—Captain Porotikov. His wingmen were Potapenko and Bulantsev. Porotikov damaged the screw and the rudder. *Storozhevoy* was dead in the water, having lost power, and began to move in a circle. When Porotikov got back to the airfield, he looked very depressed as he got out of his plane. He was awarded a medal soon after that, for his precision bombing. But he never once wore it."[32]

Cadet Valery Sablin, 1956.

Cadet Sablin learns the time-honored method of navigation with the sextant.

Sablin (*second from left*) and fellow cadets on the Neva River.

Sablin's girlfriend, Nina, wears his cadet hat, 1959.

Nina and Valery on their wedding day, November 1960.

Nina and Valery on their honeymoon, 1961.

The Sablin family in 1961. *Front row:* Valery's mother Anna, Nina, and Valery's father Mikhail. *Back row:* Valery and his younger brother Nikolai.

Fidel Castro visits the *Ozhestochenniy* in 1963 (Sablin took this photograph). On Castro's right is Adm. Sergei Gorshkov, who twelve years later would head the committee that investigated the *Storozhevoy* mutiny.

Sablin aboard *Ozhestochen-niy* as it passes through the Dardanelles, 1963.

Sablin with his antiaircraft section aboard *Ozhestochenniy,* 1965.

The brothers Sablin pose for a photo in 1967: (*left to right*) Boris, Valery, and Nikolai.

Valery, Nina, and Misha, 1970.

The officers of *Storozhevoy*, October 1973. Sablin is in the front row, fourth from the left. To his right sits Potulniy, and to Potulniy's right sits Lieutenant Firsov, who would jump ship on the night of the mutiny.

Sablin (*behind the table, center*) and Potulniy (*on his left*) host a dinner on board *Storozhevoy* with East German officers, 1974.

Storozhevoy in port, Baltiysk, 1975.

Sablin (*left*) and Potulniy (*right*) on the beach in Cuba, 1975. Their Cuban navy liaison officer sits between them.

Sablin plays dominoes with crewmen on the way back from Cuba, May 1975.

Wives and children of *Storozhevoy*'s officers greet the crew on their return from Cuba, May 1975. Nina is in the white coat and scarf facing the camera; Sablin is standing to her left, at the head of the formation. Potulniy is to Sablin's left, holding the flowers.

Sablin gives a political lecture to crewmen on board *Storozhevoy*. The men enjoyed these sessions only as a chance to write letters home or to sleep, which several of the sailors appear to be doing.

This portrait of Lieutenant Schmidt, drawn by Sablin, hung in his stateroom. Sablin saw many parallels between himself and the man who led a mutiny against the tsarist navy in 1905. The picture now sits in the Museum of the Revolution in Moscow.

Seaman Alexander Shein, Sablin's right-hand man during the mutiny.

On 8 November 1975, Soviet leader Leonid Brezhnev observes the parade for the fifty-eighth anniversary of the October Revolution. To his right is the minister of defense, Marshal Grechko. Just a few hours after this photograph was taken, both would be told that the crew of *Storozhevoy* had mutinied.

The hunt is on, 9 November 1975. A patrol craft and a Tu-16 bomber pursue *Storozhevoy* (*left*).

Storozhevoy sits dead in the water (*far right*) as smoke pours from its hull from bomb damage inflicted by attacking aircraft. Other ships of the pursuit squadron close in.

Capt. Oleg Dobrovolski, Sablin's KGB interrogator in Lefortovo Prison.

Sablin's prison picture, 1976.

Sketches of Dox Quixote that Sablin drew and mailed to Nina from prison, 1976. On the back of them he quoted the Man of La Mancha: "My intentions have always been directed towards noble deeds: namely to do good to everyone and evil to no one."

The eastern Baltic, 1975.

1. Swedish FRA communications intercept station

2. Location of the *Storozhevoy* when it was attacked and stopped by Soviet air and naval forces (57° 58′ 6″ N / 21° 02′ 9″ E).

3. Tukums Airfield

4. Skirotava Airfield

5. Liepae Naval Base

6. Baltic Fleet Headquarters and *Storozhevoy's* homeport

7. Mamonovo Airfield

8. The *Storozhevoy's* course on the night of 8-9 November 1975

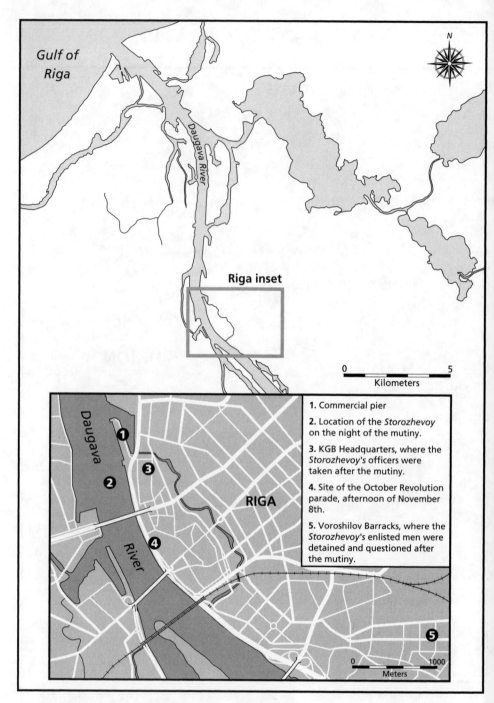

Gulf of Riga

Daugava River

Riga inset

0 _____ 5
Kilometers

Daugava

RIGA

River

1. Commercial pier

2. Location of the *Storozhevoy* on the night of the mutiny.

3. KGB Headquarters, where the *Storozhevoy's* officers were taken after the mutiny.

4. Site of the October Revolution parade, afternoon of November 8th.

5. Voroshilov Barracks, where the *Storozhevoy's* enlisted men were detained and questioned after the mutiny.

0 _____ 1000
Meters

Riga city center and surrounding region, 1975.

Chapter 5

THE AFTERMATH

After Anatoly Potulniy shot his nemesis and sent him below, he stopped engines on *Storozhevoy*. Two KGB patrol boats, their decks full of marines, came alongside port and starboard. The marines lashed the boats' hulls to the disabled BPK and came aboard, storming the bridge and forcing all the sailors to "assume the position"— feet shoulder width apart and both hands flat against the bulkhead. Even Potulniy and the officers who opposed Sablin were put up against the wall; the marines were taking no chances.

Some KGB plainclothes officers came aboard. They scoured the ship, conducting cursory interrogations and occasionally helping themselves to food in the galley. It took about three hours for them to sort things out. A prize crew came aboard to man *Storozhevoy* as it was towed to Liepae, a closed naval base about one hundred miles west of Riga, for repairs. The crew was transferred to patrol boats and landing craft for the trip back to Riga. As they left their ship for the last time, they noticed that it was listing to port; it had taken on water after being hit by 30-mm shells and 500-pound bombs.

Sablin was carried off in a stretcher to one of the adjacent patrol craft by two sailors. As he was leaving, Seaman Burov heard him say, "Don't think badly of me, boys." Burov was moved by the simple appeal. "It was said in such a matter-of-fact manner, without any drama or hand-wringing; he didn't cry out or anything," he recalled. "But it was unforgettable—you couldn't miss it. He said it man-to-man, on a very personal level to all of us, and I'll never forget it as long as I live."[1]

It took several hours for the convoy to return to Riga. *Storo-zhevoy's* vanquished crew sat out on the decks of their captors' boats under a fading twilight, surrounded by marines with Kalashnikovs trained upon them and orders to shoot them in the legs if they moved. When they got back to the city, the officers were taken to KGB Headquarters at the corner of Lenin and Engels Streets, while the enlisted men were taken to the Voroshilov Barracks near the train station. The marines stayed on to guard them all night because, in the words of one of the security officers, "the regular conscript soldiers were not trusted."

They were interrogated all night by irate KGB officers who were apparently still in holiday mode; they had been given the weekend off to celebrate the Great October Socialist Revolution and were upset at being called in. They obtained statements from everyone and told the crewmen to write out everything they remembered—not just about the mutiny but also about the days and weeks preceding it: who they had talked to, what they had said, who thought what about whom. The KGB worked quickly but thoroughly. They wanted the whole business, including signed confessions of guilt, settled as soon as possible. Warrant Officer Viktor Borodai recalled, "My first interrogator at my first interrogation announced: 'Too bad they didn't sink you!' They weren't interested in my answers. Nor were they very interested in asking questions. It soon became clear to all of us that everything was being steered in one direction—142 gullible idiots were incited to treason by an enemy of the people, Valery Sablin. They wanted any kind of information they could get from us, but only about Sablin and only the dirt that could incriminate him. At any cost. And they got it. Then they simply wrote our affidavits for us."[2]

By the following morning, Monday, 10 November, the KGB had figured out who the ringleaders were. Gorshkov and General Yepishev (the head of Sablin's chain of command at the Political Directorate) arrived in Riga with a huge entourage of other flag officers. They personally questioned nearly every one of the crew, probing to see how deeply the rebellious sentiment ran. The sailors put on a brave face, but they knew they were in serious trouble. For the most part, however, Gorshkov and his colleagues treated them leniently. The tension seemed to break when one of the sailors told them, "Well, I guess I'll never do that again!" This brought a ripple of laughter from the admirals. Gorshkov even managed a joke, asking the contrite young man, "So, you'd choose another way, would you?"[3] More laughter. At the end of questioning, it appeared that most of the crew would only receive a slap on the wrist.

It was a different story with the officers. Gorshkov came down hard on them. The sailors could be forgiven some youthful indiscretion, but the officers were ultimately responsible for everything their men did and did not do. The only junior sailor to be earmarked as a ringleader was Shein, who went out of his way to declare his support for Sablin and the mutiny's aims. On the morning of 10 November, Sablin, Shein, and twelve others were taken to Skirotava Airfield outside Riga for a direct flight to Moscow. Two An-24 transport planes were waiting for them. All the prisoners, as they now were, wore handcuffs except Sablin, who, because of his gunshot wound, was hobbling around on crutches. They were accompanied by Baltic Fleet Special Branch (KGB) troops.

When they arrived in Moscow, cars from KGB headquarters literally met the plane at its door. Sablin and his colleagues were taken to Lefortovo Prison downtown. Like its counterpart at Lubyanka, which served as KGB headquarters, Lefortovo had a grim reputation, rather like the Hotel California: you could check out any time you liked, but you could never leave. They still had execution chambers in the basements of both prisons, which had taken an uncountable toll of human lives over the previous fifty years.

Lefortovo was a compound that consisted of several buildings— prisoner quarters, interrogation rooms, and offices—surrounded by a tall wall. Sablin was taken to a solitary confinement cell in building 3A, where he would spend the next eight months. This building was about two hundred years old, constructed during the reign of Catherine the Great, and it benefited from some of the architectural styles of that era, including high ceilings and spacious corridors that were far too tasteful for a prison.

Nearly every day, Sablin was brought up from his cell by an elevator to make the short walk to Room 216, which was the office of Capt. Oleg Dobrovolski. Dobrovolski was given the unique task of finding out just what made Valery Sablin tick and why he had done the unthinkable—rebel against the Soviet system. A year younger than Sablin, Dobrovolski was an up-and-comer in the KGB who had a reputation as a skilled interrogator. He was usually given the toughest cases because of an ability to listen to the harshest criticism of the party and the state while keeping a placid look of sympathy upon his face. In the good-cop-bad-cop routine, Captain Dobrovolski was undoubtedly the good cop.

Even police in a police state occasionally hear about the hypocrisy and corruption of the system they defend. If they did not think about it themselves from time to time, they got an earful from prisoners who reminded them of why they were in a prison cell to begin with. Tough guys were a dime a dozen in the KGB; it also needed men who were more subtle, men who could probe the minds and opinions of "enemies of the people" and find out what motivated them. Did they go astray because of youthful indiscretion? Were their crimes ones of passion or calculation? Did they set out on the wrong path because of normal human emotion, or were they really the agents of a foreign intelligence service, as Stalin had always said they were?

All this presupposed that the "enemy of the people" was wrong. It took a strong interrogator to listen to anti-Communist ranting all day and still come out of it a faithful party man. Maybe that was where Sablin and Dobrovolski were so similar; faith tested was faith strengthened.

From the start, however, this case was being watched from the very top. There was already a letter of apology to Brezhnev, which each crewman had to sign, admitting to a lack of vigilance on everyone's part and begging the leader to return them to duty. Brezhnev was enraged because he had heard that this upstart *zampolit* had dared to attack him personally in a radio broadcast. Gorshkov, the country's top admiral, had already toured *Storozhevoy*, inspecting the damage and shaking his head at how such a thing could have happened in his navy.

The military and political leadership of the country was so aghast at Sablin's mutiny that they had trouble deciding exactly what they wanted to charge him with. It was almost a moot point because the real damage had already been done. One of the Communist Party's best and brightest, an officer of the Soviet Navy, had managed to convince his crew to risk their lives by taking over one of the most modern warships in the fleet, all in order to light the fires of a new Russian revolution. What could be more damning than that?

It was easier to accuse Sablin of trying to defect to Sweden, as many Soviets had done. They could write him off as another capitalist stooge selling out his country. The KGB and the navy would later make much of the 290-degree course *Storozhevoy* was holding when it was finally stopped. One of the judges at Sablin's trial would point to it as proof of his intent to flee to the West. In transcripts of his trial appearance and interrogations, Sablin must have repeated at least a dozen times that the 290-degree course was purely arbitrary; he chose it only because it seemed the best route to the open water of the Baltic. A study of the charts bears him out. If he had really intended to take *Storozhevoy* to Sweden, he could have reached its territorial waters much quicker if he had chosen a course of 270 degrees. This led straight from the Irben Channel to the island of Foryø, which he could have reached in an hour if he had wanted to.

It was more difficult to accuse him of the crime of which he was really guilty: the attempted overthrow of the Soviet government. In all the millions of people that the state apparatus had sent to their deaths over the years, how many of them had really wanted to depose the government? A few, perhaps, but not many. Most had only been guilty of holding their own political opinions, but the party had made it seem as if there were enemies everywhere.

Now they really had one—an enemy of the people in the flesh who despised Brezhnev, despised the Soviet government, and actively sought their removal from power. He made no bones about it and, in fact, had broadcast these sentiments live on the radio for five hundred miles, from a Soviet warship! And he was a Communist Party political officer. It struck a blow to the very heart of the system. Although they were not saying so, the leadership was deeply shaken.

That leadership included the seven members of the investigating committee, which was set up within hours of the mutiny's end. Minister of Defense Grechko signed Order No. 00105 on 9 November to establish this committee, chaired by Admiral Gorshkov. Its members were General Yepishev, Vice Admiral Navoitsev, Lieutenant General Romanov, Rear Admiral Sabaneyev, Major General Lyubanski, and Rear Admiral Guliayev.

Unlike his American counterpart, the secretary of defense, the Soviet defense minister was an active duty army officer. The committee members were all under Grechko in the chain of command, which even under the best of circumstances would call into question their objectivity. In any case, an investigation tends to take on a life of its own, its course becoming more complicated as more information relevant to it is discovered.

Such was not the case with the *Storozhevoy* inquiry, however, because the committee had already determined well in advance how it would proceed and how it would end. It lasted only eight days, and its objectivity was, to say the least, highly questionable. The final report that was forwarded to Grechko and Brezhnev (see Appendix F) at one point referred to Sablin as a "malicious anti-Soviet degenerate." It also explained that he was "able to persuade the psychologically unstable element of the crew that he only wanted to publicly criticize the deficiencies in the political, social and economic development of our country." The report admitted that rumors of Sablin's plans to defect with *Storozhevoy* "proved groundless." It concluded with this paragraph: "The extraordinary nature of this incident demands that the guilty parties be held criminally responsible. A party meeting was held at which those most responsible, among them Sablin, were expelled from the Communist Party. The ship's crew was disbanded, with a new one transferred to it. The BPK *Storozhevoy* is now in port, its weapons and operating systems in working order. The fleet will take all measures to keep information of this incident confidential."[4]

When Winston Churchill called Russia "a riddle, wrapped in a mystery inside an enigma," he might as well have been referring to this case. For public consumption, the Ministry of Defense would categorically deny any mutiny had taken place. For the party faithful, the story would be that Sablin had indeed mutinied and was trying to defect to Sweden. Only the very top leadership would know the real reason behind the revolt.

The party faithful were due to meet at the Twenty-fifth Party Congress in Moscow the following February. They were scheduled to receive a report on the mutiny, but the KGB, which was conducting its own investigation (see Appendix H), pressured the navy to reduce the number of crewmembers charged with treason. At the time, fourteen of them were supposed to go to trial. The KGB thought that number was too high and might alarm the congress delegates into believing that there was a serious discipline and morale problem in the fleet. As a result, criminal charges were only brought against Sablin and Shein. They would go on trial for their lives. The other twelve would be charged with "group insubordination," which carried a lighter sentence.

This concern for the reaction of the party congress delegates provides an interesting look into the dynamics of power in the Soviet

Union. Because of the political officer's dual role as a party func-
tionary and a military officer, the KGB and the navy could both lay
claim to Sablin's fate. The fact that both were willing to change the
indictments of men on trial for treason, all to appease delegates at
a Communist Party Congress, says much about who was really
pulling the strings. In the past, these congresses had been used as
mere forums in which the general secretary announced changes in
the nation's foreign and domestic policies. In Stalin's time, the KGB
had run roughshod over their ranks, imprisoning and killing congress members at will to make way for Stalin's henchmen to replace
them. In effect, the dictator had used the KGB to clean house within
the party.

Now the KGB had to tread more lightly, but the congresses were
still essentially window dressing. The fourteen-member Politburo,
at the head of which sat Leonid Brezhnev, the general secretary, was
the true seat of power in the Soviet Union. The Central Committee
just rubber-stamped whatever decrees the Politburo sent it.
Through this process, the Communist Party was able to exert total
control over the Soviet state bureaucracy. The KGB and the navy
were misleading their own government by failing to mention the
nature and extent of Sablin's mutiny. The root cause of this decep-
tion was most likely embarrassment and fear of official reprimand.
The final report to the Politburo and top-level military officers confirmed that there was no evidence Sablin was taking the ship to
Sweden. There was another report, however, which had even more
limited distribution. Marked "Top Secret—Special File," the highest
security classification in the Soviet Union, it was the full KGB transcript of the broadcast Sablin read over the radio to the Soviet people (see Appendix E). So far as anyone knows, no one outside the
KGB saw this file; it was just too inflammatory.

Captain Dobrovolski saw it, however, and heard it in person
coming from the man he was interviewing. After he found out that
only Sablin and Shein would be tried for treason, Dobrovolski spent
most of his time talking to Sablin.

It was far from a hostile interrogation. In fact, it was more like
a discussion between two colleagues, which is essentially what they
were. Dobrovolski was slightly in awe of his would-be adversary.
Sablin was so sure of himself, had such a command of Marxist-
Leninist literature, that he could pull a quote out of thin air to support what he had done. It was like playing spades with a man who

held all the trump cards. This did not just happen with Dobrovolski. General Yepishev himself, the senior *zampolit* in the Soviet armed forces, came once to talk with Sablin. It did not go well. When Yepishev attempted to scorn Sablin for the disgrace he had brought to the Soviet Navy and political officers everywhere, Sablin cut him short. He told him, "Lenin thought otherwise," and then came up with a quote from the father of the revolution, along with the page number it came from. It was uncanny and slightly unnerving to his KGB handlers. In a moment of supreme irony, Dobrovolski accused Sablin of being a fanatic, of being more Catholic than the Pope. Here was a KGB officer criticizing an accused traitor for being too Communist!

But Sablin was not all theory. Dobrovolski was amazed at the litany of scandal Valery could recite from personal experience in the navy. All those hours of talking to sailors had given him a veritable encyclopedia of anecdotal evidence: officers who embezzled party funds, sold military equipment on the black market, or pillaged food from supply dumps. The level of corruption was unimaginable, Sablin told him, finally asking Dobrovolski, "Don't you think you've had enough? Hasn't the Soviet system defrauded you for long enough?"[5]

Dobrovolski had to write down everything Sablin said in his report, which meant their conversations were taped and transcribed. For the KGB men in charge of the case, this was no easy task, not because of the volume of material, but because its content was so volatile. As Dobrovolski later remembered, "Protocol demanded that when we referred to rebellious thought in writing, it had to be written in the subjunctive tense—'The accused announced that there is supposedly no democracy in the USSR.' We were afraid to even write that, and here he was, an open book, declaring what he believed in a loud voice."[6]

Although the KGB man was fascinated by his prisoner and could admire his intelligence and determination, he was not yet ready to join Sablin's revolution. In the end, he judged his peer to be an irrational idealist. When questioned about this for Sablin's rehabilitation trial in 1992, Dobrovolski said, "I got the impression that Sablin was a man who embraced change for its own sake. He didn't have any clear understanding of how to put his plans into effect. His suggestions were very naïve and childish."[7]

When asked if Sablin was a Utopian, Dobrovolski replied, "Absolutely. He looked at everything with a childlike imagination."[8]

If this was the case, the KGB man was asked, and Valery was only a misguided idealist, why accuse him of treachery and betrayal of the Motherland? The suave Dobrovolski had a ready answer. It was one thing to be naïve, he said, but Sablin was not simpleminded. A simpleton would not plan a mutiny months, if not years, in advance, trick the captain into imprisonment below decks, persuade half the wardroom to join his revolt, and arm one of his accomplices with a pistol to preserve order. Valery Sablin was not stupid—such calculation was dangerous, Dobrovolski concluded, to the state and to the party.

All of this was probably true, and it was spoken like a true party and KGB man. For those who opposed Sablin, all the rational arguments were used: mutiny is intolerable, regardless of the motives; it was a long shot and doomed from the start; he did not have the right to risk the lives of 180 men. From their vantage points, as privileged members of the armed forces and security services, what Sablin attempted was indeed a departure from rational thought. The difference between Sablin and Dobrovolski is what has always separated supporters of the status quo from those who want to change it. What is rational is a matter of debate for both. Dobrovolski felt it irrational to expect too much from the system; Sablin felt it irrational to expect so little.

In prison, Sablin sketched to take his mind off his surroundings. Among the sketches he mailed to Nina were several of Don Quixote, the patron saint of futility, charging the windmills of La Mancha. Sablin's mutiny was certainly a quixotic adventure, but like his Spanish counterpart, he was propelled to act in order to conquer a terrible feeling of helplessness. As slim as his chances of success were, just the thought of liberation was enough to give him a new lease on life. Emboldened and exhilarated by this freedom, he felt sure his countrymen would want to share it with him.

Sablin saw the lives of everyday Soviet citizens through the eyes of his sailors. These were young men drafted from the general population that was bearing the greatest burden of Communist tyranny. He sympathized with them more than most men in his position did and sought to use that position in the name and the interests of the Russian people. Dobrovolski and the rest of Sablin's detractors probably saw the same things, the fear and the hopelessness in their countrymen, but unlike Sablin, they chose to spare themselves these indignities by becoming part of the system. This was not selfishness so much as self-interest, but the example of Valery Sablin stands in stark contrast to this "get-along and go-along" approach. Sablin felt the peace of mind and material comforts of those in power were coming at the expense of everyone else. Instead of taking the easy way out and becoming one more party bureaucrat, he sought to elevate the conditions of his men and his people at his own expense.

The accomplished film director Milos Forman, who grew up in Communist Czechoslovakia, said that the worst thing about growing up in a totalitarian environment was the self-censorship it imposed. Monitoring your own thoughts and words for fear of speaking your mind and being labeled an "enemy of the people" was the true price of authoritarian rule. Forman said that it was a way for the government to make everyone a part of the conspiracy and feel guilty. Sablin's words to his men that night on the quarterdeck broke this chain. They no longer needed to feel guilty, they just needed to feel like free men. Throughout his life, when Sablin felt that he had to impose this censorship on himself, it had always been only a temporary measure. He bided his time for many years, always knowing that once he made his statement, once he really spoke his mind, it would be in a way that was worthy of him and the cause he supported.

As strong as he was, prison began to work on Sablin's mind. Solitary confinement is solitary for a reason: it imposes the conditions that encourage prisoners to wage war on themselves. The longer someone sits in a cell and thinks about what he did, the more time he has to second-guess his actions and contemplate their consequences. Here, perhaps, is where it finally hit Sablin that he might never see his wife and son again. Romantic notions of revolution diminished and were replaced by the cold routine of prison life. After one month of this, Sablin admitted that he had violated his oath as a military officer. Reading from a transcript of the confession, Dobrovolski recounted Sablin's words: "I find my anti-government activities aboard the *Storozhevoy* regrettable, since I involved a bunch of young sailors and officers in this crime. I now see that I dragged them along without any regard to the effectiveness of this plan or their maturity level."[9]

This was fair criticism, and only an honest man could level it against himself. He held firm on two points, however: while acknowledging that he had violated his military oath, he absolutely refused to admit that he had committed treason, and he insisted that his crewmen were only following his orders and should not be held personally responsible.

Dobrovolski remains convinced that Sablin's confession was genuine and was not done in exchange for clemency. He also denied that Sablin was beaten or tortured to coerce it. Although he admitted to receiving "pressure" from his superiors to make progress on the case, he did not qualify this as political supervision. He claimed that he did his job as he would any other investigation. Dobrovolski left the case before Sablin went to trial, but he was not surprised at the death sentence. In fact, he was only surprised that Sablin found it so unlikely. "He didn't think they'd ever execute him," he recalled. "He never even considered the fact that he might be shot for what he did. He thought that he'd be reprimanded somehow, but would eventually return to the navy and continue to serve."[10]

This was obviously wishful thinking, not a crime in and of itself, but a dangerous flaw in an officer responsible for the lives of 180 crewmen. It is also a tragic flaw in a man responsible for a wife and son. As the spring of 1976 melted into summer, it became clear that Valery Sablin was eager for a return to the life he once knew. He missed his family desperately and craved details about their everyday lives. This aching for the company of his loved ones is most evident in a letter he sent to Nina just before she left to meet Valery's parents at the Sablin family *dacha* in Belyn, near Gorky. "Did you take Misha to the doctor?" he wrote.

How did it go? Draw me an outline of your new apartment. Were you able to sell some of the furniture that was broken in the move? Any luck finding work? At least you've been able to settle in a little bit. I'll send a letter right away to Belyn, as soon as I find out you've left for there. Just take the bare minimum that you need to Belyn, since I'm sure that Papa doesn't know you're coming and won't be able to meet you at the station. Leave some of your things in Moscow and some in Gorky. Do you remember the way from Dreswitz?[11]

Sablin's secret plan, and the fact that he had kept it secret from his loved ones for so long, was probably what hurt his family the most in the aftermath of the mutiny, as they contemplated the very real possibility that he would be executed. He confessed to his parents what he was going to do in a letter dated 7 November 1975 and posted it that day. They got it five days later. Not knowing it was too late, or that he was in Riga, they sent an emergency telegram to Baltiysk, begging him to come to his senses. Nina got her letter on the eighth; she read it with horror and bewilderment. Valery still did not use the word "mutiny," but he told her he was taking "the path of revolutionary struggle." It was maddening. He told her that what he wanted to do—create "a center of political activity in our country, a base on which we can build a new party"—had about a 40 percent chance of success. If he failed, the recrimination would not be pleasant, so although he wanted to, he would not give her the details. He wanted to protect her by keeping his plans to himself so the government would not think she was his accomplice.

Her confusion only intensified the next day when another officer's wife told her that something had happened aboard *Storozhevoy* but she had no specifics. All she could tell Nina was that "everything was OK, no one was killed, things could have been much worse," and then her husband told her she could no longer talk to Nina.[12]

Nina was now frantic with worry that only got worse when KGB agents came to their apartment in Baltiysk. They first came on Sunday, around the same time as her husband was being carried off *Storozhevoy* on a stretcher. The KGB men asked her a few questions about Valery's relationship with Captain Potulniy and then left. They seemed uncertain what exactly they were supposed to be investigating. When she went to work the next day, however, KGB agents were at her office. She had to leave the room while they searched her desk, and then they returned to her apartment late that night. Now they knew they were dealing with the wife of an accused traitor, and they searched her apartment for two hours, from midnight until two the next morning. Nina by this point was a nervous wreck. Even these hard-bitten men were uncomfortable searching through the personal effects of a woman who was obviously heartbroken and a son who could not understand why strange men were rummaging around their home and causing his mother such grief. Just before they arrived that night, Nina threw the letter she had received from Valery two days earlier under the bathtub behind some cans of paint. The KGB men conducted their search quickly and without much enthusiasm. They did not find the letter, but they took Valery's medals, his officer's dagger, newspaper articles he had saved, and many books in which he had made comments on the margins.

It was several weeks before she heard from Valery again. He was allowed to write his family from Lefortovo, although the letters usually took three weeks to reach them. The long turnaround time was due to the prison officials' censorship of incoming and outgoing letters. They also used them as incentives: Sablin would get them only when he agreed to sign this or admit that. Valery wrote a children's story about a dog named Dik, which he mailed to his brother Nikolai in hopes that it could be published and provide some income for Nina and Misha, but Nikolai never received it.

The Military Collegium of the Supreme Court assigned Leonid Aksyenov as Valery's defense attorney for the upcoming trial. No one in the Sablin family had any experience in retaining legal counsel, and in any case, they really had no choice. Private attorneys were unknown in the Soviet Union; all lawyers were employees of the state, and they were not nearly as numerous as their Western counterparts. Like all other professions in the country, the law was subordinate to Communist Party doctrine. In political cases, defense attorneys were mere window dressing, especially during the notorious show trials of the 1930s. Prosecutors such as Andrei Vyshinski were the golden boys of Communist jurisprudence, showmen who browbeat defendants and used the courtroom as a prop for the "purifying thunder of Soviet justice."

Unfortunately for the Sablin family, Aksyenov was not much better. Valery's father Mikhail met with him once in Moscow and told his wife, "I don't like that man one bit." Brother Nikolai felt that Aksyenov had given up on the case the moment it was assigned to him, and Nina simply wrote, "The lawyer is a coward."[13]

Their anger stemmed from the fact that there was no concept of attorney-client privilege. Aksyenov was not allowed to convey information from Valery to his family, so they were kept in the dark about how he would plead or how the evidence in his case would be presented.[14] Fifteen years later, Aksyenov did not even remember meeting Mikhail or Nina, even though the elder Sablin apparently did see him. In his defense, he claimed that the best he could do was to try to avoid the death penalty. Valery once told him, "Leonid Vasilyevich, I already have the feeling that I've got seven grams coming to me."[15] This was an old Russian saying; seven grams was the amount of lead in a bullet. Aksyenov later admitted as much. In a strange confession for a defense attorney, he said in a 1990 interview, "His case was predetermined from the very start."[16]

To occupy his time in prison, Valery wrote a lot, read a lot, and tried to rehabilitate his leg. Potulniy had shot him just below the knee, and he had to keep his whole leg straight in order for it to heal properly. Meanwhile, the KGB was trying very hard to get Valery to admit he was guilty of treason. For every "good cop" like Dobrovolski, there had to be a bad one. When Nina was finally allowed to visit her husband in prison that summer, she was horrified to find that his front teeth had been knocked out.[17] This had happened during the trial and pointed to some evidence of the KGB's use of drugs to induce Sablin's confession. As Shein recalled:

> Sablin was telling the court that I was only a "secondary partici-pant." Then, quickly turning pale, he started to shake. They dragged me out to a nearby room.
>
> I saw the following: several men ran up to Sablin, bent his arms behind his back, handcuffed him, and put a wide black muz-zle over his mouth. He tried to break free, and was snarling like an animal.
>
> The room started to smell like medicine.
>
> They hauled him through the corridor. I heard some muffled blows.
>
> Then I saw blood on the walls.[18]

Shein readily admitted that it was not difficult for the interrogators to outwit him or the other *Storozhevoy* crewmen. There was "all the fear, shame and complete helplessness that a bunch of kids felt in the hands of professionals."[19]

Few organizations had mastered the art of coercion better than the KGB. Initially, Shein refused to admit that he was guilty of betraying the Motherland. Unsatisfied with a plea of "not guilty," Shein's interrogator, Captain Kharitonov, changed his tactics from time to time to convince the twenty year old that he really was guilty. He started out by holding Shein responsible for the contin-ued detainment of his thirteen comrades. Admit your guilt, Kharitonov insisted, and the others will be set free. When this did not work, he changed tack, claiming to understand why Shein had done what he did and that all would be forgiven. In fact, said the KGB man, they already had an order from the defense minister that would discharge Shein into the reserves and allow him to return home, provided he signed an admission of guilt. "You're only hurting yourself with your stubbornness," he said.

Still Shein resisted. If Sablin could hold out, so could he. Walking in the prison courtyard one day, he spotted an inscription on the wall: "Storozhevoy." It was in Sablin's handwriting, a small reminder of support to all his shipmates. The next day it was gone.

Finally, Shein's interrogators played their trump card when Dobrovolski got Sablin to admit he was guilty of violating his military oath. "Look here," they said, "even he came around. You're the only one who's being so stupidly stubborn." The questions came faster and faster, the same ones over and over. Shein was becoming exhausted; they were gradually wearing him down. Kharitonov would bring up a particular accusation and then talk about it until he fixed on one particular thing Shein said. Then he would ask a question and keep refining it until the beleaguered sailor could only respond with a simple yes. Thus he would answer, "Yes, I admit it. I was guilty of that." His interrogator made Shein repeat this admission, which then came out in the trial as "I admit that I was guilty of violating article so and so of the criminal code, paragraph such and such."[20]

As it turned out, Shein was admitting to violating Article 64, Paragraph A of the Penal Code of the USSR, violation of the serviceman's oath. He was sentenced to eight years' imprisonment, two in Lefortovo and six at a hard labor camp. He would end up spending five and a half years in Lefortovo, two confined to his cell and three and a half as part of a prison work detail. He was then transferred to a psychiatric hospital for a short time before spending his last thirty months in a hard labor camp in Siberia's Tyumen Province.[21] After his release, he would remark bitterly upon his extra time in Lefortovo, claiming that time served there was much worse than hard labor. Adding insult to injury, he was also fined 186 rubles and 50 kopecks, the equivalent of over three years' pay for an enlisted sailor.

It became evident that Sablin had cut some sort of deal with prosecutors just before his trial on 13 July 1976. According to Shein, who was tried together with him, both of them pled guilty to treason and the judge then read out Sablin's confession that the mutiny had been a "foolish venture." After entering his plea, Sablin accepted responsibility for the incident and asked the military court not to punish any of the men who had followed him. Shein was surprised, because until that moment, his *zampolit* had steadfastly refused to admit that he was a traitor to the Motherland. Once the verdict was read, however, Shein found out why Sablin had pled guilty: he had done so in exchange for clemency.

Instead, he was sentenced to death by firing squad. As if it mattered after such a verdict, the court also stripped him of his rank, awards, and medals. Shein remembered the moment vividly: "When they read the sentence . . . Sablin turned pale and for a moment seemed to lose all awareness. Then he regained his composure. I wanted to say something, but several security guards with special gags stood behind us. They put those on us and took us out."[22]

Shein watched Sablin's reaction very closely and was sure that Valery had not been expecting a death sentence, which is what made him speculate that the prosecutor had promised to spare Sablin's life should he plead guilty to treason. If true, it meant that the court had lied to him to secure his confession; clearly, someone else was pulling the strings. Rumor had it that Brezhnev himself had insisted on the death penalty.[23] He wanted his pound of flesh. And he got it.

On 18 July, the KGB summoned Nina to Lefortovo Prison for a visit with her husband. She had flown to Moscow from Kaliningrad immediately after learning of his conviction and death sentence from Valery's family. It was the first time she had seen him since before the mutiny, and, as it turned out, it would be the last time. She brought Misha to the prison with her and saw him for no more than ten minutes. They met in a small room with a table between them, in the presence of several guards who stood ready to end the meeting abruptly should he reveal details of the case to her. Valery asked Misha how he was doing in school and joked with Nina that he wanted to see a dentist, smiling to reveal his missing teeth. Then, for the last time, he told his wife and son that he loved them and kissed them goodbye.

Neither knew this was to be their last meeting. Nina and Valery's father immediately filed an appeal with the Presidium of the Supreme Soviet for clemency on Valery's behalf. When Nina asked Aksyenov about this, she was only allowed to see one line in the indictment—the part that accused Valery of treason. The rest of the document was covered with several sheets of paper when she was brought in to view it. The chairman of the Presidium, a man named Smirnov, told Nina that the chances for clemency were slim to none;

the death sentence was final. Aksyenov nonetheless encouraged her to file. After all, he said, it could not hurt.[24]

The next day, 20 July, Mikhail Sablin saw his son for twenty minutes. The presence of guards at their meeting prohibited them from talking about anything other than personal matters. It would be the last time anyone outside the KGB saw Valery alive. From July 1976 to January 1977, a long period of silence followed during which the Sablin family heard nothing from Valery. They had not been present at his trial and only knew that he had been convicted of treason and sentenced to death. On 7 January 1977, his father wrote a letter to the KGB chief (and future Soviet leader) Yuri Andropov, asking for his help in determining his son's fate:

> On 20 July 1976, I received permission to visit my son. During our meeting we didn't talk about the charges against him. It's still unclear to his mother and I how he betrayed the Motherland.
>
> At that time, I petitioned the Presidium of the Supreme Soviet for clemency for my son. We still haven't received a response from the Supreme Soviet, nor have we received a single letter from our son since July. We believe that he has been forbidden to write us.
>
> You, Yuri Vladimirovich, understand of course how difficult these events have been for my wife and me.
>
> My wife, Anna Vasilievna, suffers from Parkinson's disease (her arms and legs don't function properly and she frequently falls down). I've suffered a myocardial infarction and have had two-thirds of my stomach removed, along with my gall bladder. I've also undergone surgery for peritonitis. Needless to say, our health has become an issue.
>
> My wife and I ask you to seek a decision from the Presidium of the Supreme Soviet in the case of clemency for our son—Sablin, Valery Mikhailovich—and to allow him to correspond with us. This would allow us some measure of relief from our deep sorrow.[25]

Mikhail Sablin also asked for assistance in helping his eldest son Boris, who was feeling the pressure as the brother of a "traitor to the Motherland." Boris was a lieutenant colonel in the Soviet Army at the time of the mutiny and was stationed in Gorky. He was abruptly transferred in August 1976 to the city of Ivanovo, about one hundred miles to the west, and attached to the military faculty of the Energy Institute. According to his father, Boris was overqualified for this position, which was already filled by another officer at the time. Ivanovo was too far away to commute, so Boris and his wife would have to leave the apartment they had just received (after waiting seven years) and move from Gorky. The elder Sablin asked Andropov to intervene with the army on behalf of Boris so he could stay where he was and help his ailing parents.

It is unknown if Andropov received this plea, but somebody in the KGB must have read it, because in February 1977, Valery's younger brother Nikolai received this notice in the mail:

Certificate of death.
Citizen Sablin, V. M. died on August 3, 1976, aged 39 years. Registered this 22nd day of February 1977. Certificate Number 344. Cause of death————[left blank]. Place of death————[left blank].[26]

They did not even get his age right; he was thirty-seven years old when he was taken to a chamber in the basement of Lefortovo Prison on 3 August 1976. He probably was not met by a firing squad but by a sole executioner with the standard issue Makarov 9-mm pistol. Then Valery Sablin was shot in the back of the head. He was the same age as his hero Lieutenant Schmidt, who met the same fate, albeit under the sunshine of a ship's main deck and before a firing squad where he could look his executioners in the eye.

Nikolai called Nina in Kaliningrad and broke the news to her. Several weeks later, she received her own copy of the death certificate in the mail. She broke the news to their old friends the Mikhalkins in a letter dated 20 March 1977:

Dear Friends,
On March 2nd, I got a telegram from Gorky that everyone there received word of Valery's death, which took place on August 3, 1976. The death certificate itself was dated 22 February. The government didn't inform me until after then, and they didn't even tell me where he was buried or how he was killed. They also said they didn't have any of his letters.

What can you say about all this? What words can describe this? I haven't said anything to Misha, of course. I want to let him grow up a little bit.

I wasn't expecting such a decision, such unprecedented cruelty from our government.

Doesn't history teach people anything?

All of this is so difficult and unbearable.

This can't be happening!

Nina.[27]

Nina and Valery's brothers were outraged that they had not been informed of his death for nearly seven months. Nikolai went to a local KGB officer to demand an explanation: "I asked him: 'Why did it happen like this, why weren't we informed of his death?' And this KGB colonel, with his radiant smile and well-rehearsed voice, told us that everything had been done according to the law. They had not informed us of his death because without our asking, they were under no obligation to do so. As soon as you sent your inquiry, he said, we sent you a copy of the death certificate, and since you made no request for his personal effects within six months, all of them have been destroyed, including his manuscripts and letters. You have no grounds for complaint."[28]

The response was the same everywhere, from everybody: "Everything was done according to the law." To this day, his family still does not know what happened to Valery's remains, and the KGB's records from Lefortovo Prison are still closed to the public. To honor him, they can only lay a wreath at a monument to political prisoners in Moscow.

Being the wife of a "traitor to the Motherland" was the mark of Cain in Soviet Russia. One disgruntled officer actually broke into their apartment and stole their furniture, convinced that a traitor's family did not deserve it. Nina did not have the heart to tell this to Valery when he was in prison, so she told him instead that several pieces of furniture had broken in the move (there is reference to this in Valery's letter to her). Misha's schoolmates chanted his last name in unison as if it was a dirty word. Captain Potulniy's son Andrei was actually in the same class as Misha and sat at the desk right next to him. Some officers and wives sympathized with the widow Sablin. *Storozhevoy*'s executive officer, Third Rank Captain Novozhilov, who was on leave when the mutiny took place, dropped by once late at night to tell her what he knew of her husband's fate. Even he had to show this sympathy with a furtive glance over his shoulder, however; the taint of betrayal might stain him, and he had a family to provide for. He never returned. Out in town one day shopping for a Christmas tree, Nina ran into one of the *Storozhevoy* officers who had been a regular visitor to their apartment. She said hello, and when the man recognized her, he ran away from her as if he had seen a ghost.[29]

Since they were no longer dependents, Nina and Misha were evicted from their apartment in Baltiysk in May 1976. They moved to nearby Kaliningrad, where Nina got another job with the building department. The extraordinary secrecy surrounding the *Storozhevoy* incident actually served to their advantage in Kaliningrad, since nobody there had heard about it. Baltiysk was a naval town where everyone knew everyone else and rumor had the force of written fact, but in Kaliningrad they were protected by their anonymity. They stayed there until Misha graduated from high school in 1980 and then moved to Leningrad to stay with her mother and blend into big city life. Nina got a job with the building inspector and Misha studied biology at the university. He wanted to follow his father into the navy but was forbidden to do so. Nina never remarried. "There's no one to marry after Valery Mikhailovich," she said. "There is no other like him."[30]

Valery's parents did not live long after their son. His father died in January 1977, just a few weeks after writing his futile letter to Andropov. Perhaps the only merciful act he received from his government, although it was purely unintentional, was that he passed away without knowing that his son had preceded him in death. He assumed the regime would have the common courtesy to provide his family one last visit with the condemned man, and at the very least to claim Valery's personal possessions. Devastated by the loss of her son and husband within six months of each other, Anna Vasilievna Sablina died eighteen months later in July 1978. Brothers Nikolai and Boris kept their jobs, but for Boris the period of constant transfers that began after November 1975 continued, and always at the last minute.

Of Sablin's thirteen conspirators, all were kicked out of the navy with the equivalent of dishonorable discharges. Viktor Borodai and the other eleven men who were charged with "group insubordination" were not released from Lefortovo Prison until March 1976. Borodai himself was demoted from warrant officer to seaman and kicked out of the Young Communist League. He was eventually discharged and sent back home. For fifteen years, he rarely spoke about the events of 8–9 November 1975 with anyone. Once, when he did let slip his role in the mutiny to someone at work, a KGB man visited him there. He gave Borodai a brusque warning to keep his mind on his work, ending the conversation with the comment, "Remember, this never happened!"

Several officers who had nothing to do with the mutiny were disciplined, including Second Rank Captain Svetlovski, the skipper of *S-263*. He was the man Firsov had told about the mutiny after jumping ship from *Storozhevoy,* the one who had been so skeptical of his story. In spite of being the first one to raise the alarm, Firsov too was punished, probably because he had first voted to support Sablin and had taken too long to change his mind.

The other blackballed officers included those responsible for the naval detachment's security in Riga. Second Rank Captain Vlasov, the chief of staff for Ship Security Brigade 78, and Second Rank Captain Yudin, head of Brigade 78's Special Detachment, were both reprimanded for failing to act quickly enough in either preventing the mutiny or bringing it to an end sooner. For all intents and purposes, their military careers were over. For his spontaneous act of defiance in refusing to fire upon *Storozhevoy* when ordered, 2nd Rank Capt. Alexei Neipert was dismissed from the service.[31]

The most dramatic public reaction to the mutiny at the time was the leadership reshuffle that occurred in the Baltic Fleet immediately following it. Adm. Vladimir Mikhailin was relieved as fleet commander within three weeks of the incident.[32] He had filled that post since 1968 and served as first deputy commander for four years before that.[33] Mikhailin was moved to Moscow to be deputy commander in chief for naval educational establishments. According to William Manthorpe Jr., former U.S. naval attaché to the Soviet Union, this job did not befit a former fleet commander, and the timing of Mikhailin's departure was abnormal.[34] Common Soviet Navy practice was to serve as first deputy commander before moving up to fleet commander. Since Mikhailin's deputy, Vice Admiral Sidorov, had been on the job only a few months and could not be promoted, Mikhailin was replaced by his chief of staff, Vice Admiral Kosov. Kosov was the man who had ordered all the ships in Riga harbor to weigh anchor and go after *Storozhevoy* early on the morning of 9 November.[35]

The commander of the Riga Naval Base, Rear Adm. I. I. Verenkin, escaped punitive action since it was thought that he was too new to receive any of the blame. He arrived at that post in May 1975, only six months before the mutiny.[36] Vice Adm. Nikolai Shabilikov, the Baltic Fleet Political Directorate chief who was above Sablin in the political chain of command, escaped the purge for reasons unknown. It would certainly seem that if blame for this event had to be placed anywhere outside of the mutineers, it belonged on the shoulders of the Political Directorates of the Baltic Fleet and the navy. That Shabilikov remained in office, given the fact that a political officer led the mutiny, shed an interesting light on the power balance between the Political Directorate and the naval high command. It suggested that the navy was paying the higher price for Sablin's insubordination.

Anatoly Potulniy, *Storozhevoy*'s ill-fated captain who did nothing more than get locked up in a compartment, was reduced in rank, thrown out of the Communist Party, and spent the rest of his naval career ashore managing a warehouse. He was accused of allowing a dangerous anti-Soviet atmosphere to infect his crew. According to his wife Nadezhda, he was tormented by nightmares for the next several years, waking up in the middle of the night shouting, "We're under fire!" and "We're sinking!" To this day, Potulniy is not bitter toward the man who ruined his career. He simply does not understand why he did it. Maybe as a man he could understand his *zampolit*'s motives, but as an officer, he felt Sablin accomplished nothing.

As of the fall of 2004, Nina and Misha still live in St. Petersburg. Nina retired from the city's building department and earns a small pension, but she still must work, as a coat check girl in the cloakroom of a museum, to support herself. Misha studied biology at university and works as a paleontologist at the Zoological Institute. Anatoly Potulniy refused to be interviewed for this book; he has not talked publicly of the events of November 1975 for twelve years and categorically refuses to grant interviews to either Russians or Americans. He regards the mutiny as a personal tragedy and prefers to leave it in the past. Oleg Dobrovolski also refused the authors' request for an interview; he is retired from the KGB and lives in Moscow. Most tragic of all, perhaps, has been the fate of Alexander Shein. After serving his eight-year sentence at Lefortovo Prison in Moscow and at a labor camp in Siberia, Shein married and settled down in Moscow. As a former convict, and a political one at that, he was not allowed to take any college entrance examinations. He started a theater design business and worked in Moscow for several years before both his business and marriage failed.[37] Unhinged by these personal failures and undoubtedly still haunted by the legacy of his role in the *Storozhevoy* mutiny, Shein suffered a nervous breakdown. He returned to his hometown of Togliatti and remains there today.

Valery Sablin's cause was not without its personal costs. He paid for it with his life, but others continue to pay for it in their lives. Nonetheless, he met his fate with courage and equanimity, and that alone marks him as an extraordinary man. He had the opportunity to go through life like the vast majority of Russians, who just got by, who survived but did not flourish. He made the choice to do otherwise and accepted the consequences of that decision. Such is the very definition of a free man, and Valery Sablin had the honorable distinction of being a free man in a world where so many avoided that responsibility or took it for granted. Sometimes a choice is not a choice at all, but the point at which a person feels he has no alternative. Valery tried to explain this in his fateful letter to Nina, written just a few days before he passed the point of no return:

My dearest Ninochka!

This is difficult for me to do, as you meet that moment when you discover that I have taken the path of revolutionary struggle. You might curse me as a man who is playing with your life. You might call me a callous man who doesn't think of his family. You might deeply resent the fact that I've kept this plan hidden from you. You might just say to me sadly: "You are and always have been a mystery!" It might turn out better than I expect.

Don't be too hard on me, and try to explain to Misha that I am not a villain nor an adventurer, nor an anarchist, but simply a man who loves his country and its people and wants to see them free— someone who couldn't find any other way to achieve this than to fight for it.

I love you and Misha very much and always have. That love has kept me honest in this life and has turned me into the revolutionary you see now. . . .

Will I find any allies in my fight? I think I will. If not, then I'll still find honor by myself. The real reason I'm doing this is because I must. If I refuse this fight, then I'll cease to be a man, stop respecting myself, and feel like I'm nothing more than an animal.[38]

Chapter 6

THE SUPPRESSION

For nearly fifteen years, the Soviet government refused to admit that a mutiny took place aboard *Storozhevoy*. The only official pronouncement on it was a denial made by Vice Adm. V. V. Sidorov, first deputy commander of the Baltic Fleet, at a Copenhagen press conference on 10 August 1976. The admiral was in Denmark commanding a five-day diplomatic port call by two Soviet warships. In reply to a question about a rumored mutiny, Sidorov stated, "Mutiny on a Soviet naval ship in the Baltic—unthinkable! It must be a hoax played by organs established for this purpose, which pursue their thwarting aims in the West. Stories of that sort, which appear in the Western world, can only invite ridicule among us. We do not believe we ever have to comment on that sort of thing."[1]

The incident was officially swept under the rug. On 18 November 1975, a *Krivak I*–class destroyer in perfect condition bearing *Storozhevoy*'s hull number (500) made a conspicuous cruise along the Soviet Baltic coast, near Götland, Utklipporna, Bornholm, and Polan. The ship participated in a number of official celebrations in order to quell the rumors of mutiny that were spreading through Western intelligence and defense circles.[2] This might have been a different ship with *Storozhevoy*'s hull number, because the Soviet Navy routinely changed their vessels' hull numbers to confuse Western intelligence. *Storozhevoy*, in fact, had appeared with different hull numbers in the past, including 203 and 626, but the fast repairs made on the ship and the unscheduled trip around the Baltic most likely were done for the sake of appearances.

On 11 April 1976, *Storozhevoy,* manned by a new crew and accompanied by a *Ropoucha*-class LST and an oiler, sailed from the Baltic. It transited the Mediterranean, passed through the Suez Canal, and entered the Indian Ocean on the twenty-fifth.[3] It operated there for two months before transiting first to Vladivostok and then to Petropavlovsk, its home port, with the Kamchatka Flotilla of the Pacific Fleet. It would remain there for nearly thirty years. Like so many other Soviet dissidents, *Storozhevoy* was banished to Siberia.

Japanese reconnaissance aircraft from Okinawa photographed the ship in 1977 wearing a distinguished citation award that had not been present before the mutiny. "Dentology" of these photos (examining them closely for dents) revealed no trace of any damage from the attack.

For many years, the fate of the crew was much less certain. Official Soviet organs were more tight-lipped than usual about this incident. When a Soviet sailor was inducted into the navy, he had to recite a military oath of strict obedience stating that should he break his vow, he would be subject "to the severe punishment of Soviet law and the general hatred and contempt of the workers."[4] To ensure this hatred and contempt, Soviet military journals and newspapers often ran stories of malefactors, complete with names and units. It was assumed that public humiliation would induce the guilty person to acknowledge his errors and prevent others from committing similar offenses. This was probably why *Krasnaya Zvezda* published its article critical of *Storozhevoy* in December 1974. After the mutiny, however, the potential for national humiliation in exposing evidence of military weakness overrode the need to make an example of the conspirators. The mutiny, the resulting trial, and the punishment were all well-guarded secrets.

There were pieces of evidence, combined with general knowledge of Soviet military jurisprudence, which led to speculation about what happened to Sablin and his co-conspirators. It was initially thought that they were brought before the procurator (prosecutor) of the Baltic Military District court in Riga, as required by Soviet law, on the morning of 10 November. Due to the nature and severity of the crime, however, it was believed that they were flown to Moscow later that day and interned at the GAPTVAK (short-term military prison) of the Moscow Military District.[5]

The chief procurator from Moscow, Anatoly Rudenko, supposedly arrived in Riga within a week to lead the investigation.[6] It initially consisted of routine discussions at all levels of the Baltic Fleet by commanders, political officers, and representatives from GLAVPUR (the political directorate to which Sablin and other *zampolits* were subordinate). Once this was finished, however, the order that no information or any responses concerning the mutiny be released was issued. All discussion of it was to cease. Not even closed letters between local party central committees were allowed to mention *Storozhevoy*.[7]

It was also thought that fifteen of the mutineers, including Sablin, were tried in May 1976 before the Military Division of the USSR's Supreme Court.[8] Because of the crime of treason and its potential for capital punishment, the two lower courts, the Military Tribunal of the Baltic Fleet and the Military Tribunal of the Navy, were bypassed. Under normal circumstances, less severe crimes committed by Communist Party members or political officers were tried outside the military system by party commissioners.[9] This was not to be in Sablin's case; he was tried by the highest court-martial in the land. The proceedings were conducted in absolute secrecy, although every possible shred of evidence was gathered in an attempt to learn the background and motivation of the mutineers.

The exact punishment meted out to the crew was unclear for many years. It was known for certain that executions were carried out, but precisely how many remained a mystery. One exaggerated source claimed that eighty-two crewmembers were executed.[10] This very high figure is possibly due to the successful suppression of information concerning the mutineers and the fact that no primary sources were available for fifteen years.

It was thought that the remainder of the crew, including Captain Potulniy, was dispersed to various locations throughout the navy. Underground sources stated that even those officers who did not participate in the mutiny were reduced in rank by one grade.[11]

In spite of the Soviet government's silence on the matter, it was clear to those who were proficient at reading between the lines of its official statements that something had happened. The Soviets changed the content of certain public pronouncements, which all but acknowledged the fact that a mutiny had occurred. At the Twenty-fifth Party Congress in February 1976, Leonid Brezhnev discussed military leadership in greater detail than ever before. This was unusual because he had not mentioned military leadership in his address to the Twenty-fourth Party Congress a few years earlier, or in his speech to the Twenty-sixth Congress later on. In his 1976 statement, he emphasized, "The modern leader must combine within himself party-mindedness and profound competence, discipline and initiative, and he must take a creative approach to matters. At the same time, on any issue the leader is obligated to take account of the sociopolitical and educational aspects, to be tactful toward people and their needs and aspirations, and to set an example at work and in his daily life."[12]

Admiral Gorshkov, referring to these comments in his Navy Day interview, said, "These high party demands apply in full to commanders of ships, units and formations." His words suggested that the time had come in the Soviet armed forces, the navy in particular, for a commander to understand and relate to his men, not just follow orders and perform "by the book" as was traditionally preached.

In an article in *Krasnaya Zvezda* on 11 February 1976, Gorshkov discussed shortcomings in the work of some party organizations in the Soviet fleets and criticized the level of efficiency attained by engineering officers: "Ship commanders and party organizations have to pay particular attention to the ideological education of junior officers. We must study in greater depth, and seek to influence the formation of the ideological and moral potential of the future commander's personality, weighing up strictly whether the officer is ready to be a military leader in the era of the scientific-technical revolution, to be a genuine innovator, whether he is capable of taking firm, scientifically based decisions from party and state positions."[13]

In the past, the admiral had seldom mentioned discipline in such specific terms, especially in terms of the ideological commitment of his officers. Such criticisms were either avoided or left for comment by lesser officials. These statements and many others reflected the frequently recurring themes in professional naval writings of discipline or ideological fervor in the period immediately following the mutiny. Such comments continued to increase after the defection of Victor Belenko in his MiG-25 aircraft in September 1976.

In the February 1976 issue of *Morskoy Sbornik* (the Soviet Navy Digest), Admiral Gorshkov again stressed the importance of discipline in command. This issue was probably the first whose content could have been affected by the mutiny, given the fifty to sixty days of preparation time for each.[14] It is interesting to note that while five articles on *Storozhevoy* appeared in the military press in the two years before the mutiny, none were published in the fifteen years after it.

Yet another clue offered credence to the evidence of a mutiny. Late in 1978, the Soviet Navy issued new shipboard regulations. This was the first major overhaul of these regulations since 1959, although minor revisions were made in 1967. The new regulations added two new shipboard departments to cope with the advancing technology of the fleet, but more important, they increased the role of the commanding officer in political indoctrination. The revised shipboard regulations "place emphasis on the duties of the commanding officers to direct the work of the political apparatus toward successful accomplishment of tasks assigned to the ship, and to strengthening the military discipline and increasing the political morale of personnel."[15] The new regulations placed greater responsibility on the ship's commanding officer for the overall direction of political work, including more supervision of the *zampolit*. Consequently, it seemed that the possibility of the ship's political officer becoming a rival to his commanding officer's authority had been duly noted and greatly reduced. Commanding officers were now expected to increase readiness and combat capability by supervising a thorough political and ideological indoctrination of their crew, both officers and enlisted men. The new regulations continued to promote the need for "exactingness" in the performance of duties on longer voyages, thereby developing a more harmonious shipboard collective.

The first hint anyone in the public had of the mutiny appeared on 22 January 1976 in the Stockholm daily *Expressen* in an article written by Alex Milits, a journalist of Estonian origin who lived in Sweden. The majority of other early news accounts used quotations from this report or from later accounts Milits would write. How he came upon the story and how it later unfolded are interesting accounts in and of themselves.

In late November 1975, Milits was visited by a Latvian émigré who had just returned from a visit to Riga. He asked the journalist why no one had written anything about the mutiny that had occurred there earlier in the month. The émigré said that he had heard of the incident from six different people while he was in Riga, and he had been told that it was a large ship, "possibly a destroyer or cruiser."[16]

Milits was unwilling to write about such an important event using only one source, so he visited the port area in Stockholm and asked about it among Soviet merchant sailors from various Baltic ports including Riga. Most had not been home for some time and knew nothing of an alleged mutiny. A few sailors promised to look into it and contact Milits when they returned to Stockholm.[17] One week later, he received a phone call. A man with a Russian accent asked if Milits was the one inquiring about the mutiny. The caller, who sounded very nervous and refused to give his name, told Milits that he had just returned from Riga and had seen a naval vessel damaged by bombing. This vessel, the caller said, had participated in the chase of the mutinous ship. When Milits asked him what sort of ship had tried to escape, the caller said, "Storozhevoy" and hung up.[18]

Milits initially misunderstood the size of the ship involved. The Russian words *storozhevoy korabl* refer to a small coastal escort ship, and he therefore thought the mutiny had occurred aboard that type of vessel rather than the much larger *Krivak*-class ship named *Storozhevoy*. With this information, he published the first account in *Expressen* of a mutiny aboard a Soviet warship.

Four days later, another seaman who had the *Expressen* article read to him by a Swedish shopkeeper called Milits. The sailor told him he was wrong; the mutiny had taken place on a destroyer. The Russian also told him to read a certain issue of *Krasnaya Zvezda*. He then said, "Someone is coming!" and hurriedly hung up. The newspaper article he was referring to was the 24 December 1974 issue about *Storozhevoy*'s serious performance problems. The information provided in that article helped along Milits's research, and after interviewing tourists, Lithuanian fishermen, and merchant sailors, he published a much more accurate account in *Expressen* in May 1976.[19]

The appearance of this article alarmed the Swedish Defense Ministry staff, who thought someone had leaked their top-secret intercepts of Soviet radio communications. They were relieved when they found out the article was built on sources outside the Swedish government. On 5 May 1976, however, a second Swedish paper, *Svenska Dagbladet,* published a similar article about the mutiny, vaguely referring to the defense staff as the source. When reporters, spurred on by Milits's story, first inquired about the mutiny in February 1976, the Swedish military high command refused to release any information to the public. Then, on 9 May 1976, after the second article appeared, they published *Defense Bulletin Number Fourteen,* which did very little to dispel the rumors. Reporters who questioned a Defense Ministry official about the incident received a bland reply: "The command staff confirms that during routine monitoring of radio traffic in this time frame, activity that deviated from the norm was noted."[20] The spokesman declined, however, to confirm that the Soviet radio traffic had pointed to a mutiny. "On the other hand, neither could he deny this supposition."[21]

Defense Bulletin Number Fourteen also stated that the information contained in the *Svenska Dagbladet* article did not originate from the defense staff. At a Swedish Foreign Ministry press conference in the middle of May, reporter Gosta Bohman asked Foreign Minister Sven Anderson if the government had received any information regarding the "destroyer fiasco in the Baltic." Anderson said it had not.[22]

In fact it had. An internal Swedish Defense Ministry document, dated 8 March 1976, gave an analysis of the mutiny. This intelligence report, which came with the understated title "Orientation Concerning an Incident in the Eastern Baltic in November 1975" (see Appendix C for the complete text) shed some light on the specifics of the hunt for *Storozhevoy:*

> At least 20 Yak-28 Brewer aircraft initiated repeated bombing assaults against the ship. Another ship also pursuing near this position was mistaken for the *Storozhevoy* during the bomb assault, and at least one bomb caused damage. Besides these aircraft a large number of ships participated in the search for the mutineers, among others:
> Two *Riga*-class frigates from Riga,
> Three *Poti*-class corvettes from Liepae,
> One *Sverdlov*-class cruiser and two *Krivak*-class guided missile destroyers from Baltiysk,
> Five similar *Stenka* patrol ships from the KGB, and possibly one *Nanuchka* guided missile corvette.[23]

The report also contained the confident assumption that "the mutineers, whose intention was to go toward Stockholm's southern archipelago, never gave up in that aim." The evidence to support this statement was rather thin, especially since Sablin was broadcasting his appeal for revolution at the same time as he was taking *Storozhevoy* into the open waters of the Baltic. If the Swedes were eavesdropping on the ship's communications, would they not know that Sablin had intentions other than defecting? Although some of the ships and planes chasing *Storozhevoy* were talking on their radios in the clear, Sablin's call for revolt was made on encrypted military channels. The Swedes might not have been able to break the Soviet military codes—or they could but did not want the Russians to know that they had deciphered Sablin's message. Such is the mental chess game that makes up so much of intelligence work.

Even without the result of a complete and careful analysis of all the taped data, Foreign Minister Sven Anderson and Defense Minister Eric Holmquist were briefed within twenty-four hours of the mutiny's end and given the Defense Staff's interpretation of what had happened.[24] Initial contact was made unofficially with the United States within two weeks to compare intelligence information. The United States only had some fragmentary information from the NATO radar station at Bornholm to add to the puzzle.

On 12 November 1975, articles in the Swedish press appeared saying that the wreck of a Soviet target ship was found abandoned in Swedish territorial waters off Götland. The Soviets apologized shortly thereafter and retrieved the hulk, saying it had been used for target practice in the Baltic on 9 November and had drifted away. A fisherman from Götland was quoted as saying that the target barge did not appear in his home waters until the eleventh. At the time very few people knew anything about the mutiny. Only a few years later was the connection made that the Soviets deliberately set the target ship adrift to provide an explanation to anyone who might have been monitoring the attack on *Storozhevoy*.[25]

Capt. Thomas Wheeler, the U.S. naval attaché in Sweden at the time, said that Swedish government officials with whom he spoke were actually very glad that *Storozhevoy* had not reached their home waters. If it had, they would have been faced with the question of granting asylum to the mutineers. The Swedes had always granted asylum on an individual basis to Soviet defectors, but mutiny was a serious crime in any navy and greatly complicated such requests. In 1981, when a Russian *Whiskey*-class submarine (which was probably carrying out surveillance operations) ran aground on the Swedish coast, it appeared that the Swedes' patience with the Soviets was wearing thin. One source stated that this incident so aggravated the Swedish government that it publicized its data on *Storozhevoy* just to spite the Russians.[26]

Soon after the mutiny, the Swedes conducted naval exercises off Götland Island. The Swedish destroyer *Smaland* played the role of an escaping ship with half the crew locked up as it entered Slite Harbor. In this training exercise, Swedish forces responded quickly to protect her.[27] All Swedish Navy vessels began to carry a thick black book titled *Action to be Taken in the Event of Violation of Swedish Territory During Time of Peace and Neutrality* (Swedish acronym IKFN). In the chapter called "IKFN Sea," the manual clearly had *Storozhevoy* in mind when it mentioned, "If, upon inspection or hearsay, it appears that fugitives have taken over the command of a foreign military vessel, the circumstances must be immediately reported to the commanding general . . . so that immediate action may be taken."[28]

The American reaction to the mutiny was even more muted than the Swedish one. According to Captain Wheeler, several State Department messages instructed U.S. Embassy personnel in Stockholm to "keep the lid on" the incident.[29] The most probable explanation for this was that the United States was still attempting to maintain some sort of détente with the Soviets and did not want to embarrass them by making the information public. The only semiofficial American reaction was a resolution by Congressman Larry McDonald (D-Ga.) calling for the U.S. government to condemn Sweden for failing to grant asylum to the ship and her crew. He made this proposal from the floor of the U.S. House of Representatives on 9 June 1976, but due to the scarcity of information on the subject, his resolution never went to a vote. As it turned out, the resolution was based on a false press account that the ship had reached Swedish territorial waters.[30]

It is possible that the U.S. government needed to protect its own intelligence capabilities and so kept quiet about what it really knew. This was refuted by intelligence personnel, however, who said, "The incident was over before we knew what was happening. . . . We had nothing focused to gather any information."[31] The P-3 Orion reconnaissance aircraft that patrolled the Baltic on a daily basis to monitor Soviet surface activity missed the incident entirely.

Taking everything into account, it appears that some Swedish Defense Ministry personnel made a concerted effort to get the actual information distributed, off the record, to various journalists. The Swedes' reluctance to make an official statement, however, could be explained by the fact that they wanted to maintain their sensitive neutral position or protect intelligence collection capabilities. But the real explanation for their evasion was not publicly disclosed until September 1976. The leftist Swedish journal *Folket I Bild-Kulturfront* accused Sven Anderson of paying a $1 million bribe to U.S. Air Force general Rocky Triantafellu, head of the Air Force Intelligence Agency, from 1970 to 1973, when Anderson was the defense minister.[32] To dissuade any more false allegations, the Swedish military was forced to explain that the four $250,000 payments were not a bribe but a perfectly legitimate business transaction to purchase electronic equipment used to eavesdrop on Soviet bloc military communications. A large part of the Swedish population and many of their Baltic neighbors were horrified over the disclosure of this classified deal with the Pentagon. To many, it was simply too naked a breach of Swedish neutrality.[33] Stig Synnergren, the armed forces chief of staff, confirmed at a press conference in September 1976 that the equipment had been used to monitor messages sent by Moscow to Soviet bombers pursuing a runaway frigate. He acknowledged that the money laundered through commercial banks to purchase the electronic eavesdropping equipment had come from a secret Defense Ministry fund.[34]

The Swedish government's purchase of this equipment from America made headlines in Sweden but was only marginally covered in the United States. Publicly, the Swedes maintained a policy of strict neutrality in the Cold War; they were not members of NATO, nor were they members of the European Union at the time. With very few exceptions, all of the FRA's intelligence production since 1945 is still classified and must remain so for seventy years after the event in question. This includes the taped intercepts from 9 November of radio communications between Soviet planes pursuing *Storozhevoy* and their ground control.

We contacted Jan-Olof Grahn, the acting head of the FRA in 2003, and invited him to comment on the *Storozhevoy* mutiny from the Swedish point of view. Grahn was a junior analyst in 1975 and worked on the case, but he could only reaffirm the official Swedish position: that its government maintained strict neutrality with regard to the Soviet-American standoff during the Cold War. The Swedes most likely passed a copy of their transcripts of Soviet pilots refusing to bomb *Storozhevoy* to the National Security Agency, but these remain classified in the United States as well. The authors' Freedom of Information Act request to NSA to declassify these documents was denied, as was their appeal. The appeals authority stated, "As a result of this review, I have concluded that the appropriate response to your request is to neither confirm nor deny the existence of responsive records. . . . I have determined that any substantive response to your request would tend to confirm or deny *specific* [NSA italics] activities."[35]

Nearly thirty years after the mutiny, Western governments remain as quiet on the subject as the Soviet government was in 1975. At that time, in the face of a total lack of information from the Soviets and only limited information from the Swedish government, rumors in the press were rampant. Milits had a head start on his colleagues with some sources no one else had and later pieced together a fairly accurate picture of the events of 8–9 November. Other newspapers competing for the story found information about the mutiny hard to obtain. In retrospect, it is evident that they often used less than reliable sources and produced wildly exaggerated accounts. For example, the *Daily Telegraph* of London reported that *Storozhevoy* actually reached Sweden but was denied asylum by the Swedish government. The report said that sailors who had jumped overboard were machine-gunned in the water by Soviet aircraft while the political officer and five co-conspirators committed suicide.[36] Other sources had their own agendas for releasing incomplete information. The *Latvian Information Bulletin,* for example, mistakenly reported that the majority of the crew were Latvian nationals and the mutiny had been part of a larger nationalist uprising in Riga. This publication, however, tended to regard anything that even hinted of anti-Soviet sentiment as being part of a larger Latvian uprising.

There was a great deal of circular reporting as well, but most of these sources were inaccurate and often contradictory. A *Dallas Times Herald* article of 7 June 1976, which was reprinted from the *Washington Post,* cited speculation that the mutiny's leader was a *zampolit* but said he was a Jewish dissident. It also claimed that the ringleaders were sentenced to death and executed, and that perhaps fifty sailors had been killed in the incident.[37] We now know that at the time this article was printed, Sablin was still in Lefortovo Prison and no one had yet been sentenced to death or executed. Furthermore, no one was killed during the mutiny, and Sablin was not Jewish.

A Russian émigré newspaper in the United States, *Novoye Russkoye Slovo,* which was always quick to assume the worst when it came to the Soviet government, claimed that 140 mutineers were shot.[38] The *Financial Times* of London was the source that put the number of executed crewmen at eighty-two.[39] An underground dissident journal in Russia, *Chronicle of Current Events,* was more restrained in its speculation but still incorrectly identified the mutinous vessel as a "patrol ship." The journal also mentioned that the ship had been towed to Liepae (true), but that it had been repainted and renamed the *Druzhba* (untrue).[40] A month later, the *Baltimore Sun* cited the *Chronicle* as its source in an article it printed on the mutiny.[41]

The U.S. government was not much better with its information, and in some respects it was the most inaccurate. A recently declassified naval intelligence report from October 1976 did not even get the year of the mutiny right, placing it in November 1974 (in three separate references). This report asserted that the political officer and the ship's executive officer had led the mutiny, throwing two men overboard in the process. This version had the ship making it all the way into Swedish territorial waters, where it was attacked by Soviet aircraft, boarded, and taken back to Riga and scrapped. The reporting officer described his source for this information as "a professional lathe operator who reportedly had learned the details provided above from his brother who worked in Riga as bus driver for the municipal transport services by which he had good contact possibilities to obtain information."[42]

Hardly a "fly on the wall" source. Meanwhile, the U.S. Defense Attaché's Office (USDAO) in Stockholm included Alex Milits's *Expressen* article, which first broke the story, in a report of the mutiny it sent to European Command Headquarters in West Germany. The USDAO officers were more careful in their evaluation, and while there was still confusion as to the type of vessel involved, one of their own sources was convinced that it was a *Krivak*-class guided missile destroyer, hull number 500. This source was only identified by a number, but according to the reporting officer, "he bases his confidence primarily on a preliminary review of sigint [signals intelligence] from the period." Most likely, then, this source worked for the FRA and had access to the transcripts of intercepted Soviet radio communications.[43]

Given all the speculation and hearsay, it is no wonder that good information was hard to come by. Until the Soviet government or an eyewitness to the mutiny came forward, it did not appear as if the mystery of what happened on *Storozhevoy* that November night would ever be solved.

Not until 1981 did a U.S. naval officer make the first attempt to bring these disparate facts together and tell the real story. Lt. Greg Young was a student at the Naval Postgraduate School in Monterey, California. A P-3 Orion aviator by trade, Young was studying for his master's degree in national security affairs. His initial thesis research sought to find more qualitative methods to assess Soviet military capability, such as evaluating Soviet military morale, training, unit cohesion, and fighting spirit. These topics had not been thoroughly researched, and his work led him to Soviet underground (*samizdat*) sources for information. He also looked into translations of foreign press accounts of Soviet military morale, and it was during this quest that he found Alex Milits's first story of the mutiny.

Since the Soviets were still denying the incident ever happened, Young had to rely on the early Swedish accounts to get started, but it was primarily his own detective work that brought the story together. He took out advertisements in Russian-language newspapers in Europe, Canada, and the United States, essentially asking for anyone with any knowledge of a mutiny in the Soviet Navy in November 1975 to contact him. One month later, the calls started coming in. Many were like the ones Alex Milits had received—quick, hushed accounts from men with heavily accented voices who called from public phone booths and refused to give their names. Nonetheless, they provided valuable information. Young clearly benefited, to some degree, from being in the right place at the right time. The first large group of Jewish émigrés, who had been allowed to leave the Soviet Union as part of détente, were just then settling in the United States and Europe.

Working through the Hoover Institute at Stanford University, he was able to tap into the vast repository of émigré and *samizdat* sources housed there. Soviet emigrant Mikhail Bernstam provided sources who were still in Russia, such as an individual who had worked in the Baltic Fleet for *Krasnaya Zvezda,* as well as someone who had seen the mutineers on their first day in holding in Riga.

Young had access to classified intelligence at the time and found almost no information to supplement what he had learned by digging through the available unclassified material. After interviewing many of these sources, along with U.S. government officials and Swedish journalists, he finished his thesis, "Mutiny on the *Storozhevoy*: A Case Study of Dissent in the Soviet Navy," in 1982. The thesis found its way, mostly unread, into government document sections of libraries throughout the country. After finishing Naval Postgraduate School, Young was transferred to the Philippines, where he was the operations officer for a P-3 wing detachment. This unit was responsible for monitoring Soviet naval activity out of the old American base at Cam Ranh Bay, Vietnam.

A year later, people began to find his research. Noted Soviet naval authority Norman Polmar wrote a summary of Young's thesis for *Sea Power* magazine.[44] An insurance agent from Owings, Maryland, who was doing some research in the basement of the Naval Academy library for a book he was writing, also came across it. After reading the thesis, he decided to write to Young and get some feedback. Once he had done a little of his own detective work and discovered that the naval officer was now stationed in the Philippines, the insurance agent wrote: "I am now working on a novel, *The Hunt for Red October*. Posit: *Red October,* a modified *Typhoon*-class SSBN is attempting to defect to the U.S. The Soviets find out. We find out. Chaos results. . . . My version has the skipper of *Red October* killing his political officer as a precondition to his defection. (I was amazed to learn that the PO lead [sic] the *Storozhevoy* incident). . . . Regards, Thomas L. Clancy Jr."[45]

Clancy requested permission to use some material from the thesis and asked Young to recommend unclassified sources on antisubmarine warfare that he could use in his research. The rest, as they say, is history. *The Hunt for Red October* was published in the fall of 1984, and by March of the following year, it had cracked the top ten on the *New York Times* bestseller list. The book became very popular among Washington's well-heeled political class. Ronald Reagan was said to have called it "a good yarn," and William F. Buckley was photographed for *Time* magazine reading it on his sailboat.

However, the book's wealth of detail on submarine operations and naval weapons technology caused great consternation among the naval leadership. Navy Secretary John Lehman supposedly gasped, "Who cleared this?" after reading excerpts from the book.

When Clancy identified Greg Young as a primary source, the news media and the naval leadership both descended upon the lieutenant commander, who was by now a Navy ROTC instructor at the University of Colorado in Boulder. The chief of naval information forbade any contacts with the media until he was assured that there was nothing classified in Young's thesis or in any other information that he had passed to Clancy. Once cleared, the first accounts of the real mutiny finally appeared in a UPI wire story, an *ABC Evening News* piece, and even a *People* magazine profile of Young, all in 1985.[46]

The biggest difference between Clancy's version and the *Storozhevoy* mutiny was that *Red October* was a submarine. Although a work of fiction, one scene in the book does mention the real-life mutiny, when CIA analyst Jack Ryan is called to the White House to brief the president on *Red October*'s flight from the Soviet Union. The president is skeptical about the possibility of an entire submarine crew defecting to the United States along with their boat:

> Ryan was ready for that. "There is a precedent for this, sir. On November 8, 1975, the *Storozhevoy,* a Soviet *Krivak*-class missile frigate, attempted to run from Riga, Latvia, to the Swedish island of Götland. The political officer aboard, Valery Sablin, led a mutiny of the enlisted personnel. They locked their officers in their cabins and raced away from the dock. They came close to making it. Air and fleet units attacked them and forced them to halt within fifty miles of Swedish territorial waters. Two more hours and they would have made it. Sablin and twenty-six others were court-martialed and shot."[47]

The fiction of mass executions seemed to reach everyone who came into contact with the story. The fact that Sablin was the only one sentenced to death surprised a lot of people, including Greg Young. Of course, Sablin never intended to defect to the West, but given the total lack of primary source information available at the time (i.e., eyewitness accounts, official Soviet investigation reports, etc.), it was remarkable that people like Young and Alex Milits got so much of the story right.

For nearly fifteen years, the Soviet government went to great lengths to hide evidence of the *Storozhevoy* mutiny. Unofficially, of course, everyone in the navy heard rumors about what happened in Riga on the night of 8–9 November 1975. One of them was another *zampolit,* Nikolai Cherkashin, who served aboard submarines for most of his career. Cherkashin recalled that the name of Valery Sablin "remained in my memory. . . . From time to time, it reappeared in idle talk among close friends, and new details, likely and unlikely, were added to it. And each time, his name was uttered sympathetically."[48]

By 1987, Cherkashin had retired from the navy and was working in Moscow as a writer. One day, purely by chance, he ran into Sablin's cousin Tamara, who had done so much to influence Valery's intellectual development. When Tamara showed him pictures of her cousin, Cherkashin's instincts told him this was not the face of a crazy man or a traitor. Tamara spoke of Valery with undisguised pride and admiration. The more Nikolai learned about the man behind the *Storozhevoy* mutiny, the more he came to realize that Sablin was only asking for the same things that Mikhail Gorbachev was: liberalization of the Communist system.

The Soviet Union was now a different place under a different leader. Inspired by glasnost and the new political climate, Cherkashin began research on the mutiny in the fall of 1988. He quickly discovered, however, that for all of Gorbachev's high-minded purpose, the Soviet Union was still a one-party state ruled by a totalitarian government. People might have been able to breathe easier, but fear that the suffocation might return was still there. Nonetheless, Cherkashin persisted in his efforts and wrote an essay that he submitted to *Pravda* for publication in November 1989. Titled "Into the Fog of Battle," it would be the first account of the mutiny published in the Soviet Union.

As it turned out, the article was still too inflammatory for *Pravda.* The paper's editorial board was locked in bitter conflict over how they were portraying a man who was still officially a "traitor to the Motherland." Unbeknownst to Nikolai, the board had decided to remove the photograph of Sablin that he had sent in with the essay and replace it with a picture of *Storozhevoy.* Cherkashin did not mind this cosmetic change, as long as the essay was printed as he originally wrote it.

The changes then became more than just cosmetic. *Pravda* pulled the story twice that November as the war in the editorial office raged on. On 17 November 1989 (the week after the fall of the

Berlin Wall), Cherkashin made his third trip to *Pravda*'s office. He was livid when he looked at an advance copy of the next day's edition and found his title had been replaced by "Crime at Sea." He refused to agree to this change, so the paper pulled the essay for the third time.

Strangely enough, these advance copies, which the pressroom printed in order to see how the next day's edition would look, were quickly stolen and ended up at various universities around Moscow. Someone also saw fit to mail copies to the KGB and GLAVPUR, the governing body for political officers in the armed forces.

This was not yet an ominous development, because Nikolai had sent GLAVPUR numerous appeals to make the events of 8–9 November 1975 public. To his pleasant surprise, he found two allies there: Col. Gen. Gennadi Stefanovski and Maj. Gen. Viktor Yakimov. Along with Viktor Verstakov, a former *Pravda* journalist, Cherkashin and the two generals went to GLAVPUR's top man, General Lizichev, to make their case. According to Cherkashin, "We tried to convince him that in the current environment, Sablin's act had taken on new significance. In keeping with our own 'Prague Spring,' the ideas, thoughts, and conclusions of the *Storozhevoy*'s political officer found complete confirmation in the speeches of the general secretary and the lead articles of *Pravda*. We mentioned the fact that the entire world was reading a novel about Sablin, published in the United States, and watching the movie version—*The Hunt for Red October*—while here in our own country, a national hero was being spoken of only in rumors and conjecture."[49]

Lizichev wavered but finally agreed and gave the green light to publish Cherkashin's essay in *Krasnaya Zvezda*. This appeared to be the victory Cherkashin had been looking for, but when he went to *Krasnaya Zvezda*'s editorial offices the next day, he found that its editor had no intention of running Cherkashin's article. In fact, he had the presses set to run an alternate article written by one of their staff columnists that described Sablin as a traitor. When Cherkashin protested that General Lizichev himself had given the go-ahead for his article, the editor replied that the general had called that morning and told him to run the negative story.

Furious, Nikolai pulled the last rabbit out of his hat. A colleague of his who was one of the country's most respected writers on military affairs, Ivan Stadnyuk, used his influence to get the *Krasnaya*

Zvezda article spiked, but at a price. Cherkashin had to agree not to publish his essay for the time being, and if it did go to press, he would have to call it "The Sablin Affair." Cherkashin accepted these conditions, and by the end of 1989, it appeared that the whole issue was deadlocked.

The KGB was then kind enough to pay a visit to Cherkashin at his apartment. Lieutenant General Sergeyev dropped by to try and convince Cherkashin that there was no need to publish anything on Sablin since it might compromise state security. Some things certainly had changed in the Gorbachev era; in the old days, whenever the KGB made house calls, it was usually late at night and without much discussion other than "You're coming with us." Now, a high-ranking official from the Committee for State Security was calmly drinking tea with Nikolai in his kitchen and suggesting that publishing an account of Sablin's mutiny might have adverse consequences in the fleet. Crews aboard ballistic missile submarines, the general pointed out, might be inspired by this true-life story and try to repeat it. This might create the very situation presented in Tom Clancy's novel, but this time with a crew that had every intention of using its nuclear payload not against the United States but against its own government.

Cherkashin easily deflected these arguments; he had heard them many times before, and after spending much of his career below the surfaces of the world's oceans, he knew how a nuclear submarine operated. It was not a motorcycle that could just be stolen off the street, he replied. This "Sablinism" would have to overcome the entire crew—from the reactor room to the engine room to the missile arming and launch sections. Besides, most skippers knew about Sablin and could have imitated him at any time in their careers. Most had not, probably because they knew he had ended up with a bullet in the back of his head, and what kind of example was that to follow?

The two men failed to convince each other, but the conversation had been pleasant enough and Lieutenant General Sergeyev left on cordial terms. Shortly thereafter, however, Nikolai noticed that whenever he spoke Sablin's name on his telephone, he would hear a click and the connection would get worse. His phone was being tapped. The KGB might be kinder and gentler, but they were still secret policemen.

The state's counterattack on Nikolai Cherkashin and the legacy of Valery Sablin intensified in early 1990, when the Soviet government finally admitted that there had been a mutiny aboard *Storozhevoy*. As with other admissions of its unappetizing past, the official state organs crafted a complex face-saving way to present it to the public. The *Izvestiya* correspondent in New York, Alexander Shalnev, wrote an article about *The Hunt for Red October* on 28 February 1990. Tom Clancy's book had been out for nearly six years, but the film, starring Sean Connery and Alec Baldwin, was due to open in American theaters that March. Shalnev used this as a pretext to comment on the true story behind the best-selling novel and the attempt to bring that story to the attention of the Soviet public.

This set the stage for a response by none other than Maj. Gen. Alexander Boriskin, the KGB judge advocate general who had presided over Sablin's case in 1976. Agreeing that the truth needed to be told, Boriskin used Shalnev's article as an opportunity to present the official party line on the mutiny. That version still had Sablin defecting to Sweden, though Boriskin made this point obliquely, only mentioning that the ship was "twenty-one miles in the direction of Swedish territorial waters."[50] He also claimed that although weapons were used to stop *Storozhevoy*, the "bombardment was not aimed at the ship but ahead of it, across its bow. Of course, there was not a single hit, nothing at all was damaged either on deck or on the superstructure."[51]

Obviously, this was not true, and in fact *Storozhevoy* suffered significant damage to its stern and rudder from Soviet Air Force bombers. Not only that, but another *Krivak*-class ship from the pursuing squadron was also damaged when it was mistakenly attacked. Whether Boriskin believed this or was just reciting the official story is not known, but he defended the Soviet government's actions and insisted that "in a breach of the military oath, [Sablin] embarked on the practical implementation of an adventurist action."[52]

This official acknowledgment signified that the taboo on discussing this subject was now removed, and *Komsomolskaya Pravda* published Cherkashin's article the next day, 1 March 1990. In Cherkashin's words, Valery Sablin now made his "appointed meeting with the country, and with the millions whom he had not been able to reach." He received a sympathetic response from the Russian people. After the story broke in the Soviet press, Nina was approached by many people who told her they thought her husband deserved a medal. It was rich vindication for the woman who had borne so much grief for so many years, but the one thought on her mind was rehabilitation. As she told the *Miami Herald* in 1993, "All I care about is rehabilitation. It's probably the way we were brought up. A piece of paper is important. The official rehabilitation is important for the others to see he did not betray his country."[53]

The first rehabilitation attempt was made in the fall of 1992 in Moscow. An unofficial trial was presided over by a local judge, Sergei Alexiev. The prosecutor, Max Khazin, presented the case against rehabilitation, while the defense attorney, Yuri Schmidt, argued for it. Testimony from dozens of sources was drawn, including eyewitness accounts from several of the mutiny participants as well as members of the pursuit force that chased *Storozhevoy*. In a nonbinding verdict, the jury found in favor of Valery Sablin's rehabilitation, but the question remained as to what kind of pardon he should be given.

In 1991, just before the fall of the Soviet Union, a commission was created to accept and process requests for the rehabilitation of victims of political persecution. Nina immediately sent in her request on behalf of Valery. In spite of all the publicity and the unofficial rehabilitation trial, the commission turned her request down in 1994. Two years later, Boris Nemtsov, the governor of the province of Nizhniy Novgorod (formerly Gorky, the city that was home to the Sablin family), publicly called on President Boris Yeltsin to pardon Valery Sablin. Finally, after numerous appeals, the Military Collegium of the Supreme Court of the Russian Federation granted Valery Sablin and Alexander Shein a partial rehabilitation on 23 June 1998. In effect, they removed the phrase "traitor to the Motherland" from their convictions. The charge of "abuse of authority" remained in effect, however, for their detention of Captain Potulniy.

Even now, full rehabilitation appears unlikely for Valery Sablin. An admission by the Ministry of Defense that his mutiny was justified, or even forgiven, would be unprecedented. Nonetheless, this admission by the Russian government that Sablin was no longer a "traitor to the Motherland" meant that Nina could be officially classified as a "victim of political persecution," entitling her to a small stipend. Ironically, Shein is not considered a victim of political persecution because he survived his prison sentence.

As Nikolai Cherkashin pointed out in his book, *Posledniy Parad* (*The Last Parade*), Sablin's military oath pledged him "to the last

breath to keep faith with our people and the Soviet Motherland."
What part of that oath did he break? American servicemen and ser-
vicewomen pledge not only to support and defend their Constitution
but also to obey the orders "of the officers appointed over me." The
Soviet military oath was much less specific. As Cherkashin also
points out, Leonid Brezhnev was subject to this oath as well, since
he was the supreme commander of the nation's armed forces. How
well did he keep faith with the "people and the Soviet Motherland"?
The invasions of Czechoslovakia and Afghanistan took place on his
orders. He pilfered money from Siberian oil contracts, smuggled dia-
monds through Central Asia, and did nothing as Russia's wealth
was squandered on endless arms production. The whole time he was
enriching himself, his countrymen lived in squalor.

In post-Communist Russia, people were being reminded on a
daily basis of the regime's past crimes. For many, it was easier to let
that past remain where it was than to dig up yet another example
of Soviet tyranny. But it was not just Sablin's rehabilitation that
mattered; it was the ability of a society to confront the ugliness in
its history. Fear and suspicion can strangle a nation just as much as
it can debilitate a human being. A Russian Orthodox priest who was
an observer at Sablin's rehabilitation trial said that from the
church's point of view, "this was a matter of conscience—a cry of the
spirit—over the future of our people. It was like a Greek tragedy.
From the Church's standpoint, and from Christianity's, it's more of
a spiritual matter. This man was killed because he wanted to do
something to end that nightmare."[54]

The *Storozhevoy* mutiny would touch a chord with many Russians. When journalist Andrei Maidanov published his book on the
mutiny, *Pryamo po Kursu—Smert (Straight on a Course for Death)*,
he included several of the letters he had received while researching
the subject, most of them expressing support for Sablin. The following came from a World War II veteran:

> Sablin realized something much earlier than the rest of us did: that
> our system was created only for the party leadership and govern-
> ment elite, which had nothing in common with the people. For this
> elite, the people were only a front, in whose name they claimed to
> be serving.
>
> I want to help, and I am not alone.[55]

One letter was sent to Maidanov from several active duty army officers, along with money to help in the rehabilitation effort. Signed "Lieutenant K., Lieutenant Colonel V., Major S., Captain B., Senior Lieutenant V., Lieutenant K., Lieutenant N.," it was posthumously addressed to Sablin:

> Forgive us, Valery Mikhailovich, for only now realizing the difference between truth and lies, hypocrisy and reality, words and action. Forgive us for being too thickheaded to see the guilt of our "leaders and mentors." It's true that we all conspired to hide our sins, in exchange for rubles, ranks, and promotions, continuing business as usual. Forgive us this as well—in the school of democracy we are only in the first grade, and as we all know, in every school there are those who excel and those who come in second.
>
> *Storozhevoy* should be a badge of honor, with a picture of Valery Sablin in the center of it.[56]

On the Neva River in St. Petersburg, the cruiser *Aurora* still sits as a museum to an earlier mutiny, the one that lit the fire of the Bolshevik Revolution in October 1917. Its crewmen were later hailed by the Communist government as heroes and awarded the Order of the Red Banner.

Storozhevoy sat, ignored and rusting, at a pier in Vladivostok in the Russian Far East for a decade. In 2004, it was sold to India for scrap metal.

Chapter 7

THE LEGACY

In the movie *The Hunt for Red October,* the final showdown takes place in the North Atlantic. Actor Sean Connery's character, Captain Marko Ramius, instructs his crew to abandon ship so that he and the submarine's other officers can take the boat down and scuttle it. Russians and Americans square off on the water's surface and below it, tensely awaiting *Red October*'s next move. Only a handful of people on both sides, including Ramius and actor Alec Baldwin's character Jack Ryan, know what is really going on. Not until the last scenes of the movie does the audience find out what happens to Ryan, Ramius, and *Red October.*

Had he known all the facts when he was writing his best-selling novel in 1984, Tom Clancy might have stuck with the true story. In many ways it is more fascinating than the fiction. Valery Sablin emerges as a more complicated hero than Marko Ramius; his motives are far more idealistic and grandiose. In the novel, the hapless Soviets are outwitted and lose their prized submarine. In real life, they recovered their fugitive vessel, but not before a few anxious minutes made it appear as if Sablin's revolt was spreading to the pilots and ships' captains chasing him. In the novel, Mrs. Ramius is the martyred wife of Sean Connery's character, a revered woman who inspires *Red October*'s skipper to do the impossible. Her real-life counterpart, Nina Sablina, is every bit her husband's inspiration, but she ends up carrying her tragic burden longer and harder than anyone in Clancy's story.

Truth is indeed stranger than fiction. The *Storozhevoy* mutiny shines a light on so many political, social, and military issues that it only grows in significance, even today. Especially today. In retrospect, it is surprising that so many people made assumptions about Sablin's imminent defection based on scant evidence. Even more surprising is that so much information was available during the Cold War indicating that the mutiny was by no means an isolated incident. The fact that this evidence was available to Greg Young and any other American with a library card begs the question: Why did we so drastically overestimate the military and economic capability of the Soviet Union? In answering this question, another one is raised: What does it take to change a government's mind about an enemy?

Nearly everyone familiar with the story assumed *Storozhevoy* was making its way to Sweden. Russian sailors had defected before, some even bringing their ships with them. They all knew the Swedish government would grant them political asylum, and there were large émigré communities in Stockholm and elsewhere. Why should they not want to leave their gray, oppressive lives in the Soviet Union for the comfort of the West? They had been through enough; why not enjoy the good life in Sweden? The government there even gave asylum seekers a stipend.

The good life, indeed, materially, but what about spiritually? Did not every émigré harbor a little guilt, no matter how misplaced, about leaving his country behind? Fleeing was the easy way out. What about their countrymen who had stayed behind and tried to change things? Most were now dead or chopping wood in Siberia. Their efforts may have been futile, but when do a million futile acts finally make a difference? It had to happen eventually, and when it did, all that futility would suddenly change and get a new name: bravery.

In his own way, Sablin confounded everyone's predictions. A life outside of Russia held no interest for him. It was his country and he wanted to take it back from Brezhnev's corrupt regime. He certainly did not fit the Western mold of Marko Ramius, and perhaps the most intriguing part of Tom Clancy's novel is the fact that Jack Ryan tries to convince his disbelieving colleagues that Ramius wants to defect to the West rather than blow it up. There was no real-life Jack Ryan in 1975, however, to make the same argument that Valery Sablin's motives were not what they appeared to be.

Sablin was remarkably clinical in his analysis of Soviet society, detaching himself and looking at it from the outside with uncanny ability. Unlike many of his countrymen, whose hopelessness turned into bitterness, Sablin believed it was imperative to channel his frustration through the supreme virtue of action. The Russian people had done nothing wrong, he wanted to tell them, and there was no reason for self-loathing. Their government had betrayed them, and like him, their redemption could come through supporting a new Russian revolution. It was one thing to hear this from an émigré talking politics in a London bar, or a university student in Leningrad who had read too much Marx, but it was quite another to hear it from a commissioned officer of the Soviet Navy who knew how to use a modern warship. Sablin was always treading on dangerous ground because he was an idealist in a profession that has traditionally been a graveyard for idealists and the men they lead.

It is interesting to note that few sources in the West, military or civilian, gave much thought to the prospects of a new Russian revolution. It was naturally assumed that any dissident living in the Soviet Union would leave it if he or she could. The refuseniks, after all, got their name from the Soviet government's refusal to grant them exit visas. So many of Russia's best and brightest had defected, it was predicted that a flood of refugees would issue forth if the doors ever opened completely.

To the American people in 1975, winning the cold war without fighting a hot war seemed improbable, especially that year, when the country's twenty-year involvement in Vietnam ended. The public had been routinely told that victory was right around the corner in Southeast Asia, only to find out that it was all a shell game. Most Americans had little patience for the argument that Vietnam could have been won if only a different strategy had been used. Nonetheless, had the U.S. government taken the initiative in Indochina in 1945, when Ho Chi Minh was still quoting Thomas Jefferson in his own declaration of independence speech, Communism might never have come to Vietnam.

Like Valery Sablin, the Vietnamese leader was motivated primarily by nationalism—the desire to see his country's interests promoted and defended. To Sablin, Russia's interests were being hamstrung by Brezhnev and his cronies, who were preventing the country from taking its rightful place as one of the world's great nations. Yet Sablin felt that this challenge had to be met within Russia by its own people, not by defecting to the West and casting stones from the comfortable existence of Stockholm or Paris.

Many Western policy makers had fooled themselves into believing that the Soviet regime, protected by a powerful police force and military, could exercise unlimited control over its citizens indefinitely. In effect, they were falling under the spell of the same Soviet propaganda that they prided themselves on being able to identify and expose. The Communists were dangerous, they said, because they were liars and subversives who were backed up by a huge and fearsome army. The possibility that the Communists may have been lying about their fearsome army did not occur to them until much later, after the Berlin Wall had fallen and everyone in the West was standing around wondering what had happened.

Sablin's revolt stunned his countrymen, but had they known about it, it also would have left many on this side of the Iron Curtain just as speechless. Here was a homegrown Soviet officer taking a course so many of them thought impossible. Who in his right mind would do such a thing? Resistance to tyranny, however, was a cornerstone of American political faith, so who in his right mind would accept it? Was it really so surprising that a Russian patriot would value liberty just as much as his American counterpart? When President John F. Kennedy gave his commencement speech at American University in June 1963, he pointed out that "no government or social system is so evil that its people must be considered as lacking in virtue."

In his independence, Valery Sablin also provided a welcome antidote to Marxist theory. To Marx, class warfare and world revolution were inescapable certainties. The most destructive aspect of this philosophy was the notion of inevitability, the idea that there is nothing an individual can do to alter events. This attitude undermined the very concept of responsibility, making committed Marxists dismissive of other theories of social development. They came to regard anyone who disagreed with the inevitability of a classless society as reactionary.

Marx no doubt would have labeled Sablin a "counterrevolutionary," and indeed he was, though not in his own mind. In his belief that Lenin's Russia could have turned out better than it did, Valery was probably mistaken. As a potential rival, and a charismatic one at that, Lenin most likely would have had someone like Sablin put up against a wall and shot. He probably did—many times.

It is doubtful that Sablin would have done likewise. A man who makes his case to his fellow officers and then simply locks up his opponents fails the ruthlessness test. Yet he passes the most important humanity test, because if history has taught anything, it is that power has to come from something more than just the barrel of a gun.

Valery Sablin proved that individuals could make history by taking their lives into their own hands. To understand the significance of what he did, consider the fact that in the space of thirty minutes, he persuaded eight officers of the Soviet Navy to commit a crime that is generally recognized as the most serious in any military unit. And these were not disgruntled has-beens but responsible officers who occupied important positions of trust on one of their country's newest and most sophisticated warships. These were men who had a stake in the system, men who had wives and children and careers to protect. They put all of that on the line and jeopardized everything, including their own lives, just so they could live like free men, if only for a few hours.

It is possible they were lying to Sablin when they chose their chess pieces at that fateful meeting on the night of the mutiny, stalling for time until they could think more clearly. They also might have been telling him only what they thought he wanted to hear. They might have changed their minds afterward, like Lieutenant Firsov, especially when the bombs began to fall.

Nonetheless, the fact that they even considered it was extraordinary, even among the enlisted men. It is true that they were part of a service that valued obedience more than initiative, but ordering a sailor to mutiny is not the same thing as ordering him to polish his boots. The men knew it was against the law, but they were motivated in part by a combination of fear, conformity, and a general "what-the-hell" attitude. Most of all, they were inspired by Sablin's speech, and the force of his words finally made them cross that invisible threshold from safe inaction into a brave new world. Although his revolt failed, how many Russians heard about it and recalled it later when the time came to decide their country's future—the old way or the new? In so doing, the average Russians might have drawn upon this and countless other memories of the daily fears they had to suffer through, finally giving them the courage to say, "Enough is enough."

Valery Sablin was only human, which meant he was flawed. It was fine if he wanted to sacrifice himself for his principles, but the moment he ordered *Storozhevoy* to weigh anchor, he was risking the lives of 162 other men. He may have persuaded them to assume that risk, but he lied to do it, assuring them that they would not be alone in their revolution. In undertaking an adventure that was at best reckless and at worst suicidal, he owed them the truth.

The men of *Storozhevoy* seem to have forgiven Sablin for this oversight. What is remarkable is that even after a quarter century, even after the prison time and ruined careers and second-guessing, the men who followed Valery Sablin into action remain loyal to him and his cause. "He was a hero and still is. My feelings haven't changed," said Viktor Borodai in 2000.[1] Nikolai Soloviev, the helmsman who piloted *Storozhevoy,* was asked in 1992 why he did not return the ship to port. "Because I supported Sablin and his plan 100 percent," he replied.[2] Perhaps the most eloquent tribute to Sablin came from the person who, outside of his wife and son, suffered the worst consequences of his aborted revolution. In a 2000 interview, Alexander Shein passionately defended his leader. "Every society needs noble spirits," he said. "Without them, no society can move forward. Sablin was that sort of noble spirit."[3]

This feeling was not unanimous among the *Storozhevoy* crewmen. Two of them testified at Sablin's rehabilitation trial that they did not believe he was justified in risking their lives the way he did. Nevertheless, the majority of them still stand behind him. They do so now, and did so then, because they recognized a responsibility to their country that was larger than themselves and more important than their own mortality. Regardless of how he motivated them, or the illusions that inspired him, Sablin appealed to their sense of duty. He offered them an opportunity to make more of themselves than they ever had before. Cynics may rest all human motives on self-interest and self-preservation, but history is full of examples where such motives have risen to a higher level. This was one of those moments.

Yet the life that he was jeopardizing did not just belong to him; part of it belonged to Nina. They had made a life together, and she deserved to know the things that affected it. If Valery failed, he would be lucky if all they did was throw him in prison. He was naïve to think that the Soviet government would spare the life of a man who advocated its overthrow, especially given its less than generous treatment of political opposition. He was practically inviting the regime to leave his wife a widow and his son fatherless. Nina knew this. For all Valery's political education, she remained the wiser judge of the political climate. Had he confided his plan to her, she most certainly would have tried to talk him out of it, and may have succeeded.

The harder question to answer is, What good did it do? The costs of the *Storozhevoy* mutiny were high, but were they worth it? At first glance, the party and state machinery remained intact and the military remained largely unaffected by the revolt.

The events of 8–9 November 1975 were indeed swept under the rug, and the Soviet government pretended it was business as usual. Yet other forces were gathering that year to expose the hypocrisy of the regime—Andrei Sakharov, another privileged son of Communism, renounced the nuclear weapons research he had performed in its service. He was convinced that those weapons were in the hands of irresponsible men. Along with refuseniks such as Anatoly Sharansky, Sakharov would use the Soviet Union's acceptance of the Helsinki Human Rights agreement in 1975 as leverage against the government, pressuring it to grant more personal freedoms.

While the *Storozhevoy* mutiny did not receive much attention in the army, the Soviet Navy was very much affected by it. Attempts by the regime to suppress information about it only went so far. Too many people were involved, and they had seen and heard too much to keep a lid on the story. Just one month after the mutiny, Alex Milits was able to piece together a rough but relatively accurate picture of what had taken place, and he did so from Sweden. Valery Sablin and *Storozhevoy* were spoken of discreetly among Soviet seamen such as Nikolai Cherkashin, but the story nevertheless spread from base to base and from ship to ship. Upon learning of it, each man instinctively asked himself the same question: Was it a good thing or a bad thing? Each had to make his own assessment of what he would do in similar circumstances. Were things so bad that such extreme measures had to be taken to draw attention to the country's condition?

If Sablin had not done it, someone else probably would have. The mutiny was not an isolated event, but the tip of a rotten, melting iceberg of dissent that was brewing below decks in the navy. Although the most dramatic, the *Storozhevoy* mutiny was by no means the only one that took place in the Soviet Union. In the spring of 1959, a large contingent of Soviet naval personnel was stationed in Gdynia, Poland, to train members of the Indonesian Navy in destroyer tactics and the use of Soviet equipment. One of their advisors was the commander of a *Skoriy*-class destroyer, Capt. Nikolai Artamonov. A seemingly brilliant product of the Communist system, Artamonov became the youngest ship captain in Soviet history at age twenty-seven. He exemplified the concept of the "New Soviet Man" and was praised by name in *Krasnaya Zvezda* and *Morskoy Sbornik*. Artamonov had also been praised for his proficiency in advocating Communist Party decisions among his officers and men.[4]

In July 1959, this golden boy gave up his glorious future in the Soviet Navy by fleeing across the Baltic to Sweden, taking his twenty-one-year-old Polish fiancée with him. He gave up his chauffeured limousine, private apartment, and other privileges to settle in the United States under the name Nicholas Shadrin. His reasons for defecting came out later in his debrief and testimony before the House Un-American Activities Committee on 13 September 1960. Underneath his good Communist exterior was a well-hidden and deep-seated hatred of the Soviet system. Shadrin testified that he was not alone in this hostility—many officers in the Soviet Navy shared it.

After years of working for the Defense Intelligence Agency and the Naval War College, Shadrin disappeared in Austria around Christmas 1975. He had been recruited as a CIA counterintelligence officer, and it was long believed that the KGB had kidnapped him on his first mission to Vienna. Twenty-five years later, the true story was finally told. As Soviet agents were bundling Shadrin into a waiting car, they put a chloroform-soaked handkerchief over his mouth and nose in an attempt to knock him out. They used more of the chemical than necessary, and Shadrin died from suffocation.[5]

In 1963, a radio operator aboard a radar patrol ship in the Northern Fleet, Vladimir Gavrilov, organized a group of sailors aboard his ship who met during movie showings. Under the guise of studying Marxism-Leninism, they were clandestinely criticizing the Soviet government and unifying the disaffected crewmen.[6] They met in the engine room so that no one else could hear their dangerous deliberations. In an attempt to express their dissatisfaction with Soviet socialism more publicly, the group wrote a letter to the

Albanian Labor Party, hoping to earn some support from a fellow Communist country. They had planned to send the letter through an intermediary, but it was intercepted and ended up in the hands of the KGB, which sent Gavrilov to a labor camp for three years before allowing him to emigrate.[7]

In June 1969, three naval officers from the Baltic Fleet were arrested in Paldiski for alleged anti-Soviet activities. They had started an organization called the Alliance of Fighters for Political Freedom and planned to begin an underground newspaper called the *Democrat,* which urged the liberalization and democratization of Soviet society. These three officers had also signed their names to an essay written by Andrei Sakharov that was critical of the Soviet Union. The essay, along with an accompanying letter, stated that "an immense amount of blood and filth has covered the banner of our society during the Bolshevik era and the only way out was through armed struggle of the masses."[8] The letter and essay were widely disseminated around the Baltic Fleet at Kronstadt, Tallinn, Paldiski, Liepae, Bolderia, and Kaliningrad.

The apparent leader of the movement was another Gavrilov (no relation to Vladimir), Capt.-Lt. Gennadi Vladimirovich Gavrilov. A contemporary of Sablin, Gavrilov graduated from the Dzerzhinski Higher Naval School as a weapons system specialist. Gavrilov was a Communist Party member and was stationed in Paldiski aboard a nuclear submarine.[9] It is not clear exactly how many followers Gavrilov had, but at the Baltic Fleet Military Tribunal in the fall of 1969, Gavrilov was sentenced to six years in prison. Two other officers were tried with him: Lt. A. Kosyrev and Lt. Alexander Gavrilovich were sentenced to two years each. A fourth officer, Lt. Georgi Paramonov, was never tried, but for the same incident he spent ten years undergoing forced treatment at a psychiatric hospital in Chernyakovsk that left him mentally crippled.[10] Sources quoted in the *New York Times* said that one of the three officers had "been engaged in political work."[11] Andrew Cockburn, in his book *The Threat,* said that all three were ultimately shot by the KGB, but *samizdat* sources never indicated this. About forty naval personnel in all were expelled from the party, demoted, or transferred to penal battalions as a result of this incident.[12]

Beyond these well-documented cases (many of which the Russian government has still not admitted to), there were rumors of mutinies throughout the Soviet Navy. We heard reports of an attempted mutiny aboard a nuclear submarine in the Baltic in 1969 and another aboard a diesel submarine in a Norwegian fjord in 1972.[13] Two other revolts were rumored to have taken place on surface ships in the early 1970s. The first occurred on the *Sverdlov*-class cruiser *Oktyabrskaya Revolyutsiya,* when a conflict arose between some enlisted men and their officers. Four conscripts and a petty officer were supposedly tried and executed for throwing several hated junior officers overboard during a storm.[14] About the same time, an intelligence collection ship (AGI) on station in the Atlantic had to leave its patrol route under escort because violence had erupted on board.

In an interview for another study, a former sailor cited an insurrection on a Pacific Fleet escort vessel in the early seventies. The crew of one hundred arrested their officers and attempted to sail their captured vessel to Japan. As with *Storozhevoy,* the ship never made its destination. Afterward, several crewmembers were diagnosed as "mentally unbalanced" and the fleet's chief psychiatrist was fired for his "alleged lack of vigilance."[15]

According to a former Soviet merchant sailor, in the mid-1970s a mutinous Pacific Fleet frigate crew armed themselves and held their ship at its pier, refusing to put to sea. Rumor had it that this insurrection was only quelled by a violent assault of Soviet Marines. Those mutineers not killed in the assault were reportedly executed. According to the same information, the commanding officer, his XO, and the *zampolit* were all relieved.

A shore-based conscript told of an attempt by two warrant officers to desert from their base near the Volga River in 1974. They killed an officer in their determination but failed to reach their objective, presumably Iran via the Caspian Sea. Both were apprehended and shot.[16]

Major reshufflings and firings in the wake of military embarrassment or failure took place in other instances after the *Storozhevoy* mutiny. In an embarrassing incident in October 1981, a Soviet *Whiskey*-class submarine ran aground in Swedish territorial waters near the Karlskrona Naval Base on which it was obviously spying. As his boat was towed out of Swedish waters, the skipper, 2nd Rank Capt. Pyotr Gushin, drew his finger across his throat in an expressive gesture to Swedish Navy vessels nearby. He obviously anticipated his fate. He was tried and sentenced to three years in a labor camp.[17]

Details are certainly meager on all these incidents, but even if only a fraction of them were true, they pointed to severe discipline problems in the Soviet Navy. In a closed society like the Soviet Union, incidents that became known to the public were only a sampling of many more that were hidden from view, like the *Storozhevoy* rebellion. The fact that an article in a military newspaper was critical of the ship's officers for their lack of ideological commitment might have indicated that the problem was not confined solely to that ship. Many analysts of the Soviet press agreed with Hedrick Smith, who wrote in his book *The Russians* that there was a policy of criticizing but not generalizing. In other words, it was all right to find fault in a particular situation, but general conclusions could not be written about because they were too politically dangerous. According to Smith, "Each case of corruption or mismanagement in some distant city or province is treated in print as an isolated shortcoming, and yet by giving it prominence in the national press, the Party bosses are signaling their nationwide apparatus that this is a general problem to be dealt with forthwith."[18]

This leads to the question of whether the 1974 article in *Krasnaya Zvezda* was signaling to all Soviet military leaders that there were widespread problems in the fleet. *Storozhevoy* was a front-line ship, supposedly manned with some of the best and brightest conscripts in the armed services. Someone must have seen enough signs of poor discipline and inadequate political zeal to convince them that an example needed to be made of it. Naval leaders must have thought that such approbation on the pages of the military's best-known journal would motivate other ships to muster the leadership necessary to deal with dissent among the ranks. Oddly enough, the day of the mutiny, the newspaper *Guardian of the Baltic* was about to print a photograph of *Storozhevoy* with the comment, "The best ship in the Baltic." Needless to say, the editorial staff hastily withdrew the photograph before it went to press.[19]

In spite of the stricter discipline and organization of the armed forces, they are still products of the society they serve. The problems affecting that society will eventually manifest themselves in the military. The drug use and racial tensions evident in the United States in the late 1960s and early 1970s did not escape the country's armed forces. In an open society, those problems come to the attention of the public, which they did in the United States in the mid-

1970s. The military took steps to address these problems and dealt with them directly with the "zero tolerance" policy toward drug use that remains in effect today.

This process was essentially absent from Soviet society. Hiding embarrassment and failure may be a common human instinct, but it was also state policy in the Soviet Union. The aims and intentions of the Communist Party were not subject to scrutiny. Having forced their way to power by styling themselves as a "vanguard of the proletariat," Lenin and his fellow Bolsheviks set the tone for their successors with their mistrust of the people. They had little confidence that they could persuade, or be accountable to, the people of Russia, who in their view were petty and ignorant. It is not surprising that such a spirit of "public service" would lead to a government that was separated from its people by a large chasm of contempt and fear.

An even larger chasm existed between the Soviet Union and the United States. This armed standoff between the superpowers continued for another sixteen years after Valery Sablin's mutiny, and as it did, each side peered intently at the other, struggling to put together the jigsaw puzzle that would reveal the enemy's true intentions and capabilities. This effort took on a life and character all its own, as analysts pored over the minutest details of their adversary's economy, government, and military establishment. By the mid-1970s, this scrutiny had become a cottage industry within the Central Intelligence Agency. In 1974, the CIA estimated that the Soviet Union spent nearly $100 billion that year on defense.[20] The official Soviet government number was just over seventeen billion rubles.[21] At the official rate of exchange, by which the Soviet National Bank estimated one U.S. dollar was worth a little more than one Russian ruble, this made seventeen billion rubles the equivalent of around $15 billion in U.S. currency. This discrepancy, $100 billion versus $15 billion, was one example of the difficulty the West had in estimating its archrival's potential.

Estimating the true cost of Soviet defense spending was an undertaking that took up a large part of the CIA's time and energies. Everyone knew the official exchange rate between the ruble and every other foreign currency was inaccurate because East and West did not even have the same banking systems. According to Karl Marx, Communist societies would not need money, banks, or interest rates because everyone would produce according to their abilities and receive according to their needs. Until one-world Communism came about, however, even a closed society like the Soviet Union needed to import things from abroad. Trade between Communist and non-Communist states was virtually nonexistent because the two sides could never agree on a common method to value their money or their goods.

As far as defense spending went, the American intelligence community decided the best way to estimate it would be as a percentage of Gross National Product (GNP), all the goods and services a nation produced. In 1974, the CIA put this number at 12–13 percent of the Soviet Union's GNP (some sources put it even higher, at 25–30 percent), compared to 7 percent in the United States.[22] No one really knew for certain, though, because it was so tough to determine Soviet GNP or defense spending or the ruble's exchange value. Even the Russians themselves were not sure, because the Communist Party would not allow accurate statistics to be published.

Another part of this whole threat assessment included evaluating the combat capability of the Soviet armed forces. It was fine if you could tell how much they spent, but this did not tell the whole story, or even most of it. Foreign powers underestimated the fighting capability of the Russian nation at their own peril, as the wars of Napoleon and Hitler demonstrated. At the same time, it was the ability of the Soviets to mass so many forces in one place that made their adversaries nervous, not necessarily the individual fighting skill of the Soviet soldier. Man for man on the eastern front during World War II, the Germans usually had the edge, since they were better trained and led. This advantage was lost, however, when fighting an enemy who used his artillery to unleash massive preassault barrages across several square kilometers of terrain. What remained were a bunch of smoking holes where German soldiers used to be. Those who survived this inferno were left to face huge waves of poorly trained Soviet conscripts who would press the attack regardless of the cost.

This philosophy was then transferred to the nuclear age. It did not matter how much damage one nuclear warhead could do; like shoe production, all that mattered were the numbers. The Soviets would not be caught off guard again as in 1941, so they equated a huge standing army with security. Yet their Cold War enemy also had painful memories of that year, specifically 7 December, when they too were hit hard by a surprise attack. The Americans swore that Pearl Harbor would not be repeated. This meant constant vigilance and a force-in-readiness that would deter any attacker.

Conventional wisdom dictated that a war between the United States and the Soviet Union would escalate into a nuclear one before long. In fact, conventional forces might not even have enough time to deploy in the field—intercontinental ballistic missiles might be streaking across the sky before the first tank ever rolled out of the motor pool. Nonetheless, the NATO and Warsaw Pact troops that faced each other in Europe still had to plan and train as if there would be a conventional war. Some saw the absurdity in trying to refight World War II, including future U.S. Marine general Anthony Zinni. In the late 1970s, Zinni attended the Naval War College in Rhode Island; he recalled the war-game scenarios he was taught there:

> Once again, we were energized to engage in global conflict against the evil Red Menace. Problem was that we never could figure just how this particular war would actually start. After playing a bazillion war games at the Naval War College and other places, I still could not come up with a logical or convincing way such a war would kick off. It was just too hard to show why the Soviets would want to conquer a burning, devastated Europe, or how that could possibly benefit the Communists in any way. So we would just gloss over the way the miserable war got started, jump into the middle of things, and play on. Deep down inside, I don't think many of us really believed it ever was going to happen.[23]

Rooted in a reasonable suspicion of Soviet Communism, this fear would take on an irrational life of its own during the Cold War. In fact, fear of Communism existed well before World War II. Its triumph in Russia, and the revolutionary movements it inspired around the world, contributed to the West's insecurity. The revulsion of Western countries to the Bolshevik Revolution and Communist power in Russia left distinct legacies on both sides that were consistently fed by fear. The Soviet Union was treated as a pariah in the interwar years, and this distorted European foreign policies to an unnatural degree. Many European countries refused to accept the Soviet Union as a continental power with interests that might coincide with their own.

Winston Churchill was one of the few who recognized the deal with the devil that Prime Minister Neville Chamberlain had made at Munich in 1938, when he allowed Hitler to absorb parts of Czechoslovakia against that country's will. It was only when Germany had consumed the rest of Czechoslovakia, conquered Poland, Norway, and Denmark, and invaded France and the Low Countries that Churchill's vision was vindicated and he became prime minister. It was almost too late for him to reverse Britain's prewar military weakness, which was a product of Chamberlain's appeasement. Disaster was averted, but only just, and Europe was at war for the second time in twenty-five years. As much emphasis as Western statesmen would place on the Munich agreement after the war, pointing to it as a textbook case of how not to conduct foreign policy, they would have done well to examine why their options were so limited by 1938. Had they adopted a more flexible diplomacy in the years leading up to it, specifically a military alliance with the Soviet Union that Josef Stalin himself favored, Munich might have been the point at which Hitler's story ended. As it was, rigid anti-Communism contributed in part to tying the hands of men who ought to have known better.

As for the Soviet Union, it took one simple lesson from the interwar period: the Western nations could not be trusted. Since the Soviets had believed that anyway, it was a moot point, but it contributed to the already dangerous paranoia that gripped Stalin, which only deepened as he got older. Stalin blamed the Western Allies for everything from selling Russia out to Hitler at Munich to delaying the invasion of France in 1944 in order to weaken the Soviet Union and delay its postwar recovery.

When the war did end, the wartime alliance quickly deteriorated. Stalin's attitude was calculating when it came to issues of European stability. Indeed, chaos on the European continent, or at least the western half of it, served Soviet interests. Communism thrived in instability, poverty, and hopelessness, and there was plenty of all three in that first winter of peace. The Red Army occupied most of the countries of Eastern Europe, but contrary to agreements Stalin had made with the Western Allies at Yalta and Potsdam, he did not allow self-government in those countries. Coups occurred all over Eastern Europe in the late 1940s, with non-Communist politicians killed, imprisoned, or forced into exile. In reaction to these events, the U.S. Congress approved $5 billion of

Marshall Plan aid in 1947 and concluded a military alliance with Canada, Britain, Belgium, France, Luxembourg, and the Netherlands in 1949 (the NATO alliance).

The American public was gradually coming around to the view that the end of the war would not bring tranquility to their lives; instead, it only meant continued international turmoil. By far the biggest shock came in the summer of 1949, when the American monopoly on the atomic bomb ended. Worse, much of the information the Soviets used to design their own bomb came from spies in the Manhattan Project, the top secret U.S. government program dedicated to building an atomic weapon. The other big political disaster that came in 1949 was the fall of China, America's Asian ally, to Communism. President Truman and the Democrats did not immediately pick up on the anxiety this was causing the American people. The Republicans did. Although he would overplay his hand and eventually be censured by his Senate colleagues, Joseph McCarthy was correct when he claimed that there were Communists in the U.S. government in the late 1940s. The Democrats casually dismissed these claims, hoping McCarthy would self-destruct. Unfortunately, the Russians had been running a spy ring in the United States since the mid-1930s, recruiting government employees with Communist sympathies. Among these Soviet agents were Julius and Ethel Rosenberg, who went to the electric chair at New York's Sing Sing Prison in 1954, becoming the only American spies ever executed in peacetime.

Ideological blinders would play havoc with statecraft during the Cold War. After the disaster in Vietnam, the lockstep anti-Communism of the McCarthy era was strongly discredited. The America of 1975 that was Valery Sablin's sworn enemy was a different country than the one he had faced at the beginning of his naval career in 1960. It was not so willing to pay any price, bear any burden, meet any hardship, support any friend, and oppose any foe to assure the survival and the success of liberty, as Kennedy had announced in his inaugural address. If other countries wanted to be Communist, so be it, said the "anti-anti-Communists." This had much to do with why détente was the default policy for the United States in the 1970s. It was more passive than containment, which had been the consensus among the American foreign policy establishment for twenty-five years. Détente fit a post-Vietnam United States that was weary of its international responsibilities and cultivated the belief that America and the Soviet Union could peacefully coexist.

This was not possible, however, and never had been. Two countries with such vastly different economic and political systems, commanding the resources they did, would eventually clash on some level. American politicians were loathe to admit it, because it threatened world war, and in the 1970s that meant only one thing—nuclear holocaust. A small clique of renegade thinkers spoke among themselves of an alternative that would win the Cold War. It was a more aggressive foreign and defense policy that would end détente and bankrupt the Soviets by forcing them to compete with America's military-industrial complex. Their time would not come until 1981, however, and until then American policy makers settled in for another long winter of the Cold War.

There was détente in 1975, but there was no peace. Hardened cold warriors, who misjudged the Communist world and assumed that it thought with one mind, limited the flexibility of American foreign policy to meet new challenges after World War II. Anti-anti-Communists, who refused to acknowledge the serious threat totalitarian regimes posed to democratic governments, failed to accept responsibility for that challenge. The two sides had been around since the very beginning of the Cold War. Their initial and reasonable disagreements would, over the next three decades, harden into bitter debate about how Soviet Communism should be countered. In 1946, when American diplomat George Kennan sent his famous cable to the State Department from Moscow, he offered his explanation of why the Soviet Union was such a dangerous threat:

In summary, we have here a political force committed fanatically to the belief that with United States there can be no permanent *modus vivendi,* that it is desirable and necessary that the internal harmony of our society be disrupted, our traditional way of life be destroyed, the international authority of our state be broken, if Soviet power is to be secure. This political force has complete power of disposition over energies of one of world's greatest peoples and resources of world's richest national territory, and is borne along by deep and powerful currents of Russian nationalism. In addition, it has an elaborate and far flung apparatus for exertion of its influence in other countries, and apparatus of amazing flexibility and versatility, managed by people whose experience in underground

methods are presumably without parallel in history. Finally, it is
seemingly inaccessible to considerations of reality in its basic reac-
tions. For it, the vast fund of objective fact about human society is
not, as with us, the measure against which outlook is constantly
being tested and re-formed, but a grab bag from which individual
items are selected arbitrarily and tendentiously to bolster an outlook already preconceived. This is admittedly not a pleasant picture. Problem of how to cope with this force is undoubtedly greatest
task our diplomacy has ever faced and probably greatest it will ever
have to face.[24]

Kennan's comments, later published in the magazine *Foreign
Policy* under the pseudonym "Mr. X," rocked the foreign policy establishment. He seemed to be suggesting that the United States was on
the losing end of a great struggle and might as well throw in the
towel because the Soviet bogeyman was just too fast, too smart, and
too sly. Just as the Communist world was not monolithic in its
thoughts or actions, however, neither was the West. A contemporary
of Kennan's who was stationed in Moscow at the same time, British
diplomat Frank Roberts, disagreed with Kennan, believing Soviet
foreign policy to be more practical: "What the Russians were thinking in terms of was that—and I think that Stalin thought in these
terms—was that Communism was one day going to be the dominant
ideology in the world, and all countries gradually were going to
become Communist. And in the meantime, you didn't, in Stalin's
idea, start dangerous wars which you might lose. But if you had a
good chance of pushing the cause along, you always pushed it
along."[25]

According to Roberts, then, there was much more of a risk
assessment procedure in the Kremlin. Still, the common denomina-
tor of both opinions was the identification of the almost evangelical
nature of Communist ideology and the faith the Soviets had in its
eventual triumph. Valery Sablin held this faith as well, but he was
much more concerned about the situation in his own country than
he was in advancing Communism around the world.

This point would have been lost on his American counterparts,
however, because in 1975 they faced the armed forces of the Soviet
Union on multiple fronts around the globe. At that time, the Soviet
military enjoyed a formidable reputation, which was part fact and
part fiction. Anyone in the West who remembers watching military

parades in Red Square on television recalls that the impression they made was of a strong, confident army at the peak of readiness. But as we now know, all the armed forces had problems with low morale caused by inadequate food and housing, ethnic tensions, and hazing. This limited the combat effectiveness of these forces, as did chronic equipment shortages and poor training.

Nonetheless, the Soviets did possess a huge army and, by the mid-1970s, a sizable navy. There was debate about the quantity and quality of these armed forces, but the fact that there was so much quantity usually blurred the importance of their quality. In a 1972 meeting with Secretary of Defense Melvin Laird and President Nixon, Adm. Elmo Zumwalt Jr., the chief of naval operations, was asked to evaluate the relative strengths of the Soviet and American Navies. Nixon and Laird expected that Congress would make deep cuts in the 1973 defense budget, and they wanted Zumwalt's opinion on how the navy would do with less money. He replied:

> Today with the existing forces . . . and based on my review of naval warfare studies and fleet exercises, I have only 55 percent confidence that we could retain control of the seas in a conflict with the Soviet Union. With the proposed cuts in forces, even with our projection forces reduced to 50 percent of their present size, including the reductions of seven carriers—the loss of sea control forces would reduce my confidence to 30 percent. I believe that similar Soviet analyses will lead them to conclude that their maritime policy can be more aggressive and their risk taking can be greater than in the past and our naval forces would no longer be adequate political-military forces or even projection forces, because the Soviets would be willing to take them on in the sea control arena.[26]

This was a grim assessment, but it certainly appeared true at the time. The year after Zumwalt made it, the Soviets seemed to confirm his judgment during the Yom Kippur War. In October 1973, Israel was attacked by Egypt and Syria on Yom Kippur, the holiest of Jewish holidays. For a week, the Israelis were locked in a desperate struggle for survival. President Nixon's decision to send direct military aid to them tipped the balance in their favor.

In sending this help, Nixon was reaffirming a longstanding American commitment to Israel, but he was also reacting to the massive assistance that Egypt and Syria were receiving from Russia. The Middle East had become a Cold War battlefield. The Soviets now had a large Mediterranean squadron, which numbered ninety-five ships at the height of the Yom Kippur War.[27] They moved most of this fleet into the eastern Mediterranean that October, standing by to support possible ground operations. Two airborne divisions were on standby in the Soviet Union, prepared to intervene on behalf of the Arabs, and a Soviet divisional staff was setting up headquarters in Damascus, Syria. Nixon sent ships from the U.S. Sixth Fleet, headquartered in Italy, into the region, and put the 82nd Airborne Division on alert.[28]

The Soviets got the message and did not send their troops into the Middle East, but another opportunity to exercise their influence came in 1975, when the Communist government in Angola declared that country's independence. It did so the very day that Valery Sablin was being flown to Moscow for interrogation, 10 November. The Soviets immediately recognized the new Angolan government. Expecting some kind of American response, they extended the service of naval conscripts that fall. In hindsight, it seems ridiculous that World War III would start over an obscure civil war in Africa, but the Russians anticipated an American reaction equal to what Nixon had given during the Yom Kippur War.

Gerald Ford was now president of the United States, and while he favored a strong response to events in Africa, Congress did not. It flatly denied Ford any money for anti-Communist forces in Angola and was even more opposed to sending American soldiers as Saigon had fallen only six months earlier. Emboldened by this indifference, Soviet support for the Angolan government became more open and involved. In at least one instance in February 1976, Soviet warships actually provided naval gunfire support to government troops.[29]

If the American public did not pay much attention to this in the late 1970s, their government did. In 1977, Adm. Stansfield Turner, the CIA director under President Carter, described the naval balance: "As a seagoing power, the U.S. is moving into a shrinking range of political options and a higher level of risk. For this there are two reasons: a major industrial power, the Soviet Union, is building up a navy with dogged determination, [and is] reacting to its perception of a threat from our once overwhelming armed superiority at sea."[30]

Four years later, that assessment had not changed. In a 1981 Department of Defense document, *Soviet Military Power,* the buildup of the Russian fleet was noted: "Over the last two decades the Soviet Navy has been transformed from a basically coastal defense force into an ocean-going force designed to extend the military capability of the USSR well out to sea and to perform the functions of tactical, theater, and strategic naval power in waters distant from the Soviet Union. The Soviets have a larger array of general-purpose submarines, surface warships and combat naval aircraft than any other nation."[31]

But just how dangerous were the Russians? Both these statements were made after the *Storozhevoy* mutiny proved that the Soviet Navy had serious discipline and morale problems. Neither account really took these problems into consideration. Although Admiral Turner and the Department of Defense did not have the full picture that we do today, they did have reports of the mutiny from the Swedes and from their own defense attaché in Stockholm. Why they did not pay more attention to them says much about the way military strength was evaluated in those days. For example, in 1979, the Soviets were thought to have 560 major surface combatants, compared with only 350 for the U.S. Navy. Another study compared major U.S. surface combatant ship tonnage to that of the Russians, in which the Americans had 2.6 million tons to the Soviets' 2.4 million tons.[32] Both of these figures were correct, but the numbers did not necessarily translate into combat effectiveness.

Determining this effectiveness is the most difficult part of intelligence work, because that is the point where number calculation ends and human factoring begins. It was this issue that Greg Young tackled in his original thesis, and it is this issue that points to another legacy of the *Storozhevoy* mutiny: cold war misperceptions. How did fear and suspicion affect the way both sides looked at each other?

Gathering information about your enemy is fairly easy. Turning it into usable intelligence is much harder. Even with perfect raw data, interpreting the intent of that enemy is always problematic. One piece of the puzzle may be accurate, but that accuracy does not necessarily translate to the whole picture. Swedish and American intelligence analysts were playing the averages when they assumed that *Storozhevoy* was defecting. When your adversary does the same thing ninety-nine times, it is reasonable to assume that, the hundredth time, he will do it again. But what if he does not?

Making your enemy out to be ten feet tall can be every bit as dangerous as underestimating him. Military officers tend to do the former because they are taught to plan for worst-case scenarios. If the enemy really is not as good as you thought, so much the better. In the case of the Cold War, however, this took on a different meaning. As the nuclear shadow lengthened, it became clear to American and Russian officers that the war-game scenarios they were planning for were becoming increasingly irrelevant. Should American soldiers ever threaten Moscow or Soviet troops ever advance on Washington, buttons on both sides would be pushed to deny the enemy total victory.

Still, having more soldiers and tanks than your enemy provides psychological consolation, even if that consolation rests on unreasonable assumptions. Of course, when numbers are used implicitly, they ignore human factors such as domestic value systems, the will to fight, ideological commitment, leadership style and ability, unit cohesion, and military esprit. War is, after all, a human activity. When it came to valuing that most elusive of human factors, fighting spirit, diehards often overestimated the threat from the other side and underestimated their own side's ability to meet it. In 1985, Daniel DaCruz wrote a book that chronicled basic training for a platoon of U.S. Marine recruits at Parris Island, South Carolina. DaCruz's conclusion is filled with accounts of foreign military training that was supposedly tougher and more intensive than the regimen given to recruits in the Marine Corps. He commented on the martial qualities of their counterparts in the Soviet Union: "These traits do not distinguish the average Soviet soldier, whose greatest military virtues are extreme hardihood and absolute obedience to orders. These are instilled from the very first day after induction at age eighteen, when recruits are chased out of their beds eighteen or twenty times a night to teach them to get into uniform quickly, clean out lavatories with their toothbrushes, and conduct nonstop sixteen-hour field exercises in the extremes of Russian weather."[33]

This was a textbook example of Cold War misperception. Contrary to DaCruz's claim, the *Storozhevoy* mutiny demonstrated that "absolute obedience to orders" was not as widespread a virtue in the Soviet military as he seemed to think. Their "extreme hardihood" came not so much from a burning desire to sacrifice for the Motherland as from the need to survive in a system that could not meet the basic needs of its people. DaCruz suggested that the Soviet soldier bore all these hardships with steely pride and determination. In fact, such hardships bred resentment and bitterness. Alexander Makushechev, a former Soviet Army sergeant, said that some troops were not given ammunition even at the practice range for fear they might turn their weapons on their officers.[34] The writer Andrew Cockburn related this story: "Veterans of the 1968 Czech invasion recall how afraid the officers were of the men once they were issued live ammunition at the border. As one man put it, 'one of my acquaintances slept with a pistol under his head and even then, only after having locked himself in the cab of his vehicle.'"[35]

As for the myths the Soviets held regarding their Cold War foe, they were part of a long continuum of Russian xenophobia that stretched back a thousand years. The fear of invasion had contributed to Russian insecurity for generations and made a large standing army a permanent part of their defense policy. Communist propaganda only contributed to their feeling that enemies surrounded them. The economic strength of the United States was eventually seen as more of a threat than its military power, but the only field in which the Soviets could compete was the latter. In the end, the Soviet myth that the United States was out to destroy it was true, but the method used was different from the one anticipated by the Communist regime. Rather than rolling across the border with tanks and planes, the Americans chose to aggravate the enduring vulnerability of the Soviet economy. President Ronald Reagan pressed forward with research on the Strategic Defense Initiative, which threatened to end détente and initiate a new arms race.

This is exactly what President Reagan and his advisors wanted, because they believed the Soviets could not afford to keep pace in this race. As it turned out, they were right. They saw an opportunity to end the Cold War by adopting a bold strategy of confrontation—not with the working end of weapons but with their price tags. This policy was risky, but the fact that nuclear war was avoided is testimony enough to its success.

Mikhail Gorbachev deserves credit for this success as well. He was the first Soviet leader from a generation that had not fought in World War II, so he did not shoulder the crushing legacy of those desperate days. To his predecessors, military force was something to be accumulated and strengthened, since enemies of the Soviet

Union were everywhere. Gorbachev, who did not look at the outside world that way, took a more traditional approach to foreign policy. Nations had interests, he believed, and sometimes the interests of a capitalist state and a Communist state coincided. In the late 1980s, Gorbachev believed reductions in nuclear and conventional forces were in the interest of the United States and the Soviet Union. He could have followed the lead of his predecessors and continued the arms race unabated, but he chose not to. Perhaps he did not really have a choice, but Gorbachev's interest in reducing tensions was nonetheless sincere. He even echoed the words of Valery Sablin when he said, "We can't go on living like this any longer."[36]

Although they took very different paths in life, Gorbachev and Sablin ultimately arrived at the same conclusion: fear of change is often worse than the change itself. The thought of what a post–Cold War world might look like was frightening to Americans and Russians alike. Would it end in nuclear war? What would happen if the Soviet Union collapsed? Would its mighty armed forces simply dissolve or would they lash out at the West in one final showdown? Without its main rival staring at it from across strands of barbed wire, what would the U.S. Army do? Who would the CIA spy on next?

Governments are not usually good at answering these kinds of questions, because their very nature works against them. Their strength in commanding great resources during times of crisis becomes a weakness when an old threat has been vanquished and a new one waits on the horizon. The drastic shift in priorities and outlook that is normally demanded by a turn of historical events is all but impossible for governments and their agencies to make quickly. In the final analysis, it might be said that neither side predicted the end of the Cold War because to do so would have required a leap of imagination that was counterintuitive. It would have meant adopting a bold vision within institutions that are slow and unresponsive by tradition and practice. Maybe, as Valery Sablin concluded, this was too much to expect.

The *Storozhevoy* mutiny touches upon many larger political, social, and military themes, but in the end, it is a story about one man's determination to live his life as he saw fit. Autocratic rule is a Russian tradition, but so is opposition to it. Russians have always had a soft spot in their hearts for the outlaw, for the lone dissenter who stands up to authority. This special brand of sympathy even has its own word in Russian: *raskolnichestvo*. It was no coincidence that in his novel *Crime and Punishment,* Dostoyevski's main character was named Raskolnikov, the gifted young student who is driven to murder by a deep-seated hatred of the existing order. He is eventually caught by the police and forced to pay for his crime. He feels remorse for what he has done, not for his victim's sake but for his own. He realizes that he has ruined his life with one decision.

Raskolnikov's tale highlights the difference between Western and Russian concepts of freedom. In the West, freedom is equated with personal liberty and nearly always placed in a positive light. The Russian meaning is much more subtle. To Dostoyevski, freedom itself was neither good nor bad, it was simply free will, the ability to choose between good and evil. Raskolnikov chose evil, only to regret it in the end.

Valery Sablin chose otherwise. He exercised his free will to take a path that his countrymen would follow a decade later. Like any good leader, he was ahead of his time. Like any good martyr, he died before it. All he could do in the end was echo the words of his hero, Lt. Peter Schmidt, who gave an impassioned statement at his trial for treason in February 1906. Schmidt denied that he had betrayed Russia when he led a mutiny against the tsarist regime the year before. In the long tradition of Russia's martyrs, he made a distinction between the mystical Russian Motherland and the government that held it by the throat:

> During the recent chaos, when the Russian government was making war on its own people, it wasn't possible to be guided by the statutes of the law. You had to find other, higher principles that everyone could recognize as legal or illegal.
>
> They spoke to me of legalisms, but I knew only one law—my duty to my people, and for three years those people have been spilling their blood.
>
> Those responsible have been a small criminal group that has seized power. Because of their predatory calculations, these people have piled up over 100,000 corpses in the war with Japan. Now they are waging their own war on Russia.
>
> Just where exactly does this treason lie? Who is the state criminal?
>
> Today, in their eyes, I am the criminal. But tomorrow, in the eyes of a future judge, they will be declared the enemy.

The years will pass and our names will be forgotten. But the names of those who found common cause with the *Ochakov* [one of the ships that participated in the mutiny] and remained true to their oaths will not be forgotten! And they will remain in the chronicles of the people.

I have done my duty! If execution awaits me, so be it. Betraying a life among the people would be more horrible than death.

A handful of sailors did indeed violate their orders so that they could remain true to their oath, and so did Citizen Schmidt before you.

Before you here . . . in the dock . . . stands immortal Russia. You will be passing judgment on her.[37]

APPENDIX A

Roster of Ship's Officers, BPK Storozhevoy, 8 November 1975

Name	*Billet*	*Status*
Captain Second Rank Potulniy	Commanding officer	Detained below decks
Captain Third Rank Novozhilov	Executive officer	On leave
Captain Third Rank Sablin	Political officer	Leader of the mutiny
Captain Third Rank Sadkov	Medical officer	Opposed mutiny
Captain-Lieutenant Kuzmin	Engineering officer	Opposed mutiny
Captain-Lieutenant Proshutinski	Communications officer	Opposed mutiny
Senior Lieutenant Dubov	Gunnery officer	On leave
Senior Lieutenant Firsov	Gunnery officer	Initially supported mutiny but changed his mind and jumped ship to warn the authorities
Senior Lieutenant Kolomnikov	Gunnery officer	On leave
Senior Lieutenant Ovcharov		On leave
Senior Lieutenant Smirnov		Opposed mutiny
Senior Lieutenant Vinogradov		Opposed mutiny

Name	Billet	Status
Lieutenant Dudnik		Supported mutiny
Lieutenant Stepanov		Not at meeting
Lieutenant Vavilkin		Supported mutiny
Warrant Officer Boganets		On leave
Warrant Officer Borodai		Supported mutiny
Warrant Officer Gindin		On leave
Warrant Officer Gomenchuk		Supported mutiny
Warrant Officer Gritsa		Opposed mutiny
Warrant Officer Kalinichev		Supported mutiny
Warrant Officer Khomyakov		Supported mutiny
Warrant Officer Khokhlov		Opposed mutiny
Warrant Officer Kovalchenkov		Not at meeting
Warrant Officer Kuteinikov		On leave
Warrant Officer Saitov		Not at meeting
Warrant Officer Smetanin	Armory officer	Not at meeting
Warrant Officer Velichko		Supported mutiny
Warrant Officer Zhitenev	Chief boatswain	Opposed mutiny

APPENDIX B

Characteristics of the Krivak I–class Destroyer

Builders: Kamysh-Burun Shipyard, Kerch; Yantar Shipyard, Kalin-ingrad; Zhdanov Shipyard, Leningrad.

Displacement: 3,075 tons standard; 3,575 tons full load.

Length: 383 feet 5 inches (116.9 meters) waterline; 405 feet 1 inch (123.5 meters) overall.

Beam: 46 feet 3 inches (14.1 meters).

Draft: 14 feet 9 inches (4.5 meters).

Propulsion: COGOG: two gas turbines; 24,200 shp + two boost gas turbines; 24,400 shp = 48,600 ship; two shafts.

Speed: 30.5 knots.

Range: 700 nautical miles at 30 knots; 3,900 nautical miles at 20 knots.

Crew: Approximately 200.

Helicopters: None.

Missiles: Two twin SA-N-4 antiair launchers.

Guns: Four 76.2-mm/59-caliber (two twin).

ASW weapons: Four SS-N-14 (one quad); two RBU-6000 rocket launchers; torpedoes.

Torpedoes: Eight 21-inch (533-mm) torpedo tubes (two quad).

Mines: Rails for twenty mines.

Radars: One Don-2 or Spin Trough (navigation); two Eye Bowl (fire control); one Head Net-C (3-D air search); one Kite Screech (fire control); two Pop Group (fire control).

Sonars: Bull Nose medium-frequency bow mounted; Mare Tail medium-frequency variable depth.

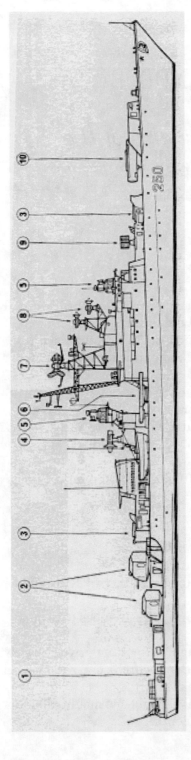

1. VDS housing
2. Twin 76.2-mm AA gun mounts
3. SA-N-4 missile launchers retracted)
4. Owl Screech radar
5. Pop Group radars

6. 533-mm torpedo tubes
7. Head Net-C radar
8. Eye Bowl radars
9. RBU-6000 rocket launcher
10. SS-N-14 missile tubes

H. Simoni

Krivak I (from Norman Polmar, ed., *The Naval Institute Guide to the Soviet Navy*, 3rd ed., Annapolis: Naval Institute Press, 1983).

EW systems: Two Bell Shroud; two Bell Squat.

Ship's departments: Command (*Boevaya Chast;* BCh): BCh-1, Navigation; BCh-2, Missile/Gunnery; BCh-3, Mine and Torpedo; BCh-4, Operations; BCh-5, Engineering; BCh-6, Air (only on ships that are capable of flight operations); BCh-7, Command and Control (only on flagships). Staff (*Sluzhba*): Sl.-R, Electronics; Sl.-Kh, Nuclear, Biological, and Chemical Defense; Sl.-M, Medical; Sl.-S, Supply.

APPENDIX C

Orientation Concerning an Incident in the Eastern Baltic

Swedish Defense Ministry
Intelligence Briefing, 8 March 1976

On the night of 8–9 November 1975, it appeared that mutiny had broken out on board the *Krivak* guided missile destroyer number 500, *Storozhevoy,* belonging to the Soviet Baltic Fleet. There is no knowledge, nor even an estimate, of what percentage of the ship's crew took part in the mutiny or who led it.

On November 7th, *Krivak* 500 took part in Riga in celebration of the anniversary of the Bolshevik Revolution. The ship remained in port thereafter in Riga. At approximately 090100 [09 refers to the date, 0100 is Greenwich Mean Time] the mutiny broke out. The ship was probably lying quietly in Riga, but it cannot be ruled out that the ship was already underway when the revolt broke out. However, with regard to the time of day and the day of the week, this appears to be rather unlikely.

Around 090600 the mutineers had been located in the Irben Straits by two ASW aircraft (Il-38 May) from Riga Airfield. About an hour later, some ten Tu-16 Badger aircraft arrived, and within an hour's time searched for and attempted to stop the ship, probably with low altitude passes, firing at will. Sometime after 090800 these aircraft prepared to use air-to-surface missiles. Some missiles were fired. However, the mutineers, whose intention was to go towards Stockholm's southern archipelago, never gave up in that aim. Around 090830, at least twenty Yak-28 Brewer aircraft initiated repeated bombing assaults against the ship. Another ship also pursuing near this position was mistaken for the *Storozhevoy* during the bomb assault, and at least one bomb caused damage to that vessel. Besides these aircraft a large number of ships participated in the search for the mutineers, among others:

Two *Riga*-class frigates from Riga
Three *Poti*-class corvettes from Liepae
One *Sverdlov*-class cruiser and two *Krivak*-class guided missile
   destroyers from the Baltic Fleet
Five similar *Stenka* patrol ships from the KGB and, possibly,
One *Nanuchka* guided missile corvette.

The mutineers, in view of the massive efforts of military forces and their intensive firepower or threat thereof, gave up at about 090900 and entered for anchorage in the Gulf of Riga. On November 10th, the *Storozhevoy* was moved to Latvian territory and was lying quietly thereafter until 18–19 November, when an unusual tour of *Krivak*-500 occurred in the Baltic—the ship passed near Götland, Utklipporna, Bornholm, and the Polish coast, and may possibly have been some sort of "exhibition" with the intention of demonstrating that the Swedish, Danish and Polish suspicions of mutiny were without substance.

Interestingly, in connection with the above-related incident, there was an article about the ship in *Krasnaya Zvezda* on 24 December 1974. There is a report in this from a visitor aboard the *Storozhevoy* that tells of certain defects aboard the ship in political training and motivation.

The activity in connection with the capture of the mutineers appears to indicate, notwithstanding whatever divided the crew, that the Soviets were prepared to sink the valuable ship rather than let it escape.

APPENDIX D

An Active Position

2nd Rank Capt. I. Lysenko
Krasnaya Zvezda, 24 December 1974

1. On being detailed to the BPK *Storozhevoy* I went happily; I had my reasons. First of all, I knew the crew well, and I always look forward to a reunion with people whom I've deployed with before. Besides this, there was to be a party election meeting aboard ship, and I expected some serious discussion on the work of the Communists on board. In the past training year, the crew of the *Storozhevoy* had made a new step forward in combat improvement, to which the crew's successful missile firing and gun shoots bear witness. The Minister of Defense, Marshal Grechko, went to sea on board this ship and gave high marks to the mastery of the anti-submariners who destroyed the targets with the first missiles. In short, the *Storozhevoy* had all the requirements necessary to win first place in the ranks of outstanding ships.

2. But at the end of the training year, it became clear that the ship could not do better than fourth place. I expected that at their party meeting, the ship's Communists would try to find out how and why they'd lost the necessary winning points. I was right.

3. One example was brought out in a speech. Senior Lieutenants I. Dubov and S. Kolomnikov command batteries in the missile/gunnery department of the ship. For Dubov, things are going well. His subdivision is outstanding and has a reputation for great seamanship. On the other hand, Kolomnikov's service has not

always been successful. In competition with its neighbors, his anti-aircraft battery lagged behind for a long time even though the "gunners" in this battery were the equal of Dubov's men. They know very well how to destroy targets in the air and yet the battery didn't compare with the other outstanding subdivisions. So what was the matter?

4. The speaker, this ship's organization secretary, Senior Lieutenant V. Firsov, tried to answer this question. He drew attention to one particular detail. Today, it's become a rule that every sailor tries his best to perform his combat duties as quickly as possible. When it came to training the crew, the *Storozhevoy*'s commanding officer and party organization were interested not in minutes but in seconds, inasmuch as these affected the crew's combat readiness. But had the Communists aboard the ship, and particularly those in the antiaircraft battery, always paid such great attention to another facet of the competition—the moral-ethical one? The chair and others who spoke at the meeting, such as Communists V. Sablin, N. Sazhin, and A. Potulniy, who analyzed the training results, were unable to give a positive answer. It appeared that this factor frequently remained unconsidered in even the outstanding departments of the ship.

5. At one point, I was told of the following episode. A sailor was released from the brig. He had only taken a couple of steps along the deck when he hears: "Hey, boys, Petrov's back!" And a minute later, the "boys" were hugging this man, who had just come out of detainment. And do you know who could be seen among them? Outstanding sailors and class-rated specialists—superior performers. They knew how to overcome adversity and carry out their duties. Everybody could see this and valued their abilities, but the fact that these same comrades have fallen down on the ethical front and have taken up a liberal position in the fight for purity is a failure that can be squarely laid at the door of the cadre [the officers aboard the *Storozhevoy* who, like Sablin, were official members of the Communist Party].

6. It is true that the sailor who slipped behind in his service should have the attention of the collective. But how? Clapping him on the shoulder doesn't help. He was returning from being under arrest. And, having arrived on deck, he should have said to his colleagues, "Comrades, I stand guilty before you, but I ask for your trust," and then to show by diligent service that he was not trusted

in vain. But if the commander and Communists didn't create such circumstance in the battery, then even the strictest rebuke loses half its force.

7. Public statement of one's attitude to a comrade's behavior is the starting point for creating a climate of opinion which will support a man's good name and preserve him from mistaken actions. Just such a climate has been created in Communist Dubov's battery. If a sailor in his section has an attitude problem he will certainly be made to feel the sharp indignation and genuine irreconcilability of his colleagues. They will also be more interested in correcting him in an effort to improve the performance of the unit as a whole.

8. In this same anti-aircraft battery, as Communists noted in their speeches, the required atmosphere was not immediately created. One can understand Kolomnikov's difficulties. He is a young officer to be in command of a battery. He doesn't have great instructional experience. This is understandable too; instructor experience doesn't come in one day. Therefore, the young officer needs help. But before he was given it, Kolomnikov managed to make a mistake and this naturally reflected negatively on the crew's final results in the competition.

9. A year of strenuous training has passed. One more page in the biography of the party organization of the *Storozhevoy* has been turned over. Every line of it tells of the deeds in which the Communists were closely involved. The majority of them played an active role in the life of the crew. I remember the words Communist N. Sazhin spoke at the meeting: "If you are a party member then it is a good thing to start off each working day by concerning yourself with the affairs of the crew. One should feel required to go to people and actively support all that is new and first-rate in service and training, and battle decisively against the outdated opinions and leftovers from the past which are in the minds of some comrades." That is, one shouldn't have a passive attitude in the process of education and training, but strenuously affirm in comrades the Communist attitude to hard work and high moral relationships. This is one of the party's important requirements, laid down in one of the decrees of the Central Committee of the CPSU, "On work in educating the ideological cadres in the Byelorussian Party organization."

10. With the requirements of this decree in mind, the ship's party organization makes great demands on the Communists, with the aim of encouraging them to be active and spirited in their work.

But what actually happened? One party member couldn't find the time from one month to another to go to the crew's quarters to have a talk with the sailors. When somebody reminded him he just clutched his hand and rushed down to the sailors with the first arbitrary theme he thought of. Naturally, an off-the-cuff talk doesn't always achieve its objective.

11. The speaker, and others taking part in the proceedings, observed that a Communist's authority is directly dependent on his deeds and on his attitude to service. He should inspire the sailors by personal example to overcome the difficulties encountered on long cruises. He has one privilege above all—to be out in front. To be first is more difficult, but it will be easier for those behind him. On the *Storozhevoy* they speak with esteem of Engineer Captain A. Ivanov. This Communist takes an active part in party political work. He often gives lectures, carries on conversations and leads a political study group that is, incidentally, the best on the ship. This party fighter is always to be found wherever the sailors' Communist outlook is being formed. It is praiseworthy that the party organization studied the experience of Ivanov on the ideological front and acquainted the crew with it.

12. But is this style of work inherent to Ivanov alone? Certainly not. *Storozhevoy*'s party organization is sufficiently strong that its Communists for the most part love, and are good at, carrying out education work in the collective.

13. Aboard ship there are now more outstanding men and class-rated anti-submariners. The crew has sailed thousands of miles over the world's oceans. These and other meritorious facts were announced at the meeting. Behind them stands a legacy of hard work and tireless people who carry their party cards close to their hearts. At their election meeting, they talked of many things, understood much, and saw clearly what they had achieved as well as their omissions. They observed, for example, that it was necessary for the party organization secretary to bring the problems of educating the sailors before the tribunal of the party collective more frequently and to meet and consult with the party and KOMSOMOL "actives" more often. There is, in short, much to take into account and lessons to be learned.

14. Right after the meeting, the Communists stepped forward to meet the tasks of the new training year, and I want to say to them "Don't dally on the way, comrades!"

APPENDIX E

Valery Sablin's Broadcast to the Soviet People

Translated by Nate Braden

The following is a KGB transcript (marked "Top Secret—Special File") of Capt. Valery Sablin's broadcast to the Soviet people on 9 November 1975, recorded on audiotape.

Attention, comrades! Attention to the words of this announcement, which we are trying to broadcast on radio and television.

First of all, many thanks to you for your support, without which I would not be able to speak to you today. Our announcement is not a betrayal of the Motherland, but a purely political, progressive declaration, and the traitors to the Motherland are those who would seek to stop us. My comrades want me to pass on to you our assurance that if our nation is attacked, we are fully prepared to defend it. Right now we have another goal: to take up the voice of truth.

We are quite certain of the necessity of setting out our views on the internal situation of our country. We want to present our criticism of the policies of the Central Committee of the CPSU [Communist Party of the Soviet Union] and the Soviet government before the honest people of the Soviet Union, who have been witness to the fact that decisions on the social, political, economic, and cultural life of our country are not made on the revolutionary principles of Marxism-Leninism, but merely on their slogans. I turn your attention to the words of Lenin in "Revolution and the State," when he noted that after the death of great revolutionaries, attempts are always made to turn them into icons—to canonize them and use their famous names for class oppression. They make fools of us all as they gut the foundations of revolutionary learning, dulling its edge and debasing it.

The teachings of Lenin deal with this in full measure. You only have to spend enough time learning them to be persuaded of just how badly they contrast with real life. Lenin dreamt of a just and free state, not a state of harsh repression and political tyranny. In one of the letters he wrote just before his death, he said, "workers who become members of the Central Committee should not, in my opinion, be drawn primarily from those who have spent a lot of time in the soviets. These workers are already biased towards a status quo that they've just recently fought against. The majority of Central Committee members should be drawn from the level of workers just below that—those who have spent five years or so working their way up through the ranks and are closer to the average worker and peasant." Lenin saw the Central Committee as a party organ by which the proletariat could control the affairs of state. Unfortunately, this didn't happen. Now the Central Committee and the government are birds of the same feather, or, more precisely, the same bird. Lenin and Marx said that every revolution was a step forward in the class struggle, and the oppressive nature of the state would gradually give way to a more open society. But as Engels pointed out, "the state keeps its official face as a servant of the people while its institutions continue to dominate over them." I don't think there's any argument that these days the servants of the state have already become the masters of the state. Everyone can see examples of this in everyday life. We see it in the parliamentary games and so-called elections of Soviet officials. The fate of the people lies in the hands of an unelected elite, in the form of the Politburo. The all-encompassing concentration of state and political power has become an established and well-known fact. In particular, the development of the revolutionary process in our country played a fatal role in crushing dissent during the cult of personality under Stalin and Khrushchev. In case you didn't know, up to seventy-five people are arrested annually for their political beliefs. Truth is something that no longer exists in our country. This is the first symptom of a seriously ill society. The attempt of the Soviet elite to create a cult of personality in a socialist society is a consequence of poor leadership. It contradicts Marxist-Leninist teachings about the role of the individual in history. These lies do nothing but embarrass the state and party leadership that hides behind them. People like Khrushchev, Beria, Malenkov, Molotov, Kaganovich, Shelest, and others mysteriously disappear from the political arena with nothing more than a short piece in the newspaper—no trial, no witnesses, nothing. They spoon-feed information to the masses and keep them in political ignorance, but the people must be politically active. They need to be aware of their significance and greatness. The people shouldn't live without political freedoms the same way they live without material comforts. Evidently, the current leadership of the CPSU has forgotten this. The people cannot forget it because they live with it. The same democratic achievements that the revolution has created over the last fifty years have been ground to dirt by the state, leaving only an empty shell. Be proud of the past as you dream of the future, but don't lose sight of the present—and don't look for the revolution in the base appeals of modern Soviet ideologues. The state teaches the people to be passive and to believe in the infallibility of its high officials.

You might be asking: where can I find such criticism of the higher-ups in the media? We are the exception. We must honestly confess that we don't have any control over the political or state institutions that might solve some of the controversial problems concerning the social, political, economic and cultural life of our country. All of this is under the influence of party and government organs. The so-called vanguard of the proletariat, who have been responsible for the development of our society over the last fifty years, have produced a system in which the people find themselves trapped in a stagnant atmosphere of blind obedience to authority. It's an atmosphere of political tyranny and censorship in which the fear of criticizing the party or other government institutions thrives, since everyone's fate is tied to it. I must recall the words of Marx when he said, "the moral state assumes its people have a sense of civic virtue, even if they protest against it." Lenin thought that any group of citizens which had attained a certain number of members or gathered a certain amount of signatures could publish their own newspaper, and he wrote about this on two occasions. Our people have already suffered much, and they continue to suffer from this political oppression. Only among the narrow circle of the Party elite is it fully known how much damage has been done, and is being done, by the deliberate interference of state and party

organs in the development of science and art, in the growth of the
armed forces and the economy, and in raising the nation's youth.

Of course, we too have laughed a million times at Raikin's
satire, *Crocodile* magazine, and *The Wick* film journal, but our
laughter is mixed with tears at the thought of the Motherland's
future. The time for laughter has passed. It's now time to win over
the people in the court of national opinion and demand that this bitter laughter be accounted for. A dangerous situation is now arising
in our country: on the one hand, there is the Party line—the out-
ward appearance of communal harmony and social consensus in a
people's state. On the other hand, there is individual dissatisfaction
with the current state of affairs. This dissatisfaction manifests
itself in the passivity of the generation now reaching middle age,
who dream of their upcoming pensions, and in the growth of that
other cult—the cult of personal success. The contradiction between
the individual and the collective grows wider, and the youth of our
country withdraws even further from the political holy ground that
we worship so much. The young people in particular sense the gap
between revolutionary slogans and revolutionary deeds. The older
generation, which for the most part still embodies the spirit of the
revolution, also senses a crisis, but there is no longer a new burst
of energy for it. We aren't condemning them, but thanking them for
what they did in the name of mankind. They were revolutionaries
in their own day, and this was their great mission.

There's currently a big theoretical examination of our society's
philosophical, economic, social and political future. In the midst of
this examination lay the seeds of a revolution, for the revolution is
a powerful movement of the community spirit, a colossal shift in
the atmosphere that challenges the masses to action. It embodies
the real change that is possible in the socioeconomic structure. Our
declaration is only one small part of it, which must serve as the
spark. We do this to inspire debate about the direction of our country. We need more than just debate; we need to really look at the
foundations of our society. I can respond right away to all opponents of Marxism-Leninism that we in no way reject the revolutionary principles of Marxist-Leninist theory—it plays a vital role
in the socialist revolution. It has been and will continue to be a reliable basis for the new revolutionary ideal that stands before us. It
just needs to progress a little further, since history has strangled

its development. We categorically reject any attempt to portray us as agents of capitalism and destroyers of socialism. No. We affirm to everyone, as we have before, that socialism is the progressive framework of all our relations. It has created the progressive social and economic relations that were a prerequisite to the Communist revolution, but it has since lost its revolutionary character and become a brake on the progressive development of our society.

Our society, on its path to Communist revolution, might only be interested in the pursuit of happiness, but happiness is the movement towards Communism. We already have an agenda set before us. Will the Communist revolution fight the class war as an armed struggle or just a political one? This depends on a number of factors. First, the people must believe in the necessity for social reform, and believe that this path can only be achieved through Communist revolution. This is a long process of social understanding and political consciousness. Second, in the very near future an organized and inspired revolutionary force must be created which will become the new revolutionary party, relying on a more progressive philosophy. Finally, as far as the senior leadership is concerned, the fact that they may offer violent resistance to our revolution, drowning it in the blood of the people, depends primarily on which side the armed forces and militia choose. It might only be a theoretical assumption, but with modern means of communication and transport, as well as the high cultural level of our people, the great experiment of social revolution in the past will enable them to come up with a government that will not resort to violent counterrevolutionary measures. Instead, they will direct the revolution along a peaceful path of development. We can never forget, however, that revolutionary vigilance provides the foundation for its very success, and therefore the people must be prepared for history's diverse turn of events. Our main problem at this moment is that until there are networks of revolutionary circles around the country, there are no trade unions, youth or community organizations free from government influence. They will grow rapidly in a free society, as mushrooms after a rainstorm, but the big problem now is to instill within the people an unshakeable faith in the vital necessity of the Communist revolution, and convince them that there is no other path—all others will lead them to larger, more complicated torment. And the doubts one generation has about the revolution only grow more destructive and severe with the next generation. This belief in the necessity of revolution will, with the fresh rain, take root in the new organizations.

Thus, we have a potential revolution that paints the following picture: the use of all kinds of media to launch a campaign of agitation and propaganda to inspire revolutionary activity among the people with the aim of creating revolutionary cells. A variety of community organizations will be created across all sections of society to fight for change—for freedom of speech, the press and assembly. A new revolutionary party will be created, willing and able to bring the masses to Communism through a new order. Finally, a just new society will be created that can bring material well-being and social equality to all of its members on the basis of the Communist principle: "From each according to his abilities—to each according to his needs." How quickly this will come about is difficult to say, but it can be significantly faster than it has been in the past. The question that comes to mind is "Which class will dominate this revolution?" It will be the working class, both the worker-peasant intelligentsia to which we belong and the engineers and technicians from industry and agriculture. The future belongs to this class, which will gradually turn into a classless society after the Communist revolution. Who will oppose this class? What does the face of the enemy look like? It's the current ruling class. They are small in number, but have the power of the economy, finance and the media concentrated in their hands. This is the foundation on which they've built the apparatus of state power that props them up. This class consists of party and union officials, along with directors of the heavy and light industrial collectives and trade centers, who use Soviet laws (they of course would never admit to breaking these laws) and industry for their own personal enrichment. They have used their positions in society to establish a state network through which they are provided special material and moral privileges. This new system of exploitation is made possible by distorting the government budget, something which needs to be looked at and exposed in greater detail.

This begs another question—what are our views on foreign policy and defense issues? I'll begin with the question of defense. We still believe that the threat of war remains, and we call upon the armed forces, especially the air defense and strategic rocket forces, to continue their defense of the Motherland from foreign aggression during the turmoil and social reforms of the revolution. We ask them to abide by their strict revolutionary principles and not turn their arms against the revolution. We approve of and support peaceful coexistence and are convinced that the Communist revolution will present great opportunities in this regard. We consider it necessary to create a national dialog so all the people can discuss the government's foreign policy, and we also think it's important to limit the role of state and party institutions in the conduct of this policy. In the field of international relations, our Communist revolution will encourage the social development of all nations on every continent. Mankind will come significantly closer to the creation of a harmonious social order all over the world.

And finally, the key question of any revolution—the question of power. First of all, we suggest that the current state apparatus will need to be thoroughly purged, the machinery smashed and thrown out onto the trash dump of history. It's thoroughly infected by nepotism, bribery, careerism and arrogance. Second, the electoral system, which has reduced the people to nothing more than a faceless mass, also needs to go. Third, all the conditions that have given birth to omnipotent and unaccountable state institutions must be removed. Can such questions be decided by a dictatorship of the proletariat? Absolutely! Otherwise, the revolution comes to an end after it seizes power. Only through the extraordinary vigilance of the people can society set out on the path to happiness. As you can see, the struggle before us is both theoretical and practical. Right now the most vital task is to rally all honest revolutionary-minded people around us, people who will be able to come together and apply their energy, dedication, and purpose to the cause. These people will form the core of our revolutionary party, and they will be extremely critical during the inevitable period of theoretical confusion that will accompany our struggle—there will be a part of our society that will reject it. This is especially true of those politically immature and irresponsible elements who favor anarchy and tyranny. It's still possible to bring about a party that has a concrete agenda and honest policies which have the people's interests at heart. The circle of history will then turn back to its proper course.

In conclusion, I want to outline our future plans. First, we are demanding that our ship be recognized as free and independent territory. Second, we are demanding daily broadcasts on radio and television for thirty minutes after the program *Vremya*. Our goal will be to use our television broadcasts as a tribune to oppose the current regime, which demands of its people a passive acceptance of the status quo in the hopes that everything will eventually turn out all right. Third, we are demanding the right to publish our own newspaper and distribute it throughout the country. Our wider political message will be addressed to people of all persuasions, and appeal to writers, poets, composers, and average citizens. Their work will serve the revolution. We want to correspond and meet with representatives from all walks of life.

Our address is: Leningrad Main Post Office, P.O. Box 49358, General Delivery.

If the government tries to crush us by force, then you will know this when we fail to appear on radio and television. In this case, only your political activity will save the revolution we have begun.

That's the end of our statement. Thank you for your attention.

[KGB comment: After a brief pause, a man's voice continues from 180 to 200 on the tape.]

And now, we bring you this radio message, addressed to the fleet commander:

I request that you report to the Politburo of the Central Committee CPSU, and the Soviet government, that the BPK *Storozhevoy* has hoisted the flag of the new Communist revolution.

We demand the following: first, to declare the *Storozhevoy* free and independent from state and Party institutions.

Second, to allow one member of the crew, a man of our choosing, to go on state radio and television for thirty minutes, from 2130 to 2200 hours Moscow time, every day.

Third, to guarantee the *Storozhevoy* the same privileges as any military base.

Fourth, to allow the *Storozhevoy* an anchorage and mooring buoy in any port in Soviet waters.

Fifth, to secure mail delivery for the *Storozhevoy*.

Sixth, to allow broadcasts from the *Storozhevoy*'s radio station on the *Mayak* network in the evenings.

Seventh, to allow members of our crew ashore unmolested.

Eighth, to use no kind of violent coercion against the crewmen's families, parents, or loved ones.

Our declaration is purely political in nature and should in no way be construed as a betrayal of the Motherland. Those who would seek to stop us are betraying the Motherland. We expect a reply to our demands within the next two hours. In the event that there isn't one, or our demands are rejected and an attempt is made to use force against us, responsibility for the consequences rests entirely with the Politburo, the Central Committee and the Soviet government.

[KGB comment: Further on the tape is one more recording, in a man's voice, from number 200 to 219 on the tape.]

I am making this broadcast to all stations that can hear me! This is the BPK *Storozhevoy*. We demand that the fleet commander, the Central Committee and the Soviet government provide an opportunity for one of our crewmen to speak on state radio and government to present our aims to the Soviet people.

We are neither traitors to the Motherland nor adventurers seeking recognition for its own sake. An extreme but necessary opportunity has come for us to openly address a range of questions about the political, social and economic development of our country. The future of our people should be discussed by everyone without pressure from the state or Party. We decided to make this announcement with a clear understanding of the responsibility we have for the fate of the Motherland, and with a sincere desire to achieve genuine Communist relations in our society. But we also recognize the danger of physical and moral destruction at the hands of state institutions or hired guns. . . . Therefore, we are turning for help to all the honest people in our country and abroad. If at 2130 Moscow time tonight you don't see a representative from our ship on your television screens, we ask you not to go to work tomorrow, and to continue this strike until the government ceases its harsh repression of free speech and you hear from us again.

Support us comrades! Goodbye.

[KGB comment: This is the end of the tape.]

After looking over the cardboard box containing the tape and listening to its contents, Sablin announced:

Having examined this cardboard box and listened to the tape contained within it, I can confirm that it was tape number 3, about which I made note during the interrogation of 25 November 1975.

On the side of the box I wrote the number of the tape and its length, along with my personal logo (three interconnected Vs).

The voice on the tape in question is mine, and I prepared this speech so it could be read on television and radio in an address I planned to give to the supreme commander of the navy and the Soviet people.

As I have already shown, I wrote out the text of these speeches beforehand. Then, in my cabin aboard the BPK *Storozhevoy* (Number 25), I recorded them on tape during our Atlantic Ocean deployment around 13 or 14 April 1975 using a Comet tape recorder. I labeled this tape number 2.

A day or two after recording this speech, I made a copy of it using the same Comet recorder, which I had borrowed from the leader of Section 4—LEVIKOV.

On the evening of 5 November 1975, I gave tape number 3 to SHEIN so he could play it to some of his trusted friends. He must have mailed the box with the tape in it when we reached Riga on 8 November.

That's all I have to say on the matter of tape number 3.

I have no other statements to add.

A copy of this tape was recorded on an **Ukher 4000 Report-L** at a speed of 9.5 centimeters a second.

The interrogation ended at 1705.

The undersigned affirm that protocol was observed during these proceedings:

The accused	SABLIN
Witnesses	RUBTSOVA
	MIKHACHEVA
Specialist	ANIKEYEV

SENIOR INVESTIGATOR FOR SPECIAL AFFAIRS, KGB INVESTIGATIONS DEPARTMENT, BY ORDER OF THE SOVIET OF MINISTERS, USSR:

Captain
DOBROVOLSKI

Typist
Kuznetsova
Folder No. 72–75.

APPENDIX F

Investigation Report to the Minister of Defense, USSR

Translated by Nate Braden

**Marshal of the Soviet Union,
Comrade Grechko, A. A.**

Our report:

The commission created by your General Order No. 00105 of 9 November 1975, has concluded its investigation into the insubordinate events of 8–9 November aboard the BPK *Storozhevoy,* 128th Brigade of Missile Ships of the Baltic Fleet.

The ship has a crew of 194 men: 15 officers, 14 warrant officers, 165 sailors and chiefs. There are also 7 members of the CPSU [Communist Party of the Soviet Union], 9 candidates for membership in the CPSU, and 164 KOMSOMOL [Young Communist League] members. Among the crewmen, eighteen nationalities are represented: 111 Russians, 22 Ukrainians, 12 Byelorussians, 5 Latvians, 5 Moldavians, 3 Lithuanians, 2 Poles and others. By social class, the breakdown is as follows: 114 workers, 19 farmers, 29 white-collar workers, and 32 students.

The ship's unauthorized departure and insubordinate command were the result of the criminal activities of its former chief political officer SABLIN, the malicious anti-Soviet degenerate. Taking advantage of his position as a commissioned officer, he made demagogic statements and temporarily managed to perpetrate his fraud by winning over some of the ship's crew.

This extraordinary incident also resulted from the poor judgment of a certain group of people who succumbed to the false and demagogic agitation of the enemy. Over an extended period of time, that enemy nurtured criminal intentions against the existing order of the party and the state. He invoked the high authority of his office and subtly played upon the emotions of many of his subordinates using distorted facts. SABLIN was able to persuade the psychologically unstable element of the crew that he only wanted to publicly criticize the deficiencies in the political, social and economic development of our country.

. . . Studying the personal notes of SABLIN along with other sources, as well as observing his conduct during the investigation makes it possible to characterize him as a man with an abnormal and obsessive ideological fixation who longs to stand out from the crowd and become an exceptional personality. One of the ways he thinks he can do this is by appearing on television.

In the course of the committee's work, the existence of a hostile anti-Soviet group aboard the *Storozhevoy* was not found in the so-called "revolutionary committee" that was mentioned in the radio message to the fleet commander. SABLIN made it seem as if he had the support of several men who were actively working behind the scenes. The assertion that SABLIN intended to take the ship to Sweden was proved groundless in the course of the investigation.

SABLIN has hidden his fervent anti-Sovietism and hostile views for a long time. Using demagogic methods and his high office to exploit the political immaturity of a certain element of the crew, he succeeded in seizing control of the ship for a short period of time.

The commander of the vessel, Second Rank Captain POTULNIY, A. V., failed to educate his crew to act as a single fighting unit that could fulfill its military duties under any conditions. This investigation also revealed a distinct passivity and confusion among the ship's officers that prevented them from recognizing the anti-Soviet content of the announcements and intentions of this traitor in time to put a stop to his actions.

With respect to the unauthorized departure of the ship, the leadership of the Riga Naval Base was also derelict in its duty. Having received the report of Senior Lieutenant FIRSOV, V. V.; Second Rank Captain VLASOV, V. S., the chief of staff for Ship Security Brigade 78; Second Rank Captain YUDIN, V. G., the head of the Brigade's Special Detachment; and Second Rank Captain SVETLOVSKI, L. V., the raid commander and skipper of the submarine *S-263*, we conclude that they all waited too long before taking proper action. This tardiness indicates to us a lack of administrative ability and indecisiveness that bordered on cowardice. . . .

Our report further determines:

During the commission's interviews of the *Storozhevoy* crewmembers, they expressed outrage at SABLIN'S treacherous actions, and wanted to assure the Minister of Defense, the Central Committee, and comrade BREZHNEV, L. I., that the sailors, chiefs, and officers deeply regret their temporary lack of vigilance and are now fully prepared to return to their military duties.

The extraordinary nature of this incident demands that the guilty parties be held criminally responsible. A party meeting was held at which those most responsible, among them SABLIN, were expelled from the Communist Party. The ship's crew was disbanded, with a new one transferred to it. The BPK *Storozhevoy* is now in port, its weapons and operating systems in working order. The fleet will take all measures to keep information of this incident confidential.

CHAIRMAN OF THE COMMISSION:

ADMIRAL OF THE SOVIET FLEET	S. GORSHKOV

MEMBERS OF THE COMMISSION:

GENERAL OF THE ARMY	A. YEPISHEV
VICE ADMIRAL	P. NAVOITSEV
LIEUTENANT GENERAL	S. ROMANOV
REAR ADMIRAL	V. SABANEYEV
MAJOR GENERAL	Y. LYUBANSKY
REAR ADMIRAL	M. GULIAYEV

17 NOVEMBER 1975

APPENDIX G

Verdict in the Case of Third Rank Captain Valery Sablin and Seaman Alexander Shein

Translated by Nate Braden

13 July 1976
Moscow

The Military Collegium of the Supreme Court of the USSR, chaired by Judge Advocate Major General G. I. BUSHUEV, and consisting of the following people's representatives:

Lieutenant General (Engineer Support) I. S. TSYGANKOV, Major General (Combat Engineer) B. V. KOZLOV, along with their secretaries: Colonel (Administrative Service) M. V. Afanasyev and, on behalf of the Soviet Army, V. S. Kuznetsov, with the participation of the state deputy chief prosecutor—Judge Advocate Major General V. S. Shanturov—and defense attorneys L. V. Aksyenov and L. M. Popov:

Have examined the criminal activities of the accused servicemen in a closed session in the Supreme Court of the USSR.

1. Third Rank Captain Sablin, Valery Mikhailovich, born 1 January 1939 in the city of Leningrad, of Russian ancestry, expelled from the Communist Party of the Soviet Union in connection with the following act, possessing higher education, married with no previous criminal record, in the service of the Navy of the USSR since July of 1956—in commission of a crime stipulated by paragraph (a), Article 64 of the Criminal Code of the Russian Socialist Federation Soviet Republic (RSFSR).

2. Seaman Shein, Alexander Nikolaevich, born 7 March 1955 in the city of Rubtsovsk, Altai District, of Russian ancestry, expelled from the Young Communist League in connection with the following act, possessing a tenth grade education, single with no recent convictions, in the service of the Navy of the USSR since May of 1973—in commission of a crime stipulated by Article 17 and paragraph (a), Article 64 of the Criminal Code of the RSFSR.

In assigning guilt to Shein and determining his punishment, the court takes into consideration his confession of guilt and remorse for his complicity, the fact that the crime he committed was done so under the influence of Sablin, his superior, as well as the degree and character of his participation in this crime, which is allowed for under Article 43 of the Criminal Code of the RSFSR and other statutes.

With regards to Sablin and the exceptional danger his crime posed, the court considers it necessary to take this into consideration when it interprets the law. By way of extenuating circumstances, Sablin fully admitted his guilt and remorse for his complicity, and the court understands that he has a child to support, as well as the fact that over the course of his service he received numerous commendations.

By the authority of Article 44 of the Criminal Code of the USSR and its republics, and Articles 301–303, 312–315 and 317 of the Criminal Code of the RSFSR, the Military Collegium of the Supreme Court of the USSR hereby finds:

Sablin, Valery Mikhailovich, guilty of treason to the Motherland, and in committing this act, in accordance with paragraph (a), Article 64 of the Criminal Code of the RSFSR and its statutes, is sentenced to death by firing squad without confiscation of belongings.

By the authority of Article 36 of the Criminal Code of the RSFSR, V. M. Sablin is stripped of his rank of Third Rank Captain. By order of the Presidium of the Supreme Soviet of the USSR, V. M. Sablin is stripped of the following award: "For service to the Motherland in the Armed Forces of the USSR—Third Class," and the following medals: "For Military Valor"; "Commemoration of V. I. Lenin's 100th Birthday"; "Fifty Year Anniversary of the Armed Forces of the USSR"; and "Twenty Year Anniversary of the Great Patriotic War, 1941–1945." The Ministry of Defense also strips V. M.

Sablin of his medals "For Impeccable Service in the Armed Forces of the USSR—Second and Third Classes."

Shein, Alexander Nikolaevich, guilty of conspiring to betray the Motherland (in the capacity of an accomplice), and in committing this act, in accordance with Article 17 and paragraph (a) Article 64 of the Criminal Code of the RSFSR and its statutes, along with Article 43 of the Criminal Code of the RSFSR, is deprived of his freedom for a term of 8 (eight) years, of which two years shall be spent in prison and the remaining time shall be spent in a hard labor camp, without exile and without confiscation of belongings.

A. N. Shein's term of imprisonment shall be calculated from the day of his initial detention on 9 November 1975.

The material evidence that was submitted in accordance with Article 39–211 (Part 1, paragraph 6) shall remain in the court's possession. That which was submitted in accordance with Articles 39-211 and 39-212 (Part 2, paragraph 6) shall be returned to the military unit from which they came: two pistols and two magazines belonging to unit 49358.

Court fees in the amount of 243 rubles and 10 kopecks shall be assigned in the following manner: Alexander Nikolaevich Shein will pay 186 rubles and 50 kopecks to the state, which will cover the remaining fifty-six rubles and sixty kopecks.

This verdict is not subject to appeal or protest.

CERTIFIED: By the court secretary of the Military Collegium of the Supreme Court of the USSR.

APPENDIX H

KGB Report on the Storozhevoy Mutiny, 18 February 1976

Translated by Nate Braden

To the Central Committee of the Communist Party of the Soviet Union:

The Committee for State Security [KGB] has finished its investigation into the criminal affair of Third Rank Captain SABLIN, V. M. and other servicemen—participants in the criminal acts of 8–9 November, 1975, that took place aboard the BPK *Storozhevoy* (fourteen men in all).

It's been established that SABLIN, the organizer of this crime, having fallen under the influence of a revisionist ideology, nurtured his hostile views of the Soviet government over a period of several years. In April of 1975, he recorded these views on tape, and during the incident aboard the *Storozhevoy,* presented them to the crew in a speech. SABLIN'S political "platform" was a collection of bourgeois propaganda and slanderous assertions made against "the obsolete Marxism-Leninism and bureaucratic degeneration" of the USSR state and party apparatus, as well as appeals for the removal of the Communist Party from power and the creation of a new, "more progressive" party.

In the spring of 1975, he was developing a detailed plan to take over his warship, which he intended to use as a "political base." He would also use it to broadcast his demands for the overthrow of the government of the USSR and wage his fight against Soviet power.

While he was preparing to put his plan into action, SABLIN studied the mood of the crew, bringing individual sailors into his plot and cultivating a negative attitude towards the Soviet system within them. However, this investigation determined that he was not successful in finding like-minded people to create an anti-Soviet group aboard the ship. Just three days prior to the incident, SABLIN brought Seaman SHEIN, A. N., into his criminal designs, obtaining his support and giving him a copy of the anti-Soviet speech on tape for distribution.

Before entering military service, SHEIN had already been convicted of theft, and during his service he received thirteen disciplinary penalties, proof of his unhealthy political opinions.

During the *Storozhevoy* incident, SHEIN, having received a pistol from SABLIN, assisted him in arresting the ship's captain, took part in detaining the officers who opposed SABLIN, resisted the efforts of several crewmembers to free the captain and arrest SABLIN, and inflicted bodily injury on Petty Officer KOPILOV.

To achieve his aims of winning over some of the crewmen and taking control of the *Storozhevoy,* SABLIN used his position as political officer and disguised his hostile intent with shrewd demagogic statements that wove in citations from the classic works of Marxist-Leninist literature.

As a result of SABLIN's criminal activities, the *Storozhevoy* was commandeered and taken from the Gulf of Riga beyond Soviet territorial waters in the direction of Sweden (to within twenty-one miles). SABLIN ignored repeated and specific orders from his superior officers to return the ship to port. Decisive action taken by the *Storozhevoy*'s captain and crew resulted in the vessel's being stopped and returned to base. The ship was gone a total of sixteen hours.

On the basis of evidence gathered over the course of the investigation, SABLIN's criminal activities qualify as treasonous—namely, his completely premeditated attempts to undermine the Soviet system and damage the military power of our country. SHEIN's crimes qualify as collaboration in betraying the Motherland.

As for the other accused: Lieutenants VAVILKIN, V. I., and DUDNIK, V. K., Warrant Officers BORODAI, V. M., VELICHKO, V. G., GOMENCHUK, A. A., KALINICHEV, V. A., and KHOMYAKOV, A. T., Petty Officer SKIDANOV, A. V., and Seamen AVERIN, V. N., BUROV, M. M., SALIVONCHIK, N. F., and SAKHNEVICH, G. V.—these are all young men, aged twenty to twenty-three, who don't have sufficient life experience or political temperament. They were provoked and deluded by SABLIN. They weren't aware of his treacherous designs, however, when they supported

SABLIN, in effect enabling him to carry out his criminal plan to seize the ship. Several of them refused to support SABLIN from the outset, and were detained by him. It is clear from the investigation's evidence that they had no intention of betraying the Motherland. In the confusion of these abrupt and short-lived events, they didn't understand the hostile nature of SABLIN's designs, which left them unable to correctly assess the situation.

In interrogations, the accused gave exhaustive testimony concerning their total violation of the law, the deep repentance they all felt, and SABLIN's criminal adventure. They had earlier taken responsibility for their crimes.

The activities of this group should be qualified as military crimes.

Now having a record of the established circumstances and motives behind this extraordinary occurrence aboard the BPK *Storozhevoy,* we consider it advisable to transfer the case of SABLIN and SHEIN, accused of betrayal of the Motherland, to the Military Collegium of the Supreme Court of the USSR.

The remaining twelve accused—having committed a military crime in accordance with the ruling of the Presidium of the Supreme Soviet of the USSR of 28 March 1958, the Decree of the Presidium of the Supreme Soviet of the USSR of 28 March 1958, and the Decree of the Presidium of the Supreme Soviet of the USSR of 26 November 1973, which regulate criminal proceedings for members of the armed forces—do not fall under the court's jurisdiction, but are instead subject to the disciplinary measures of the Minister of Defense of the USSR.

Submitted in accordance with the ruling of the Central Committee of the Communist Party of the Soviet Union.

Y. ANDROPOV   A. GRECHKO   R. RUDENKO   L. SMIRNOV

18 February 1976

APPENDIX I

Valery Sablin's Last Letters to His Wife and Son

Translated by Nate Braden

14 June 1976:

Hello, dearest Nina and Misha!

I pray for some quick decisions and actions! I hope you arrived safely in Moscow! I still don't know when I'll be able to see you next. Therefore, provided you receive this letter by June 16th, I advise you to go to Gorky on the evening of the 17th. Call Kolya [brother Nikolai] beforehand so he can buy tickets for the Meteor train for the 18th or the 19th. Before you go to Belyn [where the Sablin family *dacha* was located], send me a letter so I know you've left.

If you can, send me a care package on the 17th, but send the contents loose in a parcel, without the box. They only give us mail on Thursdays. Use the address I gave you earlier. If I can get permission, it may be possible for me to send you some of my things—I'll have to ask the duty officer.

If you don't have time to send me a care package, you can send one to Mikhalkin next Thursday [this was a childhood friend who lived in Moscow and visited Valery in prison].

Write me as soon as you get to Belyn, don't wait for my letter to arrive. Tell me how your trip was, how you're spending your time there, etc.

It's already been two months since I received a detailed letter from you, but of course we were counting on a meeting in the interim.

Did you take Misha to the doctor? How did it go? Draw me an outline of your new apartment. Were you able to sell some of the furniture that was broken in the move? Any luck finding work? At least you've been able to settle in a little bit. I'll send a letter right away to Belyn, as soon as I find out you've left for there. Just take the bare minimum that you need to Belyn, since I'm sure that Papa doesn't know you're coming and won't be able to meet you at the station. Leave some of your things in Moscow and some in Gorky. Do you remember the way from Dreswitz?

About the meeting in August—so far this isn't set in stone, so don't get your hopes up. Don't assign too much significance to these meetings—they're not the most important things in our lives, so don't wear out your nerves if they don't happen. Let's just think of this as a long voyage we have ahead of us, although I do want to see you, and soon!!

So there we have it. I agree with the motto: "Don't lose heart!"

I'll be waiting for some news from Gorky. I'll expect a detailed letter from Belyn. I hope I can get a care package either this Thursday or next.

Say hi to Mikhalkin for me. Tell him I wish him a belated happy birthday, and ask him if he can bring two or three stories from *Nedelya, Ogonyok, Literaturnaya Gazieta,* etc.

I hope you'll be able to unwind and relax a little.

Don't let your spirits get down!!

Say hi to Kolya, Irina, Mama, and Papa, and kiss them for me. 14.06 (Evening) Love and kisses from your Valery and Papa.

18 June 1976:

Ninka, Ninka, Ninka Ninka:

I have to write you separately, in order to tell you that you are my sweet, wonderful, lovely miracle! Thank you, my dear, for coming to see me!! I'm sorry if I was a little cold and calloused at our meeting. You must understand that it was difficult, shameful and awkward for me to express my love for you with three other people between us, both during the meeting and when we write each other. But I want to forget about that, and tell you once more (yet once more in our lives!) that I love you! I can close my eyes right now and see you in living color, sitting in your blue outfit and smiling that wonderful, one-of-a-kind smile, crying your tender, passionate tears. Oh, how you are my miracle! My little blue Nina! I read all your letters over again and try to remember how you look, crying and cursing me and everything under the sun—beautiful, gentle, delicate—where do you get the strength and courage that you've shown over the last six months?! So many problems, so many physical and mental trials that weigh upon you, and still you can take it!! You probably get it from your mother, who took her two kids in her arms during the Blockade, fighting hunger and rushing to find out about the fate of her husband who was lying in a hospital bed. Then the road over frozen Lake Ladoga and evacuation! Maybe you get it from your mother, but in this case, your strength is all your own!

I feel so badly for you and your suffering that no one, not even I, can blame you if you get tired of loving me and waiting for me.

How can I ever show my appreciation to you for all the wonderful things you've given me?! So far, all I've been able to give you is trouble and sorrow.

Well, I guess I've said what I wanted to say.

I look forward to our next visit.

Many kisses, your Valery.
18.06.76

GLOSSARY OF RUSSIAN TERMS

Afgantsi (Афганци). Soviet veterans of the war in Afghanistan (1979–89).

anasha (Анаша). Hashish smoked by Central Asians and Soviet forces in Afghanistan.

baychay (бч - боевая часть). Battle unit, similar to a division aboard a U.S. warship.

Bolshoi Protivolodochniy Korabl; BPK (БПК - Большой Противоло- дочный Корабль). Large antisubmarine ship. A Soviet warship class to which *Storozhevoy* belonged.

Chrezvychainoe Polozhenie; CP (Чрезвычайное Положение). Soviet naval term for a state of emergency or crisis. Literally, "extraordinary situation."

churka (чурка). Derogatory term for ethnic Central Asians meaning "block of wood" or "dense."

dacha (Дача). A country house.

dedovshchina (Дедовщина). Slang for hazing.

Duma (Дума). The Russian parliament.

feldshcher (фельдщер). Soviet military physician's assistant, similar to a hospital corpsman in the U.S. Navy.

GAPTVAK (ГАПТВАК). A military prison used for short-term incarceration.

glasnost (гласность). Term meaning "openness" used to describe Mikhail Gorbachev's political reforms (1985–91).

GLAVPUR (ГЛАВПУР). Acronym for the Military Political Directorate.

Izvestiya (Известия). One of the largest circulating newspapers in the Soviet Union. Literally, "news."

Kalashnikov (Калашников). A Soviet- or Czech-made 7.62-mm automatic rifle, also known as an AK-47.

kasha (Каша). Hot barley or oat cereal.

kazarma (Казарма). Military barracks.

kissel (Кисель). Dessert made of fruit, berries, and potato or cornstarch and served with milk.

KOMSOMOL (КОМСОМОЛ). Acronym for the All-Union Lenin Communist Youth League. Organization for those age fifteen to twenty-eight that eventually led to membership in the Communist Party.

Krasnaya Zvezda (Красная Звезда). The Soviet military newspaper. Literally, "red star."

kulak (Кулак). Nickname for landowners and well-to-do farmers in the 1930s. Literally, "fist."

michman (Мичман). A navy warrant officer; derived from the word "midshipman."

Molodye (Молодые). The "young ones." Soldiers and sailors in their first year of conscripted service.

Morskaya Aviatsiya (Морская Авиация). Naval Aviation.

Morskoy Sbornik (Морской Сборник). The Soviet Naval Digest; a monthly naval professional journal.

nomenklatura (Номенклатура). Slang for the Soviet Union's political elite.

Novoye Russkoye Slovo (Новое Русское Слово). New Russian Word; a Russian language émigré newspaper based in New York.

oblast (Область). State or province of the USSR.

otdeleniye (Отделение). Section or department aboard ship.

perestroika (Перестройка). Term used to describe Mikhail Gorbachev's economic reforms (1985–91). Literally, "restructuring."

plan (План). Opium derivative smoked by Soviet forces in Afghanistan.

pokupateli (Покупатели). Slang for officers who selected conscripts to serve in their particular branch of the military. Literally, "buyers."

porosyonok (Поросенок). The traditional roasted pig that is served to a ship's crew after returning from a successful deployment.

Pravda (Правда). A daily Soviet government newspaper. Literally, "truth."

prizovnik (Призовник). A conscript.

Protivovozdushnaya Voennaya Oborona; PVO (ПВО-Противовоздушная Военная). Soviet Air Defense Forces.

rayon (Район). County or region of the USSR.

Rodina (Родина). Refers to Great Russia or the Motherland.

salaga (Салага). Derisive nickname for first-year conscripts.

samizdat (Самиздат). Refers to various categories of underground publications in the USSR. Literally, "self-published."

samogan (Самоган). Moonshine or home-brewed alcohol.

sapogi (Сапоги). Slang term used to refer to soldiers. Literally, "high boots."

Spetsotdel (Спецотдел). Soviet Navy special shipboard KGB department.

Stariki (Старики). The "old men." Soldiers and sailors in their final year of conscripted service.

starpom (Старпом, short for Старый Помошник). A senior assistant or executive officer aboard a warship.

starshina (Старшина). Soviet Navy petty officer.

storozhevoy (Сторожевой). "Sentry" or "on guard." Also the name of the Soviet Navy ship that mutinied on the night of 8 November 1975.

storozhevoy korabl' (Сторожевой Корабль). A class of Soviet escort or coast guard ships.

Stroibati (Стройбаты). Army construction troops.

stukach (Стукач). Stool pigeon, informant.

subbotnik (Субботник). The supposedly volunteer, unpaid work soldiers and sailors had to perform on their day off, which was originally Saturday (*subbota*). Very unpopular with the troops.

Tsentr (Центр). Center; refers to Moscow.

Voenniy okrug (Военный Округ). Military district.

Voenno-Morskoi Flot; VMF (ВМФ—Военно-Морской Флот). The Soviet Navy.

voentorg (Военторг). A military store similar to an American post exchange (PX).

zampolit (Замполит). Military political officer; descended from the old military commissar.

zhopomorda (Жепоморда). An ethnic slur referring to Central Asians meaning "ass face."

NOTES

Chapter 1. THE COMMISSAR

1. Nicholas Bethell, ed., *Russia Besieged* (Alexandria, Va.: Time-Life Books, 1977): 63.

2. Ibid., 75.

3. Sumner Shapiro, "The Blue Water Soviet Naval Officer." United States Naval Institute *Proceedings* 97, no. 2 (February 1971): 20.

4. Ibid.

5. Chris Donnally, "The Soviet Soldier: Behavior, Performance, Effectiveness." In *Soviet Military Power and Performance,* eds. John Erickson and Robert Feuchtwanger (Hamden, Conn.: Shoestring Press, 1979): 114.

6. J. W. Kehoe, "Naval Officers; Ours and Theirs." United States Naval Institute *Proceedings* 140, no. 2 (February 1978): 54.

7. Norman Polmar, *Guide to the Soviet Navy.* 3rd ed. (Annapolis, Md.: U.S. Naval Institute Press, 1983): 51.

8. "Speech of Comrade Khrushchev to the Sixth Plenum of the Communist Party." *Polish Archive of Modern Records,* 1956. 8–9.

9. Nikolai Cherkashin, *Posledniy Parad* (Moscow: St. Andrew's Flag, 1992): 24.

10. Ibid., 25.

11. Ibid., 28.

12. Ibid., 28–29.

13. Andrew Cockburn, *The Threat: Inside the Soviet Military Machine* (New York: Random House, 1983): 80.

14. Harriet Scott, "The Military Profession in the USSR." *Air Force Magazine* 59, no. 3 (March 1976): 81.

15. Cockburn, *Threat,* 82.

16. Andrei Maidanov, *Pryamo po Kursu—Smert* (Riga, Latvia: Lita Publishing House, 1992): 78.

17. William Manthorpe Jr., "Attaining Command at Sea, Soviet Style." United States Naval Institute *Proceedings* 101, no. 11 (November 1975): 98.

18. Norman Polmar, *Guide to the Soviet Navy.* 5th ed. (Annapolis, Md.: U.S. Naval Institute Press, 1991): 69.

19. Cherkashin, *Posledniy Parad,* 31.

20. Nina Sablina, interview with authors. Wife of Valery Sablin. St. Petersburg, Russia, 26 and 27 June 2004.

21. Maidanov, *Pryamo po Kursu—Smert,* 75.

22. Nina Sablina, interview with authors.

23. Ibid., 76–77.

24. Nikolai Vasilievich Gogol, *Dead Souls,* translated by David Mayarshack (New York: Penguin Books, [1842] 1961): 382.

25. Nina Sablina, interview with authors.

26. Maidanov, *Pryamo po Kursu—Smert,* 76.

27. Ibid., 96.

28. Interview in *Mutiny: The True Story of Red October.* October Film Production for Channel Four Television, 2000.

29. Maidanov, *Pryamo po Kursu—Smert,* 92.

30. Ibid., 93.

31. Valery Sablin to Nina Sablina, 5 November 1975, 1–2.

Chapter 2. THE CAUSE

1. *Cold War: MAD,* episode 12, executive producer, Jeremy Isaacs, CNN, 1998.

2. Anatoly Dobrynin, interview in *The Cold War: Détente.* Episode 16. Executive producer, Jeremy Isaacs. CNN, 1998.

3. U.S. Department of Defense. "Intellectual Life and the Communist Party in the Soviet Union." Interview. FLAMRIC discussion tape (Monterey, Calif.: Defense Language Institute, 1993).

4. Richard Pipes, *The Russian Revolution* (New York: Vintage Books, 1990): 358.

5. Robert Conquest, *Harvest of Sorrow* (New York: Oxford University Press, 1986): 24.

6. *Voenniy Entsiklopedicheskiy Slovar,* edited by G. Mikhailovski (Moscow: USSR Ministry of Defense, 1984): 116.

7. Ibid., 107.

8. Maidanov, *Pryamo po Kursu—Smert,* 72.

9. Ibid., 306.

10. Vladimir Semichastny, interview in *The Cold War: Red Spring.* Episode 14. Executive producer, Jeremy Isaacs. CNN, 1998.

11. Nikolai Leonov, interview in *The Cold War: Freeze.* Episode 19. Executive producer, Jeremy Isaacs. CNN, 1998.

12. Ibid.

13. Ibid.

14. Valery Sablin to Nina Sablina, 5 November 1975, 7.

15. Alex Alexiev and S. Enders Winbush, "The Ethnic Factor in the Soviet Armed Forces." *Rand Corporation Research Report,* No. N-1486-NA (May 1980): 27.

16. Mikhail Grumman, interview with authors. Soviet Navy conscript, 1968–71. Served aboard a *K-8*-class minesweeper out of Tallinn, Estonia. Telephone interview, 5 January 1982.

17. H. R. Kaplan, "The Flawed Colossus: Problems of Soviet Military Power." *National Defense* 69, no. 46 (March 1985): 47.

18. "Ideology at Sea." *Soviet Analyst* (February 1976): 10.

19. Alexiev and Winbush, "Ethnic Factor in the Soviet Armed Forces," 13.

20. Ibid., 86.

21. Kaplan, "Flawed Colossus," 47.

22. Mikhail Grumman, interview with authors.

23. Grigori Feldman, interview with authors. Soviet Navy conscript, 1967–70. Served aboard a *Kresta I*–class cruiser out of Murmansk. Telephone interview, 9 December 1981.

Chapter 3. THE SERVICE

1. Geoffrey Ranft and Bryan Till, *The Sea in Soviet Strategy* (Annapolis, Md.: U.S. Naval Institute Press, 1984): 149.

2. "Moscow's Military Machine: The Best of Everything." *Time* (4 May 1970): 38.

3. I. Lysenko, "An Active Position." *Krasnaya Zvezda* (24 December 1974): 2.

4. Ibid.

5. William Manthorpe Jr., "The Soviet Navy in 1975." United States Naval Institute *Proceedings* 102, no. 5 (May 1976): 212.

6. "*Storozhevoy* Attacks," 2.

7. Manthorpe, "The Soviet Navy in 1975," 212.

8. Maidanov, *Pryamo po Kursu—Smert,* 28.

9. Ibid.

10. Robert Bathurst, Michael Burger, and Ellen Wolfe, "The Soviet Sailor: Combat Readiness and Morale." *Ketron Corporation Research Report* (30 June 1982): 53.

11. *USSR Naval Shipboard Regulations* (Moscow: USSR Ministry of Defense, 1976): 49.

12. Bathurst, Burger, and Wolfe, "Soviet Sailor," 54.

13. Grigori Feldman, interview with authors.

14. Ibid.

15. Mikhail Grumman, interview with authors.

16. Manthorpe, "The Soviet Navy in 1975," 212.

17. "Soviet Naval Visit to Amsterdam." *Marine Forum* 11 (1978): 308–39.

18. "Aboard the *Moskva.*" *Aviation and Marine* (December 1978): 51–60.

19. Bathurst, Burger, and Wolfe, "Soviet Sailor," 53.

20. Ibid.

21. Henry Morton, "Housing Quality and Housing Classes in the Soviet Union." In *Quality of Life in the Soviet Union,* edited by Horst Herlemann (Boulder, Colo.: Westview Press, 1987): 95.

22. Ibid., 96.

23. John Barron, *MiG Pilot: The Final Escape of Lt. Belenko* (New York: Avon Books, 1981): 97.

24. "Housing for Soviet Navy Men." *Krasnaya Zvezda* (27 March 1974): 4.

25. Barron, *MiG Pilot,* 79.

26. Nina Sablina, interview with authors.

27. Hedrick Smith, *The Russians* (New York: Ballantine Books, 1976).

28. Viktor Suverov, *Inside the Soviet Army* (New York: Macmillan, 1982): 175.

29. Richard Gabriel, *The New Red Legions* (Westport, Conn.: Greenwood Press, 1980): 51.

30. Barron, *MiG Pilot,* 97.

31. "Moscow's Military Machine," 46.

32. Mikhail Grumman, interview with authors.

33. "Moscow's Military Machine," 46.

34. Mikhail Grumman, interview with authors.

35. Capt. Richard Life, telephone interview with authors. Assistant U.S. Naval attaché to the Soviet Union, 1974–77. Boulder, Colorado, 12 October 1986.

36. Ibid.

37. Manthorpe, "Soviet Navy in 1975," 212.

38. Robert Bathurst and Michael Burger, *Controlling the Soviet Soldier: Some Eyewitness Accounts* (College Station, Tex.: Center for Strategic Technology, 1981): 9.

39. Norman Polmar, *Soviet Naval Developments* (Annapolis, Md.: Nautical and Aviation Publishing, 1979): 49.

40. Bathurst and Burger, *Controlling the Soviet Soldier,* 9.

41. Cockburn, *Threat,* 44.

42. Bathurst and Burger, *Controlling the Soviet Soldier,* 5.

43. George Feifer, "Russian Disorders." *Harper's* 80, no. 2 (February 1981): 44.

44. Andrew O'Rourke, "Justice in the Soviet Navy." United States Naval Institute *Proceedings* 207, no. 4 (April 1981): 52.

45. Interview with Alex Alexiev, Rand Corporation senior analyst and specialist in Soviet ethnic studies. Santa Monica, California, 17 November 1981.

46. Bathurst and Burger, *Controlling the Soviet Soldier,* 13.

47. Soviet Navy conscript who served 1973–75, interview with authors. Served in a naval signal battalion in Riga, Latvia. Telephone interview, 12 December 1981.

48. Ibid.

49. Cockburn, *Threat,* 431.

50. Barron, *MiG Pilot,* 82.

51. Vladislav Krasnov, interview with authors. Soviet émigré and assistant professor of Russian Studies at the Monterey Institute of International Studies. Monterey, California, 3 November 1981.

52. Mikhail Grumman, interview with authors.

53. Cockburn, *Threat,* 63.

54. Ibid., 69.

55. Ibid., 70.

56. Soviet Navy conscript who served 1973–75, interview with authors.

57. Bathurst, Burger, and Wolfe, "Soviet Sailor," 18.

58. Ibid.

59. Soviet Navy conscript who served 1973–75, interview with authors.

60. Bathurst, Burger, and Wolfe, "Soviet Sailor," 19.

61. Ibid., 18.

62. Ibid., 23.

63. Interview in *Mutiny: The True Story of Red October.*

64. Ibid.

Chapter 4. THE MUTINY

1. Kuznetsov, "Captain Sablin's Sword Bearer," 1.

2. Cherkashin, *Posledniy Parad,* 15.

3. Interview in *Mutiny: The True Story of Red October.*

4. Maidanov, *Pryamo po Kursu—Smert,* 29.

5. *Russkaya Tragediya.* Beliayev Studios. Directed by Igor Beliayev, produced by Alexander Golubov. Moscow, 1992.

6. Ibid.

7. Ibid.

8. Richard Hough, *The Potemkin Mutiny* (New York: Pantheon Books, 1961): 161.

9. Cherkashin, *Posledniy Parad,* 22.

10. Ibid., 45.

11. Ibid.

12. Ibid., 10.

13. Interview with Shein in *Kak Eto Bylo.*

14. *Russkaya Tragediya.*

15. Peter Millar, "The Truth about Red October." *London Times* (4 March 1990): 1.

16. Interview in *Mutiny: The True Story of Red October.*

17. Ibid.

18. Maidanov, *Pryamo po Kursu—Smert,* 53.

19. Ibid.

20. Cherkashin, *Posledniy Parad,* 55.

21. Ibid., 4.

22. "Case of V. M. Sablin." KGB transcript. Moscow, 12 December 1975. 2–14.

23. Ibid., 5.

24. *Russkaya Tragediya.*

25. Ibid.

26. Peter Slevin, "The True Believer." *Miami Herald* (26 September 1993): 7.

27. Ibid.

28. Interview in *Mutiny: The True Story of Red October.*

29. Maidanov, *Pryamo po Kursu—Smert,* 81.

30. Ibid., 57.

31. Ibid., 83.

32. Cherkashin, *Posledniy Parad,* 58.

Chapter 5. THE AFTERMATH

1. Maidanov, *Pryamo po Kursu—Smert,* 85.

2. Ibid., 84.

3. Interview in *Mutiny: The True Story of Red October.*

4. Cherkashin, *Posledniy Parad,* 94–95.

5. Ibid., 68.

6. Ibid.

7. *Russkaya Tragediya.*

8. Ibid.

9. Ibid.

10. Ibid.

11. Maidanov, *Pryamo po Kursu—Smert,* 303.

12. Nina Sablina, interview with authors.

13. Maidanov, *Pryamo po Kursu—Smert,* 162.

14. Ibid., 165.

15. Ibid.

16. Ibid., 252.

17. Slevin, "True Believer."

18. Maidanov, *Pryamo po Kursu—Smert,* 298.

19. Ibid., 250–51.

20. Ibid.

21. Alexander Shein, interview in *Kak Eto Bylo.* Produced by Igor Berezhkov and Tatiana Dimitrakova. Russian television series, 1995.

22. Cherkashin, *Posledniy Parad,* 82.

23. Mikhail Sablin, interviews with authors. Son of Valery Sablin. St. Petersburg, Russia, 29 and 30 October 2003 and 26 and 27 June 2004.

24. Nina Sablina, interview with authors.

25. Maidanov, *Pryamo po Kursu—Smert,* 169–70.

26. Ibid., image no. 112.

27. Ibid., 242.

28. Interview in *Mutiny: The True Story of Red October.*

29. Nina Sablina, interview with authors.

30. Slevin, "True Believer."

31. Ibid.

32. Manthorpe, "The Soviet Navy in 1976." United States Naval Institute *Proceedings* 103, no. 5 (May 1977): 209.

33. John Erickson, "The Soviet Naval High Command." United States Naval Institute *Proceedings* 99, no. 5 (May 1973): 78.

34. William Manthorpe, interview with authors. U.S. Naval attaché to the Soviet Union, 1974–77. Telephone interviews, 20 October and 15 November 1981.

35. Paul Murphy, ed. *Naval Power in Soviet Policy* (Washington, D.C.: GPO, 1978): 101.

36. Ibid., 299.

37. Valery Kuznetsov, "Captain Sablin's Sword Bearer." *Moscow News* (October 2002): 1.

38. Valery Sablin to Nina Sablina, 5 November 1975, 1–4.

Chapter 6. THE SUPPRESSION

1. "Vice Admiral Denies Baltic Mutiny Story." *Berlingske Tidende* (Copenhagen), 11 August 1976.

2. "Mutiny on the *Storozhevoy.*" *Marine Rundschau* 7 (1976).

3. Manthorpe, "Soviet Navy in 1976," 208.

4. O'Rourke, "Justice in the Soviet Navy," 52.

5. Mikhail Bernstam, interviews with authors. Soviet émigré and Hoover Institute Fellow. Palo Alto, California, 5 September 1981 and 26 February 1982.

6. "Mutiny on Russian Warship in Gulf of Riga." *Laiks,* 4 February 1976.

7. Radio Liberty/Radio Free Europe. *Samizdat* document M2767. Anonymous letter. July 1976. 3.

8. Mikhail Bernstam, interview with authors.

9. Herbert Goldhammer, *The Soviet Soldier: Military Management at Troop Level* (New York: Crane, Russak, 1975): 155.

10. "Discontent in Ranks May Be a Problem." *Financial Times,* 29 March 1978.

11. Radio Liberty. 3.

12. Manthorpe, "Soviet Navy in 1976," 211.

13. "Ideology at Sea," 15.

14. John McDonnell, "Analyzing the Soviet Press: *Morskoy Sbornik,* 1963–1975." In *Soviet Armed Forces Review Annual,* vol. 3, edited by David R. Jones (Gulf Breeze, Fla.: Academic International Press, 1979): 335.

15. G. Kostov and R. Makeyev, "New Shipboard Regulations on the Organization of Political Work." *Morskoy Sbornik* 9 (1978): 34.

16. Alex Milits to authors, 7 December 1981 and 2 February 1982.

17. Ibid.

18. Ibid.

19. Ibid.

20. "Mutiny on the *Storozhevoy*," 2.

21. "Hamburg DPA Reports Mutiny Aboard Soviet Destroyer." Broadcast in German, 1142 GMT, 5 May 1976. FBIS Report, vol. 3, no. 89, p. 6.

22. Jan-Olaf Bengtsson, "We Just Laugh at Your Stories!" *Kvallposten* (9 July 1985): 12.

23. Swedish Defense Ministry. "Orientation Concerning an Incident in the Eastern Baltic in November of 1975." Intelligence briefing, 8 March 1976. 2.

24. Bengtsson, "We Just Laugh at Your Stories!" 12.

25. Alex Milits to authors, 7 December 1981 and 2 February 1982.

26. Kenneth Robinson, interview with authors. Assistant Naval attaché to Sweden, 1975. Telephone interview, 10 June 1987.

27. Ibid.

28. Ibid.

29. Thomas Wheeler, interviews with authors. U.S. Naval attaché to Sweden, 1974–76. Telephone interview, 25 October 1981.

30. Latvian Legation, Washington, D.C. "Were Latvian Mutineers Denied Asylum in Sweden." Latvian Information Bulletin, October 1976. 12.

31. Thomas Wheeler, interview with authors.

32. Alex Milits to authors, 7 December 1981 and 2 February 1982.

33. McDonnell, "Analyzing the Soviet Press," 316–46.

34. "U.S. Helps Swedes 'Bug' Russians." *Dallas Times Herald* (15 September 1976): 4.

35. Appeals Authority, National Security Agency, to authors, 8 March 2004, 1.

36. "Russian Mutineer Sailors Denied Asylum in Sweden." *Daily Telegraph* (5 June 1976): 18.

37. Bernard Nossiter, "Mutinous Freedom Dash of Soviet Ship Told." Byline copyright *Washington Post*. Reprinted in *Dallas Times Herald* (7 June 1976).

38. "Anniversary of Revolt aboard the *Storozhevoy*." *Novoye Russkoye Slovo,* 10 November 1976.

39. Roger Boyes, "From Coastal Force to Long-Range Armada." *Financial Times* (29 March 1978).

40. Amnesty International. "Baltic Fleet." *Chronicle of Current Events: No. 43—Journal of the Human Rights Movement in the USSR,* 31 December 1976, 77.

41. "'75 Mutiny Cited in Soviet Journal." *Baltimore Sun* (5 February 1977): A2.

42. Navy Liaison Unit. "Attempted Defection by a SovBalFlt Missile Destroyer." Navy Liaison Unit, Federal Republic of Germany. Report No. 316061476. 18 October 1976.

43. "Possible Mutiny Onboard Soviet Naval Ship." U.S. Defense Attaché's Office, Stockholm. 29 January 1976.

44. Thomas B. Allen and Norman Polmar, "The Hunt for the *Storozhevoy:* Red October Almost Happened." *Seapower* (January 1985): 13–19.

45. Tom Clancy to Greg Young, 12 November 1982.

46. "A Sleuth Describes the Ill-Fated Soviet Mutiny that Inspired *The Hunt for Red October.*" *People* (16 September 1985): 133–42.

47. Tom Clancy, *The Hunt for Red October* (Annapolis, Md.: Naval Institute Press, 1984): 88.

48. Fred Hiatt, "Soviet Navy's Rebel with a Cause." *Washington Post* (18 November 1992): A25.

49. Cherkashin, *Posledniy Parad,* 85.

50. A. Shalnev, "Attempted Mutiny on Warship in 1975." *Izvestiya* (28 February 1990): 1.

51. Ibid.

52. Ibid.

53. Slevin, "True Believer."

54. *Russkaya Tragediya.*

55. Maidanov, *Pryamo po Kursu—Smert,* 271.

56. Ibid., 274–75.

Chapter 7. THE LEGACY

1. Interview in *Mutiny: The True Story of Red October.*

2. *Russkaya Tragediya.*

3. Interview in *Mutiny: The True Story of Red October.*

4. Henry Hurst, *Shadrin: The Spy Who Never Came Back* (New York: Alfred A. Knopf, 1981).

5. Bruce Kennedy, "Secret Battles, Secret Deaths." Online article. *The Cold War: Spies.* Episode 21. (CNN Interactive, 1998).

6. Vladimir Gavrilov, "What? Are You Against the Soviet Regime?" *Possev* 6 (July 1976): 2.

7. Ibid., 3.

8. Sergei Soldatov, "Plot of Baltic Fleet Officers." *Possev* 4 (April 1983).

9. Ibid.

10. Ibid.

11. Bernard Gwertzman, "Three Soviet Officers Reported Seized." *New York Times* (24 October 1969).

12. Soldatov, "Plot of Baltic Fleet Officers."

13. Grigori Feldman, interview with authors.

14. Bathurst, Burger, and Wolfe, "Soviet Sailor," 42.

15. Ibid., 33.

16. Alexander Ribowski, interview with authors. Soviet émigré and former agricultural engineer at the Riga Academy of Sciences. Telephone interview, 12 January 1982.

17. "Swedes Tow Grounded Sub into Baltic, Release It." *Monterey Peninsula Herald* (6 November 1981): 2.

18. Smith, *Russians,* 494.

19. Cherkashin, *Posledniy Parad,* 54.

20. Vasiliy Shlikov, *Shto Pogubilo Sovietskiy Soyuz?—Amerikanskaya Razvedka o Sovietskikh Voennikh Raskhodakh* (Moscow: Interregional Information Technology Fund, April 2001): 13.

21. Ibid., 5.

22. Ibid., 13.

23. Anthony Zinni, "U.S. Naval Institute Address." Transcript of Robert McCormick Tribune Foundation—U.S. Naval Institute Address. March 2000, 4. In authors' possession. 4.

24. "Telegram from Charge in the Soviet Union (George Kennan) to the U.S. Department of State." In *Foreign Relations of the United States: 1946.* Vol. 6, *Eastern Europe and the Soviet Union,* 696. Washington, D.C.: GPO, 1946.

25. Frank Roberts, interview in *Cold War: Iron Curtain.*

26. Elmo R. Zumwalt, *On Watch* (New York: New York Times Books, 1976): 291.

27. Bruce Watson and Susan Watson, ed. *The Soviet Navy* (Boulder, Colo.: Westview Press, 1986): 257.

28. Howard Sachar, *A History of Israel from the Rise of Zionism to Our Time* (New York: Alfred A. Knopf, 1996): 771.

29. Watson and Watson, *Soviet Navy,* 204.

30. Stansfield Turner, "The Naval Balance: Not Just a Numbers Game." *Foreign Affairs* (January 1977): 339.

31. U.S. Department of Defense, *Soviet Military Power* (Washington, D.C.: GPO, 1981): 39.

32. "Analysts See Little Hope of Building 600 Ship Fleet." *Navy Times* (1 February 1982): 30.

33. Daniel Da Cruz, *Boot* (New York: St. Martin's Press, 1987): 285.

34. Cockburn, *Threat,* 78.

35. Ibid.

36. Interview in *Cold War: Star Wars,* executive producer, Jeremy Isaacs, CNN, 1998.

37. Maidanov, *Pryamo po Kursu—Smert,* 288.

BIBLIOGRAPHY

"'75 Mutiny Cited in Soviet Journal." *Baltimore Sun,* 5 February 1977.

"Aboard the *Moskva.*" *Aviation and Marine,* December 1978.

Alexiev, Alex, and S. Enders Winbush. "The Ethnic Factor in the Soviet Armed Forces." *Rand Corporation Research Report,* No. N-1486-NA, May 1980.

Allen, Thomas B., and Norman Polmar. "The Hunt for the *Storozhevoy:* Red October Almost Happened." *Seapower,* January 1985.

Amnesty International. "Baltic Fleet." *Chronicle of Current Events: No. 43— Journal of the Human Rights Movement in the USSR,* 31 December 1976. London.

———. "A Meeting Before Execution." *Chronicle of Current Events: No. 48— Journal of the Human Rights Movement in the USSR,* 14 March 1978. London.

"Analysts See Little Hope of Building 600 Ship Fleet." *Navy Times,* 1 February 1982.

"Anniversary of Revolt Aboard the *Storozhevoy.*" *Novoye Russkoye Slovo,* 10 November 1976. New York.

Barron, John. *MiG Pilot: The Final Escape of Lt. Belenko.* New York: Avon Books, 1981.

Bathurst, Robert, and Michael Burger. *Controlling the Soviet Soldier: Some Eyewitness Accounts.* College Station, Tex.: Center for Strategic Technology, 1981.

Bathurst, Robert, Michael Burger, and Ellen Wolfe. "The Soviet Sailor: Combat Readiness and Morale." *Ketron Corporation Research Report,* 30 June 1982.

Bengtsson, Jan-Olaf. "Moscow Wants Results at Any Price!" *Kvallposten,* 7 July 1985.

———. "Now's Our Chance: Head for Sweden." *Kvallposten,* 6 July 1985.

———. "We Just Laugh at Your Stories!" *Kvallposten,* 9 July 1985.

———. "You Damned Idiots! You're Bombing the Wrong Vessel!" *Kvallposten,* 8 July 1985.

Bethell, Nicholas, ed. *Russia Besieged.* Alexandria, Va.: Time-Life Books, 1977.

Boyes, Roger. "From Coastal Force to Long-Range Armada." *Financial Times,* 29 March 1978.

Braden, Nate, trans. "Case of V. M. Sablin." KGB transcript. Moscow, 12 December 1975.

Cherkashin, Nikolai. *Posledniy Parad.* Nate Braden, trans. Moscow: St. Andrew's Flag, 1992.

Clancy, Tom. *The Hunt for Red October.* Annapolis, Md.: Naval Institute Press, 1984.

Cockburn, Andrew. *The Threat: Inside the Soviet Military Machine.* New York: Random House, 1983.

Conquest, Robert. *Harvest of Sorrow.* New York: Oxford University Press, 1986.

Da Cruz, Daniel. *Boot.* New York: St. Martin's Press, 1987.

"The Destroyer Had to Be Captured at All Costs." *Laiks,* 16 June 1976.

"Discontent in Ranks May Be a Problem." *Financial Times,* 29 March 1978.

Dobrynin, Anatoly. Interview in *The Cold War: Détente.* Episode 16. Executive producer, Jeremy Isaacs. CNN, 1998.

Donnally, Chris. "The Soviet Soldier: Behavior, Performance, Effectiveness." In *Soviet Military Power and Performance,* edited by John Erickson and Robert Feuchtwanger, 101–28. Hamden, Conn.: Shoestring Press, 1979.

"Drama on the Baltic Sea." *Laiks,* 12 May 1976.

Erickson, John. "The Soviet Naval High Command." United States Naval Institute *Proceedings* 99, no. 5 (May 1973).

Feifer, George. "Russian Disorders." *Harper's* 80, no. 2 (February 1981).

"Fifty Shot Immediately." *Laiks,* 15 March 1976.

Gabriel, Richard. *The New Red Legions.* Westport, Conn.: Greenwood Press, 1980.

Gavrilov, Vladimir. "What? Are You Against the Soviet Regime?" *Possev* 6 (July 1976). Frankfurt.

Gogol, Nikolai Vasilievich. *Dead Souls,* translated by David Mayarshack. New York: Penguin Books, [1842] 1961.

Goldhammer, Herbert. *The Soviet Soldier: Military Management at Troop Level.* New York: Crane, Russak, 1975.

Gwertzman, Bernard. "Three Soviet Officers Reported Seized." *New York Times,* 24 October 1969.

Hall, Ted. Interview in *The Cold War: Spies.* Episode 21. Executive producer, Jeremy Isaacs. CNN, 1998.

"Hamburg DPA Reports Mutiny Aboard Soviet Destroyer." Broadcast in German, 1142 GMT, 5 May 1976. FBIS Report, vol. 3, no. 89.

Hiatt, Fred. "Soviet Navy's Rebel with a Cause." *Washington Post,* 18 November 1992.

Hough, Richard. *The Potemkin Mutiny.* New York: Pantheon Books, 1961.

"Housing for Soviet Navy Men." *Krasnaya Zvezda,* 27 March 1974.

Hurst, Henry. *Shadrin: The Spy Who Never Came Back.* New York: Alfred A. Knopf, 1981.

"Ideology at Sea." *Soviet Analyst,* February 1976.

Kaplan, H. R. "The Flawed Colossus: Problems of Soviet Military Power." *National Defense* 69, no. 46 (March 1985): 46–48.

Kehoe, J. W. "Naval Officers; Ours and Theirs." United States Naval Institute *Proceedings* 140, no. 2 (February 1978): 50–60.

Kennedy, Bruce. "Secret Battles, Secret Deaths." Online article. *The Cold War: Spies.* Episode 21. CNN Interactive, 1998.

Kostov, G., and R. Makeyev. "New Shipboard Regulations on the Organization of Political Work." *Morskoy Sbornik* 9 (1978): 28–31.

Kuznetsov, Valery. "Captain Sablin's Sword Bearer." *Moscow News,* October 2002.

Latvian Legation, Washington, D.C. "Were Latvian Mutineers Denied Asylum in Sweden." Latvian Information Bulletin, October 1976.

Leites, Nathan. *Soviet Styles in War.* Rand Corporation report. Santa Monica, California, 16 November 1981.

Leonov, Nikolai. Interview in *The Cold War: Freeze.* Episode 19. Executive producer, Jeremy Isaacs. CNN, 1998.

Lysenko, I. "An Active Position." *Krasnaya Zvezda,* 24 December 1974.

Maidanov, Andrei. *Pryamo po Kursu—Smert.* Nate Braden, trans. Riga, Latvia: Lita Publishing House, 1992.

Manchester, William. *The Last Lion.* Vol. 1, *Visions of Glory, 1874–1932.* Boston: Little, Brown, 1983.

———. *The Last Lion.* Vol. 2, *Alone, 1932–1940.* New York: Dell, 1988.

Manthorpe, William, Jr. "Attaining Command at Sea, Soviet Style." United States Naval Institute *Proceedings* 101, no. 11 (November 1975): 97–98.

———. "The Soviet Navy in 1975." United States Naval Institute *Proceedings* 102, no. 5 (May 1976): 205–15.

———. "The Soviet Navy in 1976." United States Naval Institute *Proceedings* 103, no. 5 (May 1977): 203–14.

McDonnell, John. "Analyzing the Soviet Press: *Morskoy Sbornik,* 1963–1975." In *Soviet Armed Forces Review Annual,* vol. 3, edited by David R. Jones. Gulf Breeze, Fla.: Academic International Press, 1979.

Millar, Peter. "The Truth about Red October." *London Times,* 4 March 1990.

Morton, Henry. "Housing Quality and Housing Classes in the Soviet Union." In *Quality of Life in the Soviet Union,* edited by Horst Herlemann. Boulder, Colo.: Westview Press, 1987.

"Moscow's Military Machine: The Best of Everything." *Time* (4 May 1970): 36–47.

Murphy, Paul, ed. *Naval Power in Soviet Policy.* Washington, D.C.: GPO, 1978.

"Mutiny on Russian Warship in Gulf of Riga." *Laiks,* 4 February 1976.

"Mutiny on the *Storozhevoy.*" *Marine Rundschau* 7 (1976).

Mutiny: The True Story of Red October. October Film Production for Channel Four Television, 2000.

Navy Liaison Unit. "Attempted Defection by a SovBalFlt Missile Destroyer." Navy Liaison Unit, Federal Republic of Germany. Report No. 316061476. 18 October 1976.

Nossiter, Bernard. "Mutinous Freedom Dash of Soviet Ship Told." Byline copyright *Washington Post*. Reprinted in *Dallas Times Herald,* 7 June 1976.

O'Rourke, Andrew. "Justice in the Soviet Navy." United States Naval Institute *Proceedings* 207, no. 4 (April 1981): 51–57.

Pipes, Richard. *The Russian Revolution.* New York: Vintage Books, 1990.

Polmar, Norman. *Guide to the Soviet Navy.* 3rd ed. Annapolis, Md.: U.S. Naval Institute Press, 1983.

———. *Guide to the Soviet Navy.* 5th ed. Annapolis, Md.: U.S. Naval Institute Press, 1991.

———. *Soviet Naval Developments.* Annapolis, Md.: Nautical and Aviation Publishing, 1979.

"Possible Mutiny Onboard Soviet Naval Ship." U.S. Defense Attaché's Office, Stockholm. 29 January 1976.

Radio Liberty/Radio Free Europe. *Samizdat* document M2767. Anonymous letter. July 1976.

Ranft, Geoffrey, and Bryan Till. *The Sea in Soviet Strategy.* Annapolis, Md.: U.S. Naval Institute Press, 1984.

Roberts, Frank. Interview in *The Cold War: Iron Curtain.* Episode 2. Executive producer, Jeremy Isaacs. CNN, 1998.

"Russian Mutineer Sailors Denied Asylum in Sweden." *Daily Telegraph,* 5 June 1976.

Russkaya Tragediya. Beliayev Studios. Directed by Igor Beliayev, produced by Alexander Golubov. Moscow, 1992.

Sachar, Howard. *A History of Israel from the Rise of Zionism to Our Time.* New York: Alfred A. Knopf, 1996.

Sakharov, Vladimir, and Umberto Tosi. *High Treason: Revelations of a Double Agent.* New York: G. P. Putnam's Sons, 1980.

Scott, Harriet. "The Military Profession in the USSR." *Air Force Magazine* 59, no. 3 (March 1976): 76–81.

Semichastny, Vladimir. Interview in *The Cold War: Red Spring.* Episode 14. Executive producer, Jeremy Isaacs. CNN, 1998.

Shalnev, A. "Attempted Mutiny on Warship in 1975." *Izvestiya,* 28 February 1990.

Shapiro, Sumner. "The Blue Water Soviet Naval Officer." United States Naval Institute *Proceedings* 97, no. 2 (February 1971): 19–26.

Shein, Alexander. Interview in *Kak Eto Bylo.* Produced by Igor Berezhkov and Tatiana Dimitrakova. Russian television series, 1995.

Shlikov, Vasiliy. *Shto Pogubilo Sovietskiy Soyuz?—Amerikanskaya Razvedka o Sovietskikh Voennikh Raskhodakh.* Moscow: Interregional Information Technology Fund, April 2001.

"A Sleuth Describes the Ill-Fated Soviet Mutiny that Inspired *The Hunt For Red October.*" *People,* 16 September 1985, 133–40.

Slevin, Peter. "The True Believer." *Miami Herald,* 26 September 1993.

Smith, Hedrick. *The Russians.* New York: Ballantine Books, 1976.

Soldatov, Sergei. "Plot of Baltic Fleet Officers." *Possev* 4 (April 1983). Frankfurt.

"Soviet Naval Visit to Amsterdam." *Marine Forum* 11 (1978): 308–39.

"Speech of Comrade Khrushchev to the Sixth Plenum of the Communist Party." *Polish Archive of Modern Records,* 1956.

"The *Storozhevoy* Attacks." *Krasnaya Zvezda,* 18 December 1974.

"Storozhevoy Sent to Vladivostok." *Laiks,* 3 July 1976.

Sullivan, Mark. *Our Times.* New York: Scribner's, 1996.

Suverov, Viktor. *Inside the Soviet Army.* New York: Macmillan, 1982.

"Swedes Tow Grounded Sub into Baltic, Release It." *Monterey Peninsula Herald,* 6 November 1981.

Swedish Defense Ministry. "Orientation Concerning an Incident in the Eastern Baltic in November of 1975." Intelligence briefing, 8 March 1976.

"Telegram from Charge in the Soviet Union (George Kennan) to the U.S. Department of State." In *Foreign Relations of the United States: 1946.* Vol. 6, *Eastern Europe and the Soviet Union,* 696. Washington, D.C.: GPO, 1946.

Turner, Stansfield. "The Naval Balance: Not Just a Numbers Game." *Foreign Affairs,* January 1977.

U.S. Department of Defense. "Intellectual Life and the Communist Party in the Soviet Union." Interview. FLAMRIC discussion tape. Monterey, Calif.: Defense Language Institute, 1993.

———. *Soviet Military Power.* Washington, D.C.: GPO, 1981.

"U.S. Helps Swedes 'Bug' Russians." *Dallas Times Herald,* 15 September 1976.

USSR Naval Shipboard Regulations. Moscow: USSR Ministry of Defense, 1976.

"Vice Admiral Denies Baltic Mutiny Story." *Berlingske Tidende* (Copenhagen), 11 August 1976.

Voenniy Entsiklopedicheskiy Slovar. Edited by G. Mikhailovski. Moscow: USSR Ministry of Defense, 1984.

Watson, Bruce, and Susan Watson, ed. *The Soviet Navy.* Boulder, Colo.: Westview Press, 1986.

Young, Gregory D. "Mutiny on the Storozhevoy: A Case Study of Dissent in the Soviet Navy." Master's thesis. Naval Postgraduate School, Monterey, California, March 1982.

Zinni, Anthony. "U.S. Naval Institute Address." Transcript of Robert McCormick Tribune Foundation—U.S. Naval Institute Address. March 2000, 4. In authors' possession.

Zumwalt, Elmo R. *On Watch.* New York: New York Times Books, 1976.

Author Interviews

Alexiev, Alex. Rand Corporation senior analyst and specialist in Soviet ethnic studies. Santa Monica, California, 17 November 1981.

Bernstam, Mikhail. Soviet émigré and Hoover Institute Fellow. Palo Alto, California, 5 September 1981 and 26 February 1982.

Cherkashin, Nikolai. Author and former Soviet Navy *zampolit.* St. Petersburg, Russia, 27 October 2003.

Feldman, Grigori. Soviet Navy conscript, 1967–70. Served aboard a *Kresta I*–class cruiser out of Murmansk. Telephone interview, 9 December 1981.

Freidkin, Vasily. Served on staff of *Krasnaya Zvezda* (Riga), 1975. Telephone interview, 16 December 1981.

Grumman, Mikhail. Soviet Navy conscript, 1968–71. Served aboard a *K-8*-class minesweeper out of Tallinn, Estonia. Telephone interview, 5 January 1982.

Krasnov, Vladislav. Soviet émigré and assistant professor of Russian Studies at the Monterey Institute of International Studies. Monterey, California, 3 November 1981.

Life, Capt. Richard, USN. Assistant U.S. Naval attaché to the Soviet Union, 1974–77. Boulder, Colorado, 12 October 1986.

Manthorpe, Capt. William, Jr. USN. U.S. Naval attaché to the Soviet Union, 1974–77. Telephone interviews, 20 October and 15 November 1981.

Ribowski, Alexander. Soviet émigré and former agricultural engineer at the Riga Academy of Sciences. Telephone interview, 12 January 1982.

Robinson, Capt. Kenneth, USN. Assistant Naval attaché to Sweden, 1975. Telephone interview, 10 June 1987.

Sablin, Mikhail. Son of Valery Sablin. St. Petersburg, Russia, 29 and 30 October 2003 and 26 and 27 June 2004.

Sablina, Nina. Wife of Valery Sablin. St. Petersburg, Russia, 26 and 27 June 2004.

Soviet Navy conscript who served 1973–75 (anonymous). Served in a naval signal battalion in Riga, Latvia. Telephone interview, 12 December 1981.

Wheeler, Capt. Thomas, USN. U.S. Naval attaché to Sweden, 1974–76. Telephone interview, 25 October 1981.

INDEX

ABOUT THE AUTHORS

Gregory D. Young retired from the U.S. Navy in 1998. His twenty-four years were split evenly between flying P-3s and academic pursuits. Memorable tours included commander, Indian Ocean Air Patrol Group/CTG 72.8, and senior naval officer at the U.S. Air Force Academy. Greg is now an instructor of political science and is completing his doctorate at the University of Colorado at Boulder.

Nate Braden served in the Marine Corps for eight years as an intelligence officer, including several tours of duty in the Middle East and Far East. He is the founder and owner of America and the World, Inc., an online publishing company in Denver, Colorado.